ROUGH GUIDES

KT-416-463

POCKET ROUGH GUIDE
BERLIN

written and researched by
PAUL SULLIVAN

04493971

CONTENTS

Clockwise from top: East Side Gallery; Memorial to the Murdered Jews of Europe; Kaiser Wilhelm Memorial Church; Badeschiff

BERLIN

Of all today's European capitals, Berlin carries the biggest buzz. In the two and a half decades since it was reunified, the city has developed into a heady meld of grit and glamour that's vastly different from anywhere else in Germany – or the rest of the world for that matter. Its edgy cultural and fashion scenes, unsurpassed nightlife and radical anti-gentrification agenda regularly make global headlines, as does its reputation as "poor but sexy" – a term coined by former mayor Klaus Wowereit and quickly adopted as the city's unofficial motto.

Hackescher markt

When to visit

Berlin is a great city to visit at any time of year with plenty to do and see – but like most places, it really comes alive in the warmer months. If you're not a fan of cold weather, be warned that the winter months can be brutally chilly thanks to winds blowing in from the east. In general though, the city enjoys a cool and humid climate with an average summer temperature of around 25°C as well as the occasional heatwave. Spring and autumn are often lovely seasons.

The crackle of youthful energy that characterizes much of the inner city – especially areas such as trendy Mitte (Spandauer Vorstadt and around), student-heavy Friedrichshain and artist and expat haven Neukölln – mingles incongruously with the scars of Berlin's less glamorous past. Holocaust memorials, concentration camps and a wealth of thought-provoking museums, such as Daniel Libeskind's celebrated Jewish Museum, join bullet holes and empty spaces to provide visitors with constant reminders of the horrors of National Socialism and World War II. The fragments of the Berlin Wall, scattered around the city like broken concrete teeth, testify to its painful division – sometimes still reflected in the mindsets of the city's formerly divided neighbourhoods, many of which have retained their pre-reunification identities.

So overwhelming is Berlin's twentieth-century history and its twenty-first century grab for the future, that it's easy to forget that the city has a longer and more illustrious history. Originally two cities – Cölln, an island in the middle of the city, now the site of the Museum Island, and Alt Berlin, formerly a fishing village – Berlin was formed in 1237. Located at the intersection of significant trade routes, it quickly prospered, rising to power as the seat of the Hohenzollern dynasty following the Thirty Years' War. During the eighteenth century, Frederick the Great (1712–86) established Berlin – and neighbouring Potsdam, with its magnificent summer palace Sanssouci – as a grand capital for the Prussian monarchy; it was during this time that many of the buildings on Unter den Linden were constructed. When Germany was united in 1871, Berlin became its capital.

Following the defeat of World War I, during the Weimar Republic (1919–33) the city rivalled Paris as a centre for the cultural avant-garde, the legacy and spirit of which live on in contemporary Berlin. World War II reduced seventy percent of the city to ruins, and it was partitioned into American, British and French zones in the West and a Soviet zone in the East. The three Western-occupied zones eventually merged into West Berlin, while the Soviet zone in the East remained defiantly separate – the city's division was fully realized with the building of the Berlin Wall in August 1961 by the East German government.

The fall of the Wall in 1989 provided a rare opportunity for a late twentieth-century rebirth. Berlin still carries an unfinished air and change remains an exciting constant in the city, though it's not without its growing pains, with gentrification a red-hot

What's new

Berlin has taken up the craft beer 'n' burgers craze with real zest. For artisan brews, check out *Kaschk* (p.38) – particularly strong on Nordic ales – and *Vagabund Brauerei* (p.95), which was in the vanguard of Europe's crowd-sourced breweries. When the time comes to soak it all up, we heartily recommend *The Bird* (p.88), which offers a greasy slice of US-style goodness, or *Marienburgerie* (p.89), a little venue with a lot of big burgers.

topic: Prenzlauer Berg and Mitte have been yuppified beyond recognition, while in Friedrichshain, Kreuzberg and Neukölln cars are torched, windows smashed in and hip cafés spray-painted with graffiti in an effort to resist.

Political forces and ideals continue to battle it out in Berlin, rendering the city a vibrant and vertiginous place to be: an irresistible combination of entrepreneurial possibility and creative energy rubbing shoulders with a fully developed tourist destination overflowing with museums, sights and events. What's not to like?

Cyclists at Tempelhofer Park

Where to...

Shop

Despite Karl Lagerfeld's public dismissal of it back in 2010, Berlin's fashion scene has been going from strength to strength in the past decade or so, with a string of local designers constantly upping the ante. The city is awash with small boutiques, with clusters around Neue Schönhauser Strasse and Münzstrasse in Spandauer Vorstadt (Mitte) and between Kantstrasse and Ku'damm in Charlottenburg, while Kreuzberg and Friedrichshain have a surfeit of street fashion stores. More commercial shopping can be found around Hackescher Markt and along Ku'damm.

OUR FAVOURITES: do you read me? p.33. Mall of Berlin p.56. Voo Store p.114,

Eat

The dining scene in Berlin has come on leaps and bounds since the Wall fell. Cheap eats are abundant all over the city, with snack stalls – *Imbisse* – hawking everything from burgers and *Currywurst* to Asian food. At the other end, you can dine in style at a decent selection of high-end, Michelin-starred spots – particularly in upscale areas such as Unter den Linden, Potsdamer Platz and Charlottenburg. The area in between – mid-priced restaurants – make up the majority of eating options, again all over the city, and vary from authentic and traditional German restaurants to stylish dens of cool. A particular Berlin favourite is the weekend brunch buffet, served in cafés across the city – Prenzlauer Berg is a good bet for these.

OUR FAVOURITES: Cocolo p.115. Katz Orange p.36. I Due Forni p.35

Drink

The majority of bars are independent, and relaxed licensing laws means they can usually close when they like. Though there are a decent spread of bars everywhere, the biggest concentration is around Mitte, Prenzlauer Berg, Kreuzberg and Neukölln, with many operating as cafés during the day serving snacks and light meals, and then as bars later on, staying open all the way through to the early hours.

OUR FAVOURITES: Schwarze Traube p.118. Weinerei Forum p.39. Vagabund Brauerei p.95

Party

Berlin's nightlife scene is the envy of, well, most of the world, and its large creative scene means that people have fairly flexible schedules. The city's nightclubs not only stay open later than most (some don't close for days) but also purvey some of the most cutting-edge house and techno around, attracting clubbers from around the globe who come to the city just to party the weekend away at heavyweight places like *Berghain* and *Watergate*. There's a strong concentration of clubs in Friedrichshain and East Kreuzberg, particularly along the River Spree, which divides these two neighbourhoods.

OUR FAVOURITES: Berghain p.103. Clärchens Ballhaus p.40. B-Flat p.40.

Berlin at a glance

WEDDING

Spandauer Vorstadt p.26.
Dense with boutiques, bars and
restaurants, this is the heart of
Berlin's Mitte district.

Charlottenburg p.124. Chic West
Berlin, with Ku'damm, Schloss
Charlottenburg, the Zoo and Kaiser-
Wilhelm-Gedächtnis-Kirche.

Museum fi
Naturkund

MOABIT

Hauptbahnhof

CHARLOTTENBURG

**Unter den Linden and the
government quarter** p.48.
Berlin's grandest boulevard
culminates in the imposing
Brandenburg Gate and Reichstag.

Reichsta

Brandenburg
Gate

T i e r g a r t e n

Sony
Center

POTSDAME
PLATZ

Kulturforum

Potsdamer Platz and Tiergarten
p.68. Commercial Potsdamer Platz
borders the vast Tiergarten and the
Kulturforum, home to galleries and
the Berlin Philharmonic.

Schöneberg p.136.
Residential neighbourhood
with a low-key charm.

SCHÖNEBERG

West Kreuzberg p.104. Bohemian
quarter with a few major sights –
Checkpoint Charlie and the Jewish
Museum among them.

Viktoria-
park

Rathaus
Schöneberg

Prenzlauer Berg and Wedding p.80. Prenzlauer Berg appeals thanks to its leafy squares filled with cafés and boutiques. Neighbouring Wedding has an edgier sort of charm.

The Museum Island p.42. Five world-class museums, impressively renovated and housing collections of art and antiquities.

PRENZLAUER BERG

Alexanderplatz and the Nikolaiviertel p.60. The main square of old East Berlin and neighbouring Nikolaiviertel, a reconstruction of a medieval quarter.

Gedenkstätte
Berliner Mauer

SPANDAUER
VORSTADT

Neue
Synagoge ✡   Hackesche
Höfe

ALEXANDER-
PLATZ

Volkspark
Friedrichshain

Pergamon-
museum

Fernsehturm

UNTER
DEN LINDEN

NIKOLAIVIERTEL

Nikolaikirche

FRIEDRICHSHAIN

MUSEUM
ISLAND

Ostbahnhof

East Side Gallery

Checkpoint
Charlie

Friedrichschain p.96. East Berlin district that's home to an alternative bars and club scene.

WEST
KREUZBERG

Jewish
Museum
Berlin

EAST
KREUZBERG

Kottbusser
Tor

East Kreuzberg p.112. The more counter-cultural half of Kreuzberg, with a series of superb independent bars.

Neukölln p.120. Berlin's fastest-changing district is a hipster haven of bars, galleries, cafés and lots of buzz.

NEUKÖLLN

TEMPELHOF

Volkspark
Hasenheide

17

Things not to miss

It's not possible to see everything that Berlin has to offer in one trip – and we don't suggest you try. What follows is a selective taste of the city's highlights, from eye-catching architecture to exceptional art.

∨ Gemäldegalerie
p.70
The undisputed heavyweight of the Kulturforum boasts hundreds of exquisite Old Masters.

∧ Berliner Fernsehturm
p.61
Buy an online fast track ticket to beat the queues and better enjoy the peerless city views from this Berlin landmark.

> Memorial to the Murdered Jews of Europe
p.54
Nineteen thousand square metres of dramatic, disorienting concrete stelae, plus a highly emotive underground museum.

< Reichstag
p.54
Having survived fascism, revolution, bombardment and neglect, the Reichstag is today a symbol of the city's reunification.

∧ **Schloss Charlottenburg**
p.128
The largest palace in Berlin is also a fine example of Prussian-era architecture, built in stunning Rococo and Baroque style.

< **Jewish Museum**
p.107
Daniel Libeskind's Jewish Museum is notable not only for its content but also for its architectural prowess.

> **Berlin Zoo & Aquarium**
p.124 & p.125
One of the largest zoos in Europe, with pandas, elephants, giraffes and more plus a comprehensive aquarium around the corner.

∨ **Hamburger Bahnhof**
p.32
This former train station now houses Berlin's largest collection of cutting-edge international art.

∧ Panoramapunkt
p.69
Take a high-speed ride to the top of the Art Deco Kollhoff Tower for soaring vistas over Potsdamer Platz and beyond.

⟨ Berliner Dom
p.42
The interior of Berlin's neo-Renaissance cathedral is as dramatic as its outsized exterior.

⟩ Deutsches Technikmuseum
p.107
A jaw-dropping ensemble of German technical innovations, past and present.

< Gedenkstätte Berliner Mauer
p.80
The Wall memorial on Bernauer Strasse has fascinating indoor and outdoor exhibitions for free.

∨ Strandbad Wannsee
p.145
The most popular lakeside retreat in the city, Wannsee also has one of the largest lidos in Europe.

THINGS NOT TO MISS

∧ **Topography of Terror**
p.106
Located where the SS headquarters used
to be, this museum unflinchingly explores
the rise of the Nazi party and its atrocities.

> **Museum Island**
p.42
A treasure trove of ancient and modern art
spread over five world-class museums.

‹ Brandenburger Tor
p.53
One of Berlin's most iconic
landmarks now comes with a
multimedia museum that
showcases its fascinating history.

⌄ East Side Gallery
p.96
This significant remaining stretch
of the Berlin Wall doubles as one
of the world's longest open-air art
galleries.

Day one

Breakfast p.48. The café of the Deutsches Historisches Museum is a refined and classic place to start the day with a hearty breakfast before throwing yourself into the museum.

Deutsches Historisches Museum p.48. Check out two thousand years of German history neatly and thoughtfully arranged throughout this beautiful museum, spread across two contrasting buildings.

Neue Wache p.49. Visit Schinkel's famous Neoclassical monument and its moving tributes to victims of wartime, including the emotive Käthe Kollwitz sculpture *Mother with her Dead Son*.

Lunch For a tasty budget option in the area try sushi at *Ishin* (p.57); for classic Austro-Hungarian dishes opt for *Café Einstein* (p.58).

Brandenburg Gate p.53. Berlin's foremost landmark and one of its biggest tourist attractions. A must see for first-time visitors, either with a leisurely stroll via Unter den Linden or with a visit to the neighbouring museum.

Reichstag p.54. Climb the Norman Foster-designed dome of this historic building to find great views across the city. Make sure you book a guided tour ahead.

Memorial to the Murdered Jews of Europe p.54. Visit the controversial memorial with its rows of stelae above ground and sobering visitor centre below.

Dinner p.56. End the day with high-quality Italian cuisine and a warm welcome at *Bocca di Bacco*.

Deutsches Historisches Museum

Brandenburg Gate

Reichstag

Day two

Breakfast p.135. West Berlin's *Schwarzes Café* is a vaguely bohemian 24-hour café with a relaxed, spacious interior upstairs (more of a "Black Café" downstairs) and decent breakfasts.

Berlin Zoo and Aquarium
p.124 & p.125. One of the biggest zoos in Europe – hippos are among the celebrated residents – with an equally comprehensive aquarium right around the corner.

Kaiser-Wilhelm-Gedächtnis-Kirche p.128.
Don't let the shattered spire put you off, this memorial church has a wonderful interior to investigate.

Käthe Kollwitz Museum
p.128. The biggest collection of work from Berlin's pre-eminent sculptor displayed in a lovely villa on Fasanenstrasse.

Lunch p.134. Linger over coffee or lunch right next door at elegant café/restaurant *Café im Literaturhaus*, nabbing a table outdoors if the sun's shining.

Story of Berlin p.128.
This museum does precisely what it says on the tin, covering eight centuries of Berlin's history in an insightful and impressive manner.

Shopping on Ku'damm
p.130. Since you're on the mighty Kurfürstendamm it'd be a shame not to indulge in some retail therapy. Don't forget to check the side streets too for a host of excellent, independent boutiques.

Dinner p.132. Try some thoroughly old-fashioned Silesian and Pomeranian food at *Marjellchen*, a marvellous timewarp.

Berlin Zoo

Kaiser-Wilhelm-Gedächtnis-Kirche

Käthe Kollwitz Museum

GDR Berlin

Take an "Ostalgie" tour through former East Berlin, its monumental sights, kitsch icons and memorials to the city's divided past.

DDR Museum p.62. Get hands on with GDR culture at this interactive museum, which evokes both the lighter and darker sides of life in communist East Germany. Nearby stand statues of Marx and Engels, tucked into a corner of the Marx-Engels-Forum park.

Berliner Fernsehturm p.61. Gape at the bleak GDR architecture of Alexanderplatz before taking a trip up the Fernsehturm for tremendous views over the city.

East Side Gallery

Lunch p.31. For the complete television tower experience, book ahead for a meal in the revolving restaurant, *Sphere*.

Karl-Marx-Allee p.97. Admire the Soviet architecture along this impressive historical boulevard, formerly known as Stalinallee, including the original Kino International, as featured in the film *Good Bye Lenin!*

Coffee p.101. Grab coffee and cake (or ice cream) at *Café Sybille*, which also hosts a small but informative museum about Karl-Marx-Allee.

East Side Gallery p.96. Finish up at the largest remaining section of the Berlin Wall, also one of the world's largest open-air galleries.

Café Sybille

Sleep p.151. For a complete Ostalgie experience, book a night at the GDR-themed *Ostel* in Friedrichshain, which is also well placed for the neighbourhood's nightlife.

Ostel

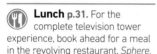

ITINERARIES

Budget Berlin

Berlin's not necessarily an expensive city, and there are plenty of fun ways to explore on the cheap.

Breakfast p.93. Tuck into the weekend veggie breakfast at *Morgenrot* in Prenzlauer Berg, where the amount you pay depends on your income.

Take the bus p.156. Public buses #100 and #200 will give you a guided tour of some of the city's main sights at a fraction of the cost.

Free art p.70 & p.50. For free contemporary art, check out Daimler Contemporary (always free) and DB Kunsthalle (free Mon).

Lunch p.77. *Joseph Roth Diele*, a charming restaurant near Potsdamer Platz, is dedicated to the Jewish author and has excellent lunch deals.

Topography of Terror p.106. Built on the grounds of the former SS Headquarters, this memorial of Gestapo horrors will leave you reeling.

Gedenkstätte Berliner Mauer p.80. The Wall memorial on Bernauer Strasse has fascinating indoor and outdoor exhibitions for free.

Cheap and quirky museums p.113 & p.114. You can access the delightful Museum der Dinge (Museum of Things) for just €6 while the Ramones Museum (€4.50) is the only one of its kind in the world.

Drinks p.39. Drink and make merry at one of the *Weinerei* bars, low-key, hipster hangouts where you pay what you feel is fair for the wine.

Museum of Things

Joseph Roth Diele

Weinerei

Berlin nightlife

Berlin's nightlife is justifiably renowned around the globe, with several distinct nightlife districts making it easy to spend an evening – or even an entire weekend – exploring the city's multitude of bars and clubs.

Clärchens Ballhaus p.40. Start the night with a pizza and Pilsner at this charming century-old ballhouse, which hosts a variety of nights from Tango to classical concerts.

B-Flat p.40. One of the newer jazz spots in the city, B-Flat is also one of the most dynamic with regular international guests and weekly jam sessions. A great place to get into the swing of things.

Schokoladen p.41. For more live music, head to intimate Schokoladen which hosts indie-pop and upcoming acts in a bare brick (former squat, former chocolate factory) interior.

Club der Visionaere p.117. A top pre-club spot, this CdV has the advantage of being mostly set outdoors on a floating deck. The dancefloor is small but the vibes can be big on the right night.

Salon zur Wilden Renate p.103. One of the most reliably fun nightspots in the city, the parties have an arty aesthetic and favour a house and disco soundtrack over the usual techno.

Rosi's p.103. Upbeat and oddball, a visit to Rosi's feels like crashing a house party – you can even chill out in the kitchen, or over a game of ping pong, in between sessions on the dancefloors, where indie, punk and electro pound.

Berghain p.103. It's notoriously tough to get into, but if you can penetrate Berlin's world-famous techno temple you'll realise why it's considered one of the best in the world. The Saturday night party runs until Monday morning.

Club der Visionaere

Clärchens Ballhaus

Salon zur Wilden Renate

Open spaces

Although it's known more for its urban thrills, the German capital is a surprisingly green city. Its many parks are not only easy to get to, but often come with plenty of options for activities (jogging, volleyball, barbecues, rowing on lakes), along with lots of history.

Mauerpark p.81. Salvaged by local residents after the fall of the Wall, this scruffy but popular park was once the Wall's "death strip" between East and West Berlin. Visit on a Sunday to find life-affirming public karaoke and a popular flea market.

Viktoriapark p.108. This much-loved Kreuzberg park is famous for having the tallest peak in the city. It also offers a pretty waterfall in summer and lots of hills for winter sledging.

Tiergarten p.75. The city's most famous park used to be a hunting ground for the Kaiser and his cohorts. Nowadays it provides ample running and walking tracks, lakes and a couple of great beer gardens.

Tempelhofer Park p.108. One of the largest and most unique parks in Europe, this former Nazi airport is now a vast community space where residents and visitors can rollerblade and kite-surf along the former runway.

Volkspark Friedrichshain p.96. GDR-era memorials abound at this sprawling city park, which also offers a picturesque nineteenth-century fountain, a great recreational area with climbing walls and sandy volleyball courts, and a couple of beer gardens.

Pfaueninsel p.144. Take to the water to escape the city for a fantasy island getaway – now a car-free nature reserve, stalked by a flock of peacocks, Pfaueninsel also features a mini-Schloss and gardens landscaped by the original designer of the Tiergarten.

Mauerpark

Tempelhofer Park

Viktoriapark

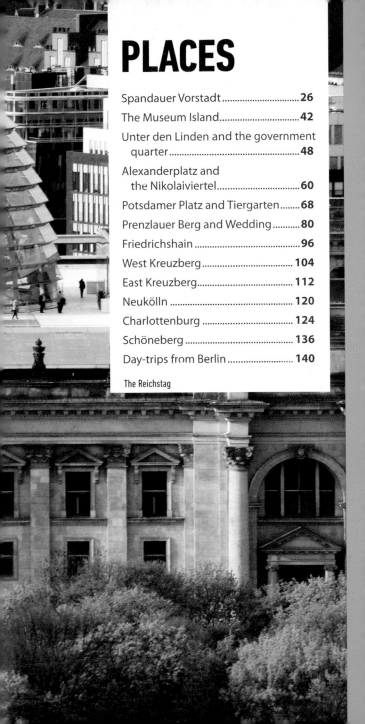

PLACES

The Reichstag

Spandauer Vorstadt

Arcing elegantly above the Spree between Friedrichstrasse and Alexanderplatz, the Spandauer Vorstadt was an eighteenth-century suburb that today serves as Berlin's primary "downtown" area, and is the heart of the Mitte district. Before World War II it was a significant hub for Jewish and French Huguenot exiles; after the Wall fell it became an artists' enclave, playing a vital role in the transferral of the city's art scene from West to East. Two decades of commercialization have resulted in a vibrant but touristic part of the city that's dense with boutiques, bars and restaurants, mainly around Hackescher Markt and the adjacent Oranienburger Strasse, as well as galleries, along Auguststrasse and Torstrasse. Key insights into local Jewish life remain at the Neue Synagoge, the Jewish cemetery on Grosse Hamburger Strasse, and a trio of museums in the Haus Schwarzenberg.

Hackesche Höfe

MAP p.28, POCKET MAP E12
Rosenthaler Str. 40/41 & Sophienstr. 6
Ⓢ Hackescher Markt ☎ 030 28 09 80 10,
Ⓦ www.hackesche-hoefe.com. Open various hours (residential parts close 10pm).

Hackesche Höfe

The extensive series of interconnected courtyards known as the Hackesche Höfe, located just across from S-Bahn station Hackescher Markt, are one of the best-known sights in this area. Having formerly hosted a Jewish girls' club, ballroom, factories, apartments – even a poets' society – the courtyards were remixed post-Wall into a more commercial enterprise, albeit with a vaguely arty twist. Today you'll find a cinema, several theatres, a jumble of smart restaurants and shops – and a throng of tourists, attracted by the impressive Art Nouveau restoration.

Haus Schwarzenberg

MAP p.28, POCKET MAP E12
Rosenthaler Str. 39 Ⓢ Hackescher Markt
Ⓦ www.haus-schwarzenberg.org.
Haus Schwarzenberg is the grungy alternative to gentrified Hackesche Höfe, located just a couple of doors away. It has only been minimally refurbished and at least part of its allure is its wonderful crumbling facades. Inside is an

Along the River Spree

aptly unpretentious selection of cafés, bars and shops plus a cinema and galleries (street-art lovers will want to visit Neurotitan Gallery), as well as the **Monsterkabinett**, a collection of moving mechanical monsters (Ⓦ www.monsterkabinett. de; check website for opening times; €8). Of particular interest is a trio of small museums that explore Jewish life in the area during the Third Reich. The **Gedenkstätte Stille Helden** (Ⓣ 030 23 45 79 19, Ⓦ gedenkstaette-stille-helden.de; daily 10am–8pm; free) commemorates local residents who risked their lives to rescue persecuted Jews, documenting both heroic successes and tragic failures via photographs, documents and oral testimonies. Among the heroes is Otto Weidt, a German entrepreneur who helped save a number of his blind Jewish employees at his workshop. Now called the **Museum Blindenwerkstatt Otto Weidt** (Ⓣ 030 28 59 94 07, Ⓦ museum-blindenwerkstatt. de; daily 10am–8pm; free), it preserves photographs and personal mementoes of Weidt and his workers and the claustrophobic, hidden room, located behind a backless wardrobe, where he hid

Jewish families when the Gestapo came knocking. Finally, the **Anne-Frank-Zentrum** (Ⓣ 030 28 88 65 600, Ⓦ www.annefrank.de; Tues–Sun 10am–6pm; €5) is a modern, surprisingly engaging exhibition on her life.

Sammlung Hoffmann

MAP p.28, POCKET MAP D11
Sophie-Gips-Höfe, Sophienstr. 21
Ⓢ Hackescher Markt Ⓣ 030 28 49 91 20,
Ⓦ www.sammlung-hoffmann.de. By appointment only: Sat 11am–4pm; closed Aug. €10.

Started by avid art collectors Erika and Rolf Hoffmann, this sizeable private museum displays their personal collection of contemporary art, which spans painting, sculpture, photography and video over two floors filled with natural light. Organized subjectively – there are no names, descriptions or over-arching curatorial themes – the exhibition features internationally renowned names such as Jean-Michel Basquiat, Andy Warhol and Bruce Nauman. The collection is rearranged every year. Entry is by guided tour (English tours available) – a pleasantly interactive and informative way of experiencing such major works.

SPANDAUER VORSTADT

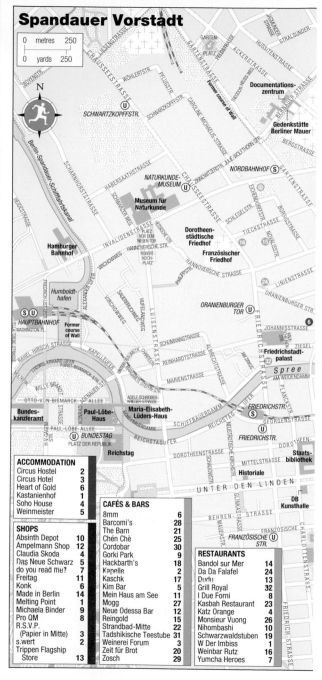

Spandauer Vorstadt

ACCOMMODATION

Circus Hostel	2
Circus Hotel	3
Heart of Gold	6
Kastanienhof	1
Soho House	4
Weinmeister	5

SHOPS

Absinth Depot	10
Ampelmann Shop	12
Claudia Skoda	4
Das Neue Schwarz	5
do you read me?	7
Freitag	11
Konk	6
Made in Berlin	14
Melting Point	1
Michaela Binder	9
Pro QM	8
R.S.V.P. (Papier in Mitte)	3
s.wert	2
Trippen Flagship Store	13

CAFÉS & BARS

8mm	6
Barcomi's	28
The Barn	21
Chén Chè	25
Cordobar	30
Gorki Park	9
Hackbarth's	18
Kapelle	2
Kaschk	17
Kim Bar	5
Mein Haus am See	11
Mogg	27
Neue Odessa Bar	12
Reingold	15
Strandbad-Mitte	22
Tadshikische Teestube	31
Weinerei Forum	3
Zeit für Brot	20
Zosch	29

RESTAURANTS

Bandol sur Mer	14
Da Da Falafel	24
Dudu	13
Grill Royal	32
I Due Forni	8
Kasbah Restaurant	23
Katz Orange	4
Monsieur Vuong	26
Nihonbashi	10
Schwarzwaldstuben	19
W Der Imbiss	1
Weinbar Rutz	16
Yumcha Heroes	7

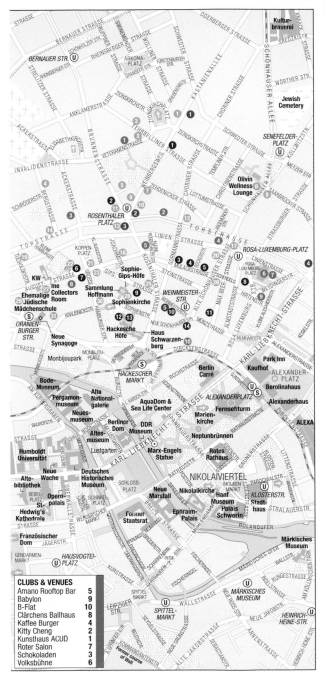

CLUBS & VENUES

Amano Rooftop Bar	5
Babylon	9
B-Flat	10
Clärchens Ballhaus	8
Kaffee Burger	4
Kitty Cheng	2
Kunsthaus ACUD	1
Roter Salon	7
Schokoladen	3
Volksbühne	6

SPANDAUER VORSTADT

Neue Synagoge

MAP p.28, POCKET MAP D12
Oranienburger Str. 28–30 ⓢ Oranienburger
Str. ☏ 030 88 02 83 00,
ⓦ centrumjudaicum.de. April–Sept: Mon–
Fri 10am–6pm, Sun 10am–7pm; Oct–March
Mon–Thurs 10am–6pm, Fri 10am–3pm, Sun
10am–7pm. Permanent exhibition €5;
temporary exhibitions €3.50; entry to the
dome €3.

Topped with a golden, glittering
dome that almost rivals the
Reichstag's for prowess and
recognition, the Moorish Neue
Synagoge (New Synagogue) is a
building with a long and largely
brutal history. Consecrated
on Rosh Hashanah in 1866,
it quickly became the most
important synagogue in Berlin;
in its prime it could house over
three thousand worshippers. Its
fortunes changed under the Nazis
and the synagogue was heavily
vandalized during *Kristallnacht*
(1938), bombed by Allied planes
(1945) and demolished by the
GDR in the 1950s. Rebuilt and
restored in the 1990s, it stands
proudly today both as a memorial
to Jewish suffering in Germany
and a depository of local Jewish
culture. Sadly it wasn't possible to
restore all of the synagogue and
its interior, so the front section
(or **Centrum Judaicum**) displays
the oldest surviving elements
– original carvings, entrance
vestibules and anterooms – and
hosts exhibitions, which mostly
focus on the history of the
building and Jewish Berlin. You
can get an idea of the building's
former dimensions by visiting
a gravel-covered area outside,
which marks the original layout
of the synagogue. Note that the
permanent exhibition is set to
change during 2018.

Neue Synagoge

Me Collectors Room

MAP p.28, POCKET MAP D11
Auguststr. 68 ⓢ Oranienburger Str. ☏ 030
86 00 85 10, ⓦ www.me-berlin.com. Tues–
Sun noon–6pm. €8.

Me Collectors Room – a platform
for international private art
collections – was conceived
and built by chemist and
endocrinologist Thomas Olbricht
to showcase his private art
collection – which happens to be
among the most comprehensive in
Europe, including works by John
Currin, Franz Gertsch, Marlene
Dumas and Gerhard Richter – via
a series of alternating exhibitions.
The "me" stands for "moving
energies": the collection spans
painting, sculpture, photography,
installation and new media
works from the early sixteenth
century to the present day. A
permanent part of the museum
is the **Wunderkammer**, which
rekindles an older tradition,
popular during the Renaissance
and Baroque periods, of bringing
together eccentric curiosities and
"wonders" from around the world.
The spacious café downstairs
serves lunches, snacks and coffee
(Tues–Sun noon–6pm).

KW Institute for Contemporary Art

MAP p.28, POCKET MAP D11
Auguststr. 69 ⓢ Oranienburger Str.
ⓣ 030 24 34 590, ⓦ www.kw-berlin.de.
Mon–Wed & Fri–Sun 11am–7pm, Thurs
11am–9pm. €8.

The KW Institute for
Contemporary Art was one of the
prime movers in the post-*Wende*
(reunification) transformation of
Auguststrasse into what has been
dubbed Berlin's "art mile". Once
a nineteenth-century margarine
factory, KW was turned into
a dedicated art space by Klaus
Biesenbach and a group of fellow
art-lovers in the early 1990s. The
elegant facade leads into a lovely,
tree-filled courtyard surrounded
by artist studios, the glass-
walled *Café Bravo* (designed by
American artist Dan Graham)
and a series of modern, white
spaces that include an exhibition
hall by Berlin architect Hans
Düttmann. The institute
mainly exhibits cutting-edge
international works from both
up-and-coming and major names
such as Doug Aitken, Dinos
and Jake Chapman and Paul
Pfeiffer. KW also runs Berlin's
immensely popular Biennale for
Contemporary Art.

Ehemalige Jüdische Mädchenschule

MAP p.28, POCKET MAP D11
Auguststr. 11–13 ⓢ Oranienburger Str.
ⓣ 030 33 00 60 70,
ⓦ maedchenschule.org. Daily 8am–
midnight; specific opening hours vary
according to venue.

Built in the late 1920s as one
of the last major Jewish
structures before the Nazis took
over, this charming, former
Jewish girls' school opened as a
space for art and cuisine in 2012
following a sensitive restoration. The former classrooms
and corridors are now used
for cultrual venyes such as the
Camera Work and Michael
Fuchs galleries, and Museum
The Kennedys, which documents
the lives of the Kennedy
family. As for cuisine, the one-
Michelin-star *Pauly-Saal* offers
an ambitious menu made from
the best of the region, the more
relaxed (and affordable) *Mogg*
Jewish deli brings NYC flavour,
and the cultivated *Pauly Bar*
provides some evening buzz.

Me Collectors Room

Hamburger Bahnhof

Friedrichstadt-Palast

MAP p.28, POCKET MAP C12
Friedrichstr. 107 ⓢ Friedrichstr. ☏ 030 23
26 23 26, ⓦ www.palast.berlin.
Founded in the 1860s,
this theatre has a long and
distinguished history, having
been a market hall, circus,
theatre and, during the Nazi era,
the Theater des Volkes when
it staged bourgeois operettas.
Its current incarnation – an
imposing GDR-style block – was
opened in 1984. The stage is a
whopping 2800 square metres
and the main hall holds up to
two thousand people for its
programme of revue shows.

Museum für Naturkunde

MAP p.28, POCKET MAP A10
Invalidenstr. 43 ⓤ Naturekundemuseum
☏ 030 20 93 85 91, ⓦ naturkunde
museum-berlin.de. Tues–Fri 9.30am–6pm,
Sat & Sun 10am–6pm. €8.
Inaugurated in 1889 by Emperor
Wilhelm II, Berlin's natural history
museum is the largest of its kind
in Germany, counting some
thirty million objects within its
collections. Highlights include the
largest mounted dinosaur in the
world – a *Brachiosaurus brancai*
composed of fossilized bones –
plus a 2015 T. rex skeleton found
in Montana and an impressive
room of stuffed animals that
showcase biodiversity.

Hamburger Bahnhof

MAP p.28, POCKET MAP A11
Invalidenstr. 50 ⓢ/ⓤ Hauptbahnhof ☏ 030
39 78 341, ⓦ www.smb.museum. Tues,
Wed & Fri 10am–6pm, Thurs 10am–8pm,
Sat & Sun 11am–6pm. €14. Free guided
tours (in English) Sat & Sun noon.
Occupying a capacious and
architecturally interesting space
(formerly one of the city's first
terminal stations), Berlin's
contemporary art museum
(Museum für Gegenwart) is one
of the city's major modern art
venues. Its permanent collection,
which features holdings from
the Nationalgalerie, focuses on
the major movements of the
late twentieth century up to the
present day, with an emphasis on
installation art and a number of
large-scale sculptures by Joseph
Beuys, to whom the entire west
wing is dedicated. The museum's
Marx Collection has works by
Anselm Kiefer and Andy Warhol,
while Friedrich Christian Flick's
collection, donated in 2004, added
works by artists like Isa Genzken,
Bruce Nauman, Pipilotti Rist and
Wolfgang Tillmans. The museum
also hosts temporary exhibitions
by international artists at the
forefront of their respective
fields. The adjacent restaurant,
an elegant affair run by German
celebrity chef Sarah Wiener, is a
good lunch spot.

Shops

Absinth Depot

MAP p.28, POCKET MAP E11
Weinmeisterstr. 4 Ⓤ Weinmeisterstr. ☏ 030
28 16 789. Mon–Fri 2pm–midnight, Sat
1pm–midnight.

The place not only to find all kinds
of "Green Fairy" liquor but also a
wide variety of props for the true
absinth experience. You can even
have a little taste.

Ampelmann Shop

MAP p.28, POCKET MAP D11
Rosenthaler Str. 40–41 Ⓤ Weinmeisterstr.
☏ 030 44 72 65 15, Ⓦ ampelmann.de.
Mon–Sat 9.30am–10pm, Sun 10am–7pm.

Everything here is based on the
Ampelmännchen – the distinctive
(and stylish) traffic light men
once present on all East German
traffic lights, who were saved from
extinction after the Wall fell by
various high-profile campaigns.

Claudia Skoda

MAP p.28, POCKET MAP E11
Mulackstr. 8 Ⓤ Weinmeisterstr. ☏ 030 40
04 18 84. Mon, Tues, Fri & Sat
12.30–6.30pm.

Skoda's renowned knitwear
is unapologetically chic (and
correspondingly expensive). The
clothes are geared mostly for
women but there's a small men's
section too.

Das Neue Schwarz

MAP p.28, POCKET MAP E11
Mulackstr. 38 Ⓤ Weinmeisterstr. ☏ 030 27
87 44 67, Ⓦ www.dasneueschwarz.de.
Mon–Sat 10.30am–8.30pm.

"The New Black" stocks innovative
garments for men and women,
often from previous seasons to
keep the prices down. Expect
handbags, shoes, suits and jackets
from top designer brands.

do you read me?

MAP p.28, POCKET MAP D11
Auguststr. 28 Ⓤ Rosenthaler Platz ☏ 030
69 54 96 95, Mon–Sat 10am–7.30pm.

A magazine lover's paradise,
this multilingual store offers a
vast assortment of magazines
and reading material from
around the world, covering
fashion and photography, art
and architecture, culture and
literature.

Freitag

MAP p.28, POCKET MAP E11
Max-Beer-Str. 3 Ⓤ/Ⓢ Alexanderplatz
☏ 030 24 63 69 61, Ⓦ www.freitag.ch.
Mon–Fri 11am–8pm, Sat 11am–7pm.

The Mitte flagship store features
concrete, couches and catwalk
lighting – all of which provides
the perfect backdrop for Markus
Freitag's creations: 1600 colourful,
durable bags in every shape
imaginable.

Konk

MAP p.28, POCKET MAP D11
Kleine Hamburger Str. 15 Ⓢ Oranienburger
Str. ☏ 030 28 09 78 39. Mon–Fri
noon–7pm, Sat noon–6pm.

Featuring collections from
many of Berlin's esteemed labels
(Anntian, Boessert/Schorn,
Marina Hoermannseder), this
women's boutique features
cutting-edge fashions, jewellery
and other glamorous accessories
that flit between fashion and art.

Ampelmann Shop

Made in Berlin

MAP p.28, POCKET MAP E12
Neue Schönhauser Str. 19
Ⓤ Weinmeisterstr. Ⓣ 030 21 23 06 01,
Ⓦ picknweight.de. Mon–Sat noon–8pm.

One of four shops that sell cutting-edge, mostly vintage clothes for girls and boys. Tuesday noon till 3pm is happy hour (20 percent off all vintage).

Melting Point

MAP p.28, POCKET MAP E10
Kastanienallee 55 Ⓤ Rosenthaler Platz
Ⓣ 030 44 04 71 31. Mon–Sat noon–8pm.

Opened in the mid-1990s, Melting Point records has stayed true to Berlin's techno and house culture, though it also sells funk, Afro, Latin and more. Masses of vinyl.

Michaela Binder

MAP p.28, POCKET MAP E11
Gipsstr. 13 Ⓤ Weinmeisterstr. Ⓣ 030 28 38
48 69. Tues–Fri noon–7pm, Sat noon–4pm.

Michaela Binder's smart shop stocks her stylish rings, bracelets, ear studs and necklaces in clean, basic shapes, from silver and gold. There's also a line of (cheaper) steel and stone vases.

Pro QM

MAP P.28, POCKET MAP F11
Almstadtstr. 48 Ⓤ Rosa-Luxemburg-Platz
Ⓣ 030 24 72 85 20, Ⓦ pro-qm.de. Mon–
Sat 11am–8pm.

Run by an artist and an architecture professor, this smart and surprisingly spacious store specializes in books and magazines dedicated to these subjects, as well as design and craft, and spans lifestyle as well as academic publications.

R.S.V.P. (Papier in Mitte)

MAP p.28, POCKET MAP E11
Mulackstr. 14 Ⓤ Weinmeisterstr. Ⓣ 030 28
09 46 44. Mon–Sat 11am–7pm.

From rare international notebooks to the store's own unique cards and journals, R.S.V.P. sells elegant stationery and related products

Made in Berlin

from international artists. A new shop at no. 26 sells wrapping paper, boxes and envelopes.

s.wert

MAP p.28, POCKET MAP D10
Brunnenstr. 191 Ⓤ Rosenthaler Platz
Ⓣ 030 40 05 66 55. Mon–Fri 11am–7pm,
Sat 11am–6pm.

Interested in special Berliner "architecture pillows", or unique designs of wrapping paper? s.wert sells all this and more, including stylish drinking cups, dresses and curtains.

Trippen Flagship Store

MAP p.28, POCKET MAP D11
Hackesche Höfe, Hofs 4 & 6, Rosenthaler
Str. 40/41 Ⓢ Hackescher Markt (also Alte
Schönhauser str. 45 in Spandauer
Vorstadt) Ⓣ 030 39 13 37. Mon–Fri
11am–8pm, Sat 10am–8pm.

Trippen sells men's and women's shoes for every occasion. There are several branches around, but this flagship store has the best range. Footwear also made to order.

Restaurants

Bandol sur Mer

MAP p.28, POCKET MAP D11
Torstr. 167 Ⓤ Rosenthaler Platz Ⓣ 030 67
30 20 51. Mon–Thurs & Sun 6pm–late.

A former kebab kiosk refurbished into a tiny, Michelin-starred French restaurant. The menu, chalked up on the all-black walls, consists of regional French cuisine like snails, entrecote and foie gras. As well as à la carte options (mains around €32), there are also five-course menus available for €82. The sister restaurant next door, 3 minutes sur mer (W 3minutessurmer.de), serves more typical French cuisine.

Da Da Falafel

MAP p.28, POCKET MAP C11
Linienstr. 132 Ⓤ Oranienburger Tor Ⓣ 030 27 59 69 27, W www.dadafalafel.de. Mon–Wed & Sun 10am–1am, Thurs–Sat 10am–2am.

Berlin isn't exactly short of falafels but *Da Da* stands out thanks to their fresh salads and an excellent array of sauces. The Dada Teller (€8) will set you up for a day's sightseeing, though expect long queues at lunchtimes.

Dudu

MAP p.28, POCKET MAP D11
Torstr. 134 Ⓤ Rosenthaler Platz Ⓣ 030 51 73 68 54, W www.dudu-berlin.de, Mon–Sat noon–midnight, Sun 1pm–midnight.

This trendy Asian spot, hidden away behind a walled garden on Torstrasse, draws a cosmopolitan Mitte crowd. The menu includes very good Japanese dishes alongside flavoursome Vietnamese soups, and you can sit inside the chic, minimal interior or at picnic tables in the cosy garden area.

Grill Royal

MAP p.28, POCKET MAP C12
Friedrichstr. 105b Ⓤ Oranienburger Tor Ⓣ 030 28 87 92 88, W www.grillroyal.com. Daily from 6pm.

The steaks are definitely high end at this celeb-friendly restaurant. Some of the best Argentine, German and French cuts in town

are served, as well as excellent seafood and wines. In summer try and reserve a seat out on the Spree-facing terrace. Steaks from €29 to – wait for it – €125.

I Due Forni

MAP p.28, POCKET MAP F10
Schönhauser Allee 12 Ⓤ Senefelderplatz Ⓣ 030 44 01 73 33. Daily noon–midnight.

This famous Italian joint serves up cheap and tasty brick-oven pizzas (€5.50–8.50) and pasta dishes, in an idiosyncratic atmosphere, aided by the punk staff (all Italian) and – in summer – a large beer garden. Service is appropriately blasé.

Kasbah Restaurant

MAP p.28, POCKET MAP D11
Gipsstr. 2 Ⓤ Rosenthaler Platz Ⓣ 030 27 59 43 61, W www.kasbah-berlin.de. Tues–Sun 6pm–midnight.

One of the few spots in Berlin to find authentic Moroccan cuisine, *Kasbah* has the experience down to a tee, from the rose-water hand-rinsing ritual and flickering lanterns to the tasty tagines and couscous dishes (from €12).

Bandol sur Mer

Katz Orange

MAP p.28, POCKET MAP D10
Bergstr. 22 ⓤ/Ⓢ Nordbahnhof ☎ 030 98
32 08 430, ⓦ www.katzorange.com. Daily
from 6pm.

Tucked away in a restored,
nineteenth-century brewery in
Mitte, the (slightly) glamorous
"orange cat" offers a pleasant blend
of casual and fine dining with an
international menu that runs from
salads to quality fish and meat
dishes. There's also a cocktail bar
and a lovely courtyard terrace for
warmer weather.

Monsieur Vuong

MAP p.28, POCKET MAP E11
Alte Schönhauser Str. 46
ⓤ Rosa-Luxemburg-Platz ☎ 030 99 29 69
24, ⓦ www.monsieurvuong.de. Mon–Thurs
noon–11pm, Fri–Sun noon–midnight.

The light, simple and cheap
Vietnamese food served at
Monsieur Vuong has made it one
of the most popular dining spots
in Mitte. The menu changes every
few days but there's always good
fresh soups, noodle salads and
fruit cocktails. You may have to
wait for a table, especially at peak
times. Specials from €7.80.

Nihombashi

MAP P.28, POCKET MAP E10
Weinbergsweg 4 ⓤ Rosenthaler Platz
☎ 0176 222 234 15, ⓦ nihombashi.de.
Daily noon–midnight.

Brightly decorated Japanese spot
that serves good-quality sushi
(with red rice as well as white),
soups and sashimi, plus tasty
kushiyaki skewers with meat,
vegetables and fish. The basketball
hoops in the toilets are a cute
touch.

Schwarzwaldstuben

MAP p.28, POCKET MAP C11
Tucholskystr. 48 Ⓢ Oranienburger Str.
☎ 030 28 09 80 84. Daily 9am–midnight.

This Mitte mainstay doubles
as a casual restaurant serving
hearty Swabian food – think
Sauerkraut, *Maultaschen*
(filled pasta) and *Flammkuchen*
(a type of thin-crust pizza, from
€7.50) – and a friendly bar in the
evenings with decent German
beers on draught.

W Der Imbiss

MAP p.28, POCKET MAP H2
Kastanienallee 49 ⓤ Senefelderplatz
☎ 030 43 35 22 06, ⓦ w-derimbiss.de.
Mon–Thurs & Sun noon–10pm, Fri & Sat
noon–11pm.

Easily identified by its cheekily
inverted *McDonald's* sign (and
orange tables), *Imbiss W* serves
up fusion food that includes such
unusual items as naan pizza and
other bright ideas. The results can
be a bit hit and miss, but they're
generally good and the reasonable
prices (items begin at €2) and
outdoor seating make this a good
budget option.

Weinbar Rutz

MAP p.28, POCKET MAP B11
Chausseestr. 8 ⓤ Naturkundemuseum
☎ 030 24 62 87 60, ⓦ rutz-restaurant.de.
Tues–Sat: wine bar 4–11pm; restaurant
6.30–10.30pm.

Double-Michelin-starred cuisine
on the second floor and over eight
hundred wines on offer make this
a de rigueur stop for foodies. It's
expensive – six-course menu €129
or nine courses for €169 – but the
bar sells slightly cheaper (but still
great) home-style dishes.

Yumcha Heroes

Yumcha Heroes

MAP p.28, POCKET MAP E16
Weinbergsweg 8 ⓤ Rosenthaler Platz
ⓣ 030 76 21 30 35, ⓦ yumchaheroes.de.
Daily noon–midnight.

With the same owners as nearby
Portuguese café *Galao*, *Yumcha
Heroes* is *the* place in Mitte for
dumplings – steamed, baked
or in a tasty broth. The food is
handmade and MSG-free, cooked
in an open kitchen and served in a
small, but stylish interior.

Cafés and bars

8mm

MAP p.28, POCKET MAP F10
Schönhauser Allee 177b ⓤ Senefelderplatz
ⓦ 8mmbar.com. Mon–Fri from 7pm, Sat &
Sun from 8pm.

It's just a small, blacked-out room
with a small bar, a DJ spinning
anything from rock to northern
soul and 8mm films projected
onto one wall – but it's a superb
place for low-key, late-night
hedonism.

Amano Rooftop Bar

MAP P.28, POCKET MAP E11
Auguststr. 43 ⓤ Rosenthaler Platz ⓣ 030
80 94150, ⓦ www.amanogroup.de.
May–Sept: Mon–Fri from 4pm till late, Sat
& Sun from 2pm till late.

The rooftop bar at the *Amano*
hotel has become a firm summer
favourite, not only for the see-
and-be-seen ambience and views
across Mitte's rooftops but also
for its excellent array of summery
wines and cocktails.

Barcomi's

MAP p.28, POCKET MAP D11
Sophienstr. 21, Sophie-Gips-Höfe
ⓤ Weinmeisterstr. ⓣ 030 28 59 83 63,
ⓦ www.barcomis.de. Mon–Sat 9am–9pm,
Sun 10am–9pm.

This second outlet from American
baker Cynthia Barcomi is tucked
away in a lovely courtyard (with
a new extension) and offers

Barcomi's

excellent bagels, brunches, coffee
and cakes – the cheesecake is
justly famous. Reservations
essential at weekends.

The Barn

MAP p.28, POCKET MAP D11
Auguststr. 58 ⓤ Rosenthaler Platz
ⓦ thebarn.de. Mon–Fri 8am–6pm, Sat &
Sun 10am–6pm.

Wooden shelves stacked with
delicious products for sale, some
of the best coffee in town, home-
made cakes, and sandwiches
using bread from local artisan
bakeries all make *The Barn*
well worth a visit. They also
have a spacious roastery-café in
Prenzlauer Berg (Schönhauser
Allee 8) and a couple of other
locations in the city.

Chén Chè

MAP p.28, POCKET MAP E11
Rosenthaler Str. 13 ⓤ Rosenthaler Platz
ⓣ 030 28 88 42 82, ⓦ chenche-berlin.de.
Daily noon–midnight.

This charming Vietnamese tea
room, with its high ceilings and
elegant, handmade lanterns, has
a small but considered menu
featuring a selection of starters
and mains as well as great teas
and coffees. Try one of the
weekend breakfasts for something
a bit different.

Cordobar

MAP p.28, POCKET MAP D11
Grosse Hamburger Str. 32 ⓢ Oranienburger
Str. ⓣ 030 27 58 12 15, ⓦ cordobar.net.
Tues–Sat 7pm–2am.

Berlin has finally overcome its
dearth of serious wine bars,
and *Cordobar* is a refreshing
mix of high-end viticulture and
accessible atmosphere. There are
over nine hundred selections
on the menu, including many
rarities, plus a small, creative
food menu.

Gorki Park

MAP p.28, POCKET MAP E10
Weinbergsweg 25 ⓤ Rosenthaler Platz
ⓣ 030 44 04 65 19, ⓦ www.gorki-park.de.
Mon–Fri 8am–1am, Sat & Sun 9am–1am.

A network of lounge-style rooms
decked out with interesting
furniture and retro wallpaper.
Despite the Russian theme,
mostly evident in the name and
the blini and borscht available,
there's a very Berlin-esque
"Wohnzimmer" (living room)
feel to the place.

Hackbarth's

MAP p.28, POCKET MAP D11
Auguststr. 49a ⓤ Rosenthaler Platz ⓣ 030
28 27 704. Mon–Sat from 9am.

With its simple wooden interior
and crowd of regulars, *Hackbarth's*
is a casually tasteful option.
Snacks and freshly baked cakes are
offered during the day.

Kaschk

Kapelle

MAP p.28, POCKET MAP H2
Zionskirchstr. 22 ⓤ Rosenthaler Platz
ⓣ 030 44 34 13 00, ⓦ cafe-kapelle.de.
Daily 10am–late.

Taking its name from the Red
Orchestra, an anti-capitalist
group who held clandestine
meetings in the café's basement
throughout the 1930s and 1940s,
this mellow space serves a solid
(and mostly organic) selection
of breakfasts, soups, smoothies
and cakes.

Kaschk

MAP P.28, POCKET MAP F11
Linienstr. 40 ⓤ Rosa-Luxemburg-Platz
ⓦ kaschk.de. Mon–Thurs 8am–2am, Fri
8am–3am, Sat 10am–3am, Sun 10am–2am.

This hip place serves top-notch
third-wave coffee, a great selection
of local and international
(especially Nordic) craft beers
and – downstairs – Germany's first
ever shuffleboards.

Kim Bar

MAP p.28, POCKET MAP D10
Brunnenstr. 10 ⓤ Rosenthaler Platz
ⓦ kim-bar.com. Tues–Sat 8pm–late.

Art space, bar and locals'
hangout, *Kim* is a firm favourite
among Mitte's trend-conscious
residents. There's no sign on the
door, just a glass facade (the
entrance is through the adjacent
courtyard). The dark, grey-walled
space hosts an array of art, film
and DJ nights.

Mein Haus Am See

MAP p.28, POCKET MAP D16
Brunnenstr. 197–198 ⓤ Rosenthaler Platz
ⓣ 030 27 59 08 73, ⓦ mein-haus-
am see.blogspot.com. Open 24hr.

A spacious café/bar, stumbling
distance from Rosenthaler Platz,
Mein Haus am See is filled with
comfy flea-market furnishings
and is as good a spot for reading
a book as it is for a drink late at
night, when DJs play anything
from disco to Latin.

Mogg

MAP P.28, POCKET MAP D11
Auguststr. 11–13 Ⓢ Oranienburger Str.
ⓣ 030 330 06 07 70, Ⓦ moggmogg.com.
Mon–Fri 11am–10pm, Sat & Sun
10am–10pm.

Breezy and chic deli, located
inside the former Jewish Girls'
School (see p.31) that serves
up delicious, Jewish-inspired
food, including one of the best
pastrami sandwiches in the
city (€9.50/€13.50) and a range
of delicious salads, lentil and
hummus dishes (from €7).

Neue Odessa Bar

MAP p.28, POCKET MAP E10
Torstr. 89 Ⓤ Rosenthaler Platz/
Rosa-Luxemburg-Platz ⓣ 0171 839 89
91, Ⓦ www.neueodessabar.de.
Daily from 7pm.

Neue Odessa Bar is now
something of a place-to-be
thanks to a well-thought-out
combination of attractive,
swanky interior, reasonably
made cocktails and table service.
Perpetually busy.

Reingold

MAP p.28, POCKET MAP C11
Novalisstr. 11 Ⓤ Oranienburger Tor ⓣ 030
28 38 76 76, Ⓦ www.reingold.de. Tues–Sat
from 7pm.

Featuring one of the most
impressive bars in town –
certainly one of the longest – this
classy 1920s-themed watering
hole offers impeccably attired
waiters who make meticulous
cocktails.

Strandbad-Mitte

MAP p.28, POCKET MAP D11
Kleine Hamburger Str. 16 Ⓢ Oranienburger
Str. ⓣ 030 24 62 89 63, Ⓦ strandbad-
mitte.de. Daily 9am–1am.

This laidback café, with breezy,
green-tiled, seaside-themed
decor, is slightly off the tourist
routes and has a correspondingly
local vibe. The food and coffee
and cakes are good and the staff
friendly.

Mogg

Tadshikische Teestube

MAP p.28, POCKET MAP D11
Oranienburger Str. 27 Ⓢ Oranienburger Str.
ⓣ 030 20 41 112, Ⓦ www.tadshikische-
teestube.de. Mon–Fri 4–11pm, Sat & Sun
noon–11pm.

Though it's moved from its
original Unter den Linden
location, the delightful "Tajik
Tea Room" still features the same
Oriental cushions-and-carpets
interior, a vast tea menu (tea
ceremony around €8) and a kids'
storyteller on Mondays spinning
fairytales in German.

Weinerei Forum

MAP p.28, POCKET MAP E10
Shop: Veteranenstr. 14; bar: Fehrbellinr
Str. 57 Ⓤ Rosenthaler Platz ⓣ 030 44 06
983, Ⓦ weinerei.com. Shop: Mon–Fri
1–8pm, Sat 11am–8pm; bars 10am–
midnight.

This "underground" members-
club-style wine shop and bar
operates on an honesty-box
system after 8pm: you pay what
you feel is fair for your drinks.
As such it's popular with a mix of
leftie sympathizers, students and
freeloaders. The wine is decidedly
average but the atmosphere is
friendly. The owners run other
ventures nearby.

Zeit für Brot

MAP p.28, POCKET MAP E11
Alte Schönhauser Str. 4 Ⓤ Rosa-
Luxemburg-Platz Ⓣ 030 28 04 67 80,
Ⓦ zeitfuerbrot.com. Mon–Fri
7.30am–8pm, Sat 8am–8pm, Sun
8am–6pm.

This café offers a mellow, pastel-
coloured interior, large windows
and an eye-catching assortment
of artisanal breads (you can
see the bakers working away
through a Perspex window).
The quiches, sandwiches and
sweets are organic and delicious.
There is another branch in
Charlottenburg.

Zosch

MAP P.28, POCKET MAP C11
Tucholskystr. 30 Ⓤ Oranienburger Str.
Ⓣ 030 280 76 64, Ⓦ zosch-berlin.de. Daily
4pm till late.

Alternative place that started
as a squat when the Wall came
down, and has retained an
early 90s feel. A good place for
gigs and club nights in the cellar,
where a fun-loving local Creole
jazz band often plays amid the
smoky ambience and constant
chatter.

Clubs and venues

Babylon

MAP p.28, POCKET MAP F11
Rosa-Luxemburg-Str. 30
Ⓤ Rosa-Luxemburg-Platz Ⓣ 030 24 25
969, Ⓦ www.babylonberlin.de.

This striking Berlin *Kino* opened
in 1929 and remains one of the
defining architectural landmarks
of Rosa-Luxemburg-Platz. Today
the cinema shows a mix of indie,
trash, silents with live organ music
and cult movies, as well as hosting
concerts and over forty film
festivals annually.

B-Flat

MAP p.28, POCKET MAP E11
Dircksenstr. 40 Ⓤ Rosenthaler Platz Ⓣ 030
28 33 123, Ⓦ b-flat-berlin.de. Daily from
8pm; concerts start at 9pm.

This cosy jazz club offers a mix of
local musicians and the occasional
international act. There's a free
jam session on Wednesdays (from
9pm).

Clärchens Ballhaus

MAP p.28, POCKET MAP D11
Auguststr. 24 Ⓤ Rosenthaler Platz dor

Babylon

Amano Rooftop Bar

Weinmeisterstr. ☎ 030 28 29 295, ⓦ www.ballhaus.de. Daily noon–late.
This authentic prewar ballroom still hosts dance classes, but at weekends the downstairs is taken over by one of the most diverse crowds (young, old, straight, gay) in Berlin, drawn by the unique atmosphere of a live covers band and an unpretentious good time. Tasty pizzas too.

Kaffee Burger

MAP p.28, POCKET MAP E11
Torstr. 60 ⓤ Rosa-Luxemburg-Platz ☎ 030 28 04 64 95, ⓦ www.kaffeeburger.de. Daily from 9pm.
Kaffee Burger has been throwing parties and events beloved of students and culture vultures for years. In recent years, its programme has become less cultural and more focused on DJ and live music events that span hip-hop and disco to world music.

Kitty Cheng

MAP p.28, POCKET MAP E10
Torstr. 99 ⓤ Rosa-Luxemburg-Platz ☎ 030 89 64 56 55, ⓦ kittycheng.de. Wed–Sat 9pm–6am.
With its vague Renaissance theme – red-and-white-striped walls, regal furnishings – and lengthy drinks list, this slightly under-the-radar spot manages to attract the attention of Mitte's buzzy (and spoiled-for-choice) party crowd. The best parties are at the weekend and the music is refreshingly diverse.

Kunsthaus ACUD

MAP P.28, POCKET MAP D10
Veteranenstr. 21 ⓤ Rosenthaler Platz ☎ 030 98 35 26 13, ⓦ acud.de. Entry and opening times vary.
One of the few cultural spaces left from the immediate post-Wall era, ACUD contains a theatre, cinema, club, bar and studio, and puts on regular concerts.

Roter Salon

MAP P.28, POCKET MAP F11
Rosa-Luxemburg-Platz 1
ⓤ Rosa-Luxemburg-Platz ☎ 030 24 06 55, ⓦ volksbuehne.berlin. Wed–Sat 11pm–4am.
Set within the Volksbühne theatre, this long-running venue's lurid red decor and chintzy furniture give it the feel of a cultured 1950s brothel. Readings, concerts and talks are held here. Entry varues according to event.

Schokoladen

MAP p.28, POCKET MAP D10
Ackerstr. 169 ⓤ Rosenthaler Platz ☎ 030 28 26 527, ⓦ www.schokoladen-mitte.de. Daily from 9pm.
A small live venue (in a former chocolate factory) that is a bit like visiting a private lounge – albeit one with cheap drinks, a friendly atmosphere and a consistently good line-up of indie-pop bands and upcoming singer/songwriters.

Volksbühne

MAP p.28, POCKET MAP F11
Rosa-Luxemburg-Platz
ⓤ Rosa-Luxemburg-Platz ☎ 030 24 06 57 77, ⓦ www.volksbuehne-berlin.de.
Built just before World War I, the Volksbühne ("People's Theatre") has its origin in the free people's theatre movement. Damaged during World War II, it was rebuilt in the 1950s and is now established as one of Germany's most experimental theatres. The venue also hosts club nights and concerts.

The Museum Island

The world-renowned Museum Island (Museumsinsel) comprises five of Berlin's most famous museums and is an absolute must for any visitor to Berlin, if only to stroll around and take in the lovely buildings and waterside atmosphere. Friedrich Wilhelm III commissioned the Royal Museum (now the Altes Museum) in 1830, but the plan for an island of museums – intended as the embodiment of Enlightenment ideas about culture – came to fruition under Friedrich Wilhelm IV of Prussia. The site was further developed under successive Prussian kings. The range of artwork and architecture is startling, spanning two thousand years and featuring such treasures as the Roman gate of Miletus and the bust of Nefertiti as well as a dizzying range of paintings and sculptures. Though badly damaged during World War II, with the collections divided during the Cold War, sensitive renovations have seen the buildings revived.

Berliner Dom (Cathedral)

MAP OPPOSITE, POCKET MAP D13
Am Lustgarten 1 ☏ 030 20 26 91 36,
Ⓦ berlinerdom.de. Mon–Sat 9am–8pm, Sun
noon–8pm, Oct–March closes 7pm. €7,
audioguide €3. Guided tours of the dome
are available (☏ 030 20 26 91 19).

Designed by Julius Raschdorff in Baroque style with Italian Renaissance influences, Berlin's Protestant cathedral was intended as a counterpart to St Peter's Basilica in Rome. The present structure dates from

Berliner Dom

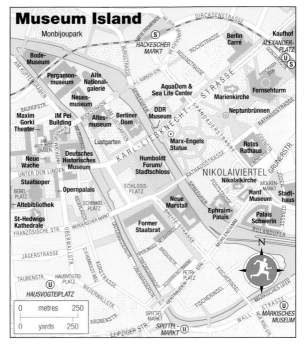

Museum Island

1905, but stands on the site of several earlier buildings, including the St Erasmus Chapel and a Neoclassical design by Schinkel dating from 1822. Restoration of the current interior began in 1984 and in 1993 the church reopened. It's a handsome and interesting building to explore, with notable eye candy including Sauer's organ, stained-glass windows designed by Anton von Werner and a marvellous dome intricately decorated with mosaics. You can get an excellent close-up view of the dome – and the entire interior – by climbing the 270 steps to the gallery. The most historically significant feature of the cathedral is its crypt, which holds more than eighty sarcophagi of Prussian royals, including those of Friedrich I and his queen, Sophie Charlotte.

Lustgarten

MAP ABOVE, POCKET MAP D13

Berlin's "Pleasure Garden" is a fundamental part of the Museum Island landscape. It's difficult to believe that this charming rectangular park, a great spot for picnics or taking a pause between museum visits, has been used variously as a military parade ground (for Wilhelm I and Napoleon), mass protests (a huge anti-Nazi demo here in 1933 prompted the banning of demonstrations) and rallies (Hitler addressed up to a million people here). Bombed in the War and renamed Marx-Engels-Platz by the GDR, its current incarnation harks back to Peter Joseph Lenné's early nineteenth-century design with a central 13m-high fountain, as re-envisioned by German landscape architect Hans Loidl.

Museum Island practicalities

The **phone number** and **website** for all Museum Island enquiries are: ☎ 030 26 64 24 242 (Mon–Fri 9am–4pm), Ⓦ www.smb.museum. The nearest **station** for all museums is Ⓢ Hackescher Markt.

Three-day tickets for all state museums (including those in the Kulturforum, see p.68) and a wealth of private museums can be bought for €29 (discounted €14.50), though these do not include special exhibitions. Note that entrance is always free for anyone under 18.

The **Berlin Welcome Card Museum Island** includes admission to many museums including the Museum Island, travel for up to 72 hours and up to 50 percent discount on many top attractions in Berlin for €40.50. See Ⓦ www.visitberlin.de.

A new visitor centre, the **James Simon-Galerie**, opens in 2018 between the Neues Museum and Kupfergraben.

Altes Museum

MAP p.43, POCKET MAP D13
Am Lustgarten. Tues–Sun 10am–6pm (Thurs till 8pm). €10. Guided tours by arrangement.

The Altes Museum, built between 1823 and 1830 after a design by Karl Friedrich Schinkel, is Berlin's oldest museum. It's also one of the city's most

important Classicist statements and a marvellous piece of architecture, all fluted Ionic columns, a beautiful rotunda filled with sculptures of Greek gods and a grand staircase that more than nods to Athens and Rome. As well as Greek statues downstairs, the upper floor contains a colossal range of Roman and Etruscan art – urns, shields, sarcophagi, friezes – all chronologically and thematically arranged.

Neues Museum

MAP p.43, POCKET MAP D13
Ⓦ www.neues-museum.de. Daily 10am–6pm (till 8pm Thurs). €12.

One of the Museum Island's undoubted highlights, the misleadingly named Neues Museum was opened in 1859 to cater for the overspill of the by-then overcrowded Altes Museum. Largely destroyed during World War II, it was only reopened in 2009, fully restored by British architect David Chipperfield, whose distinguished makeover has melded the old with the new, maintaining traces of war damage. Over three floors you'll find no less than twenty exhibition halls, each impressively designed and

Neues Museum

Market Gate of Miletus, Pergamonmuseum

connected via a stunning winding staircase. As well as the archeological collections of the Egyptian museum and papyrus collection, there's plenty of pre- and early history, as well as works from classical antiquity. The big draw is the bust of Egyptian Queen Nefertiti – famously described as "the world's most beautiful woman" – but you could happily spend an entire day absorbing the endless exhibits. Note that due to the popularity of the exhibitions you need to reserve a time slot, either by purchasing one from the nearby sales cabin or on the museum's website in advance.

Pergamonmuseum

MAP p.43, POCKET MAP D12
Am Kupfergraben 5. Daily 10am–6pm (Thurs till 8pm). €12. Guided tours by arrangement.

The Pergamonmuseum was built by Alfred Mussel in 1930 to house the artefacts from the nineteenth-century excavations of German archeologists in Pergamon and Asia Minor, perhaps most famously the controversial "Priam's treasure" – a cache of gold and other artefacts discovered by classical archeologist Heinrich Schliemann, but whose authenticity and relationship to Homeric king Priam has long been in doubt. Essentially three museums in one, the museum offers a collection of Classical antiquities (part of which is also on display in the Altes Museum); the museum of the Ancient Near East; and the museum of Islamic Art. As with the Neues Museum, you can spend a day here easily, though some of the main highlights – specifically the reconstructed (and mind-bogglingly large) Pergamon Altar from the second century BC and the Gallery of Hellenistic Art – have been affected by current renovations that are expected to last until 2019. Depending on what's on display at the time, check out the facade of the throne hall of King Nebuchadnezzar, the Market Gate of Miletus (an important example of Roman architecture) or the bright blue, glazed-brick Ishtar Gate of Babylon from the sixth century BC instead.

Alte Nationalgalerie

Alte Nationalgalerie

MAP p.43, POCKET MAP D12
Bodestr. 1–3. Tues–Sun 10am–6pm (Thurs until 8pm). €10.

The Neoclassical Alte Nationalgalerie (Old National Gallery), designed to resemble a Greek temple, houses one of the country's most significant collections of nineteenth-century painting. Built between 1866 and 1876, the museum reopened in 2001 to showcase its wealth of Classical, Romantic, Impressionist and early Modernist masterpieces. Highlights include the Goethe-era landscapes, works by Jakob Philipp Hackert and Anton Graff and Romantic paintings by the

Schlossplatz

The reconstruction of Berlin's **Stadtschloss** (City Palace) is just one of the many controversial components of Berlin's cityscape – not least because of its projected €590 million cost. The original palace, which featured architectural elements designed, built and inspired by Schlüter, Stüler, Schinkel and Goethe was the seat of the Prussian rulers (Hohenzollerns) from the fifteenth century onwards. The Stadtschloss was at the centre of the Revolution of 1848 and its last resident, Kaiser Wilhelm II, quit the palace and throne in 1918 following Germany's surrender in World War I.

The palace was damaged during World War II and pulled down in 1950 by the GDR, who replaced it with their own **Palast der Republik**, a bronze-tinted, blocky behemoth that became surprisingly popular with many East Germans. Nonetheless, after reunification this building was also pulled down, leaving a vast empty space and a lot of heated discussion about whether to rebuild the original palace or something more suited to the modern city. In 2007, the Bundestag (parliament) reached a compromise of sorts by deciding to rebuild the exterior facade with a modern interior – the new building is to be called the **Humboldt Forum** and will house parts of Humboldt University, two museums relocated from Dahlem (see p.143) and various shops and restaurants. The empty space will remain for a while yet, however, since budget cuts have delayed the project until at least 2019, several years later than planned.

likes of Caspar David Friedrich and Karl Friedrich Schinkel (a gifted landscape painter as well as Berlin's foremost architect). The Impressionist section, with its international "big guns" Manet, Monet, Renoir and Rodin, is worth the visit alone.

Bode-Museum

MAP p.43, POCKET MAP D12
Am Kupfergraben 1. Tues–Sun 10am–6pm (Thurs till 8pm). €10.

The stately Bode-Museum, with its recognizable dome, was originally called the Kaiser Friedrich Museum, and was renamed in 1956 after its inaugural curator Wilhelm van Bode. Opened after extensive refurbishments in 2006, the building is notable for its refined architectural details – the opulent staircases, monumental pilasters and demi-columns – as well as a wealth of art and artefacts from the Byzantine and Medieval periods. These are mainly from Germany but also come from major European art centres such as the Netherlands, Italy, France and Spain, and are culled from three major state museum collections: the sculpture collection, with highlights including the terracotta statues from Luca della Robbia, the Madonna from Donatello and the sculptures of Desiderio da Settignano; the Museum of Byzantine Art – the only one of its kind in Germany; and the Numismatic Collection, a vast and impressive collection of coins (and other forms of currency) that range from the seventh century BC to the twenty-first century.

On summer Sundays, the Bode-Museum hosts popular outdoor classical concerts. Entry is free (donations welcome) and the setting, on the elegant Monbijou Bridge, spectacular.

THE MUSEUM ISLAND

Bode-Museum

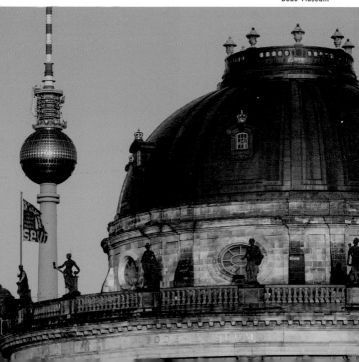

Unter den Linden and the government quarter

Berlin's grand boulevard, named for the Linden (lime) trees that line it, runs east–west from the site of the former royal palace to the Brandenburg Gate. The road originated as a bridle path for Duke Friedrich Wilhelm in the seventeenth century; by the nineteenth century it was a popular gathering place for many Berliners and Unter den Linden was furnished with new buildings, including the Neoclassical Neue Wache. Despite appearances, most of the buildings are reconstructions. Nonetheless it maintains its upscale aura, reflected in the fine-dining restaurants and expensive shops that predominate. Beyond the Brandenburg Gate lies the modern, yet no less authoritative Regierungsviertel ("government quarter"), a cluster of buildings starting with the Reichstag that stretch along the Spree. A stroll along the river past the striking Paul Löbe Haus and the Bundeskanzleramt, towards the Hauptbahnhof, is a pleasant and architecturally interesting way to pass a couple of hours.

Deutsches Historisches Museum

MAP p.50, POCKET MAP D13
Unter den Linden 2 Ⓤ/Ⓢ Friedrichstr.
Ⓣ 030 20 30 40, Ⓦ dhm.de. Daily
10am–6pm. €8.

The German Historical Museum (Deutsches Historisches Museum) is spread across two buildings: the unique Baroque Zeughaus (armoury) and a modern exhibition hall designed

Deutsches Historisches Museum

Neue Wache

by Chinese-American architect I.M. Pei. The **Zeughaus** was first used as a museum for German history during the years of the GDR (1952–90), essentially to espouse the Marxist-Leninist concept of history. In 2006 a permanent exhibition "German history in images and artefacts" was inaugurated in the three-hundred-year-old building (the oldest on Unter den Linden), which showcases two thousand years of German history via eight thousand objects from the museum's extensive collections. Supplementing this are special temporary exhibitions displayed on the four floors of the spacious **Pei building**, with its glass-and-steel lobby and winding staircase. There's also a very tasteful and little-known **cinema**, entered from the Spree side of the museum, with a historically protected interior, and a refined **café** serving great breakfasts, lunches and cakes.

Neue Wache

MAP p.50, POCKET MAP D13
Unter den Linden 4 ⓤ/Ⓢ Friedrichstr.
☏ 030 25 00 25. Daily 10am–6pm.
The Neue Wache (New Guard House) was Karl Friedrich Schinkel's first major commission in Berlin – he rose to the occasion by building a leading example of German Neoclassicism. Originally constructed as a guardhouse for the troops of the crown prince of Prussia, the building became a memorial to the Wars of Liberation (Napoleonic Wars) until 1918. From 1931 onwards it was a memorial for World War I, and the inner courtyard was covered over, apart from a small opening in the roof letting through a slither of symbolic light. Post World War II, the GDR leadership turned it into the monument for the victims of fascism and militarism. An eternal flame was placed in a cube above the ashes of an unknown concentration camp prisoner and an unknown fallen soldier. After German reunification, the GDR memorial piece was removed and replaced by an enlarged version of Käthe Kollwitz's sculpture *Mother with her Dead Son* (*Pietá*). This sculpture is directly under the oculus, its exposure to the elements a metaphor for the suffering of civilians during World War II.

Bebelplatz

MAP BELOW, POCKET MAP C13
Ⓤ Französische Str.

This historical square on the south side of Unter den Linden was constructed between 1741 and 1743 and was originally known as Opernplatz. Though framed by the opulent **Staatsoper** (see p.59), a library and the swanky *Hotel de Rome* (see p.149), it remains best known for the 1933 Nazi book burning that took place here, as instigated by propaganda minister Joseph Goebbels. The Nazis burned some twenty thousand books, including works by Thomas Mann, Erich Maria Remarque, Heinrich Heine and Karl Marx. At the centre of the square is a **memorial** of the burning by Micha Ullman, which consists of a glass-covered view into an underground chamber of empty bookshelves. Nearby, an engraving of a line from Heinrich Heine translates as: "Where they burn books, they ultimately burn people".

DB KunstHalle

MAP BELOW, POCKET MAP C13
Unter den Linden 13/15 Ⓢ Französisches Str. ☎ 030 20 20 930, Ⓦ www.deutsche-bank-kunsthalle.de. Daily 10am–8pm. €4, free on Mon.

Located on the ground floor of the Deutsche Bank – where it replaced the highly successful Deutsche Guggenheim in 2013 – the DB Kunsthalle presents contemporary art from all corners of the globe (Asia, Africa, South America), running collaborations with local museums and galleries such as the Neue Nationalgalerie and international institutions like London's Tate Modern. The Kunsthalle's opening exhibition in 2013 was a retrospective of Pakistani artist Imran Qureshi,

ACCOMMODATION

Adlon Kempinski	3
Arcotel John F	5
Arte Luise Kunsthotel	1
Hotel de Rome	4
Westin Grand	2

SHOPS

Ampelmann Shop	2
Dussmann das KulturKaufhaus	1
Galeries Lafayette	3
Mall of Berlin	5
Quartier 206	4

CLUBS & VENUES

Komische Oper	4
Konzerthaus Berlin	5
Maxim Gorki Theater	2
Staatsoper	3
Tausend	1

Bebelplatz

whom they proclaimed as "Artist of the Year", while other exhibitions have celebrated South American magical realism and the art of painting. The gallery café serves tapas created by food artists and hosts weekly lunchtime lectures (Wed at 1pm): free guided tours through the current exhibition followed by a vegan lunch (not free) based on fresh farm produce.

CAFÉS & BARS

Café Einstein	4
Café Nö!	11
Newton Bar	12
Windhorst	2

RESTAURANTS

Bocca di Bacco	7
Borchardt	9
Cookies Cream	5
Crackers	6
Fischers Fritz	8
Ishin	3
Käfer Dachgarten	1
Lutter & Wegner	10

Unter den Linden and the government quarter

Gendarmenmarkt

MAP p.50, POCKET MAP C14
Ⓤ Hausvogteiplatz/Französische Str./
Stadtmitte.

The Gendarmenmarkt, one of Berlin's most beautiful squares, was created at the end of the seventeenth century as a market place (then called the Linden Markt) but its current name comes from the Regiment Gens d'Armes that had their stables here from 1736 to 1773. Despite its inherent grandness, it's a surprisingly quiet place defined by three landmark buildings: the **Französischer Dom**, **Deutscher Dom** and the **Konzerthaus** (Concert Hall, see p.59), which frame a central statue of Friedrich Schiller. The **Französischer Dom** and **Deutscher Dom** are two seemingly identical churches facing each other across the square, poised in a standoff for visitor attention. The Französischer Dom (French Cathedral) is older, built between 1701 and 1705 by the Huguenot community, and contains a Huguenot museum, a restaurant on the top floor and a viewing platform. The pentagonal

Deutscher Dom (German Cathedral), at the southern end of the square, was designed by Martin Grünberg, built in 1708 by Giovanni Simonetti and modified in 1785 after a design by Carl von Gontard, who added the domed tower. A popular Christmas market is held on the square during the holidays.

Akademie der Künste

MAP p.50, POCKET MAP B14
Pariser Platz 4 (and Hanseatenweg 10, Tiergarten) Ⓤ/Ⓢ **Brandenburger Tor**
ⓣ 030 20 05 71 000, Ⓦ www.adk.de.
General visits daily 10am–8pm; exhibitions Tues–Sun 11am–7pm. Admission varies.

Founded as the Prussian Academy of Arts in 1696 by Friedrich III, this public corporation continues its original mission to support and foster the arts. Its prestigious members have included Goethe, Mendelssohn-Bartholdy and Brecht; Max Liebermann headed the institution in the 1920s after the academy introduced a literature section. Under Hitler it was used as a headquarters for architect Albert Speer to redesign Berlin into "Germania",

Akademie der Künste

Brandenburg Gate

before being bombed almost to the ground (only the exhibition halls remained intact). During the GDR era it was turned into studios for Academy members like the sculptor Fritz Cremer and several master scholars such as Wieland Förster and Werner Stötzer. The glass-facade building, designed by Günter Behnisch, lies directly in front of what's left of the original academy, and its current members include German Nobel laureate Günter Grass, architects Daniel Libeskind and Sir Norman Foster and composer Sir Harrison Birtwistle. The venue holds a number of lectures, exhibits and workshops.

Brandenburg Gate

MAP p.50, POCKET MAP A13
Pariser Platz ⓤ/Ⓢ Brandenburger Tor
ⓣ 030 25 00 23 33.

A former city gate (the only remaining of the period), the Brandenburg Gate (Branden-burger Tor) is one of the most recognizable icons of Berlin, if not Europe. Commissioned by Friedrich Wilhelm II of Prussia as a sign of peace, and built by Carl Gotthard Langhans in 1788 from a design based upon the Propylaea (the gateway to the Acropolis in Athens), the gate has at various times been a symbol of victory, peace, division and unity. After the 1806

Prussian defeat at the Battle of Jena-Auerstedt, Napoleon took the Quadriga (added in 1793 by Johann Gottfried Schadow) to Paris. After Napoleon's defeat in 1814 and the Prussian occupation of Paris by General Ernst von Pfuel, the Quadriga was restored to Berlin. The Gate survived World War II and was one of the damaged structures still standing in the ruins of Pariser Platz in 1945. In December 2000, the Branden-burg Gate was closed for a €4 million private refurbishment by the Stiftung Denkmalschutz Berlin (Berlin Monument Conservation Foundation), reopening less than two years later. Today, it still draws punters by the busload. The best way to enjoy it is to stroll towards it via Unter den Linden, taking in the trees and run of shops, glamorous theatres and excellent museums along the way. It's a very touristy spot, so for a bit of peace and quiet pop into the Room of Silence on the north side, built specifically for visitors to rest and reflect. Since 2016, a museum right next to the Brandenburg Gate on Pariser Platz has offered a 300-year history of the city as witnessed via its iconic gate (ⓣ 030 236 078 366, ⓦ brandenburggate-museum.com; admission €9; daily 10am–6pm).

Memorial to the Murdered Jews of Europe

MAP p.50, POCKET MAP A14
Cora-Berliner-Str. 1 ⓤ/ⓈBrandenburger Tor ☎ 030 26 39 430, ⓦ holocaust-mahnmal.de. Guided tours: ☎ 030 26 39 43 36; memorial open 24hr; information centre Tues–Sun: April–Sept 10am–8pm (last entrance 7.15pm), Oct–March 10am–7pm (last entrance 6.15pm).

Peter Eisenman's hugely controversial 2711 sombre concrete slabs (stelae) are arranged in a neat grid spread across 19,000 square metres of prime Berlin real estate near the Brandenburg Gate, the memorial's grand scale intended as a reminder of the magnitude of the Holocaust. The slabs are purposefully varying in height to give visitors walking among them a sense of disorientation and confusion, though from above the slabs appear to make a wave-like form. Soon after construction began in 2003, a Swiss newspaper reported that a subsidiary of the company hired to produce the anti-graffiti substance to cover the stelae, Degussa, had created the poison gas used to exterminate so many in the Nazi death camps of the Holocaust. Rather than spend an additional €2 million to undo the work and hire another company, work continued.

As impressive as the memorial is, it's really the 800-square-metre underground **information centre** (located in the southeastern corner) that leaves you reeling. The centre holds factual exhibits to balance the abstract memorial above, including personal information about many of the victims and a video archive ("Voices of Survival") where you can listen to Holocaust survivor testimonies in many languages, or even search for specific places, people or events in the database.

The Reichstag

MAP p.50, POCKET MAP A13
Platz der Republik 1 ⓤ Bundestag ☎ 030 22 73 21 52, ⓦ bundestag.de. Roof terrace and dome accessible on prearranged guided tours only (daily 8am–midnight, last entry 10pm; free) or with a restaurant reservation (daily 9am–4.30pm & 6.30pm–midnight; ☎ 030 22 62 99 33).

The Reichstag, the seat of the German Parliament, has played a crucial role in several of the city's most significant historic events. After the founding of the German Empire in 1872, German architect Paul Wallot was commissioned to create this imposing neo-Renaissance parliament building. It was constructed between 1884 and 1894, mainly funded with wartime reparation money from France – following Prussia's defeat of France in 1871. The famous inscription "Dem Deutschen Volke" (To the German People) was added in 1916 by Wilhelm II. In 1933 a fire destroyed much of the Reichstag. Though it remains uncertain how the fire started, the Communists were blamed, giving a boost to Hitler and the Nazis, who would soon come to power. The building was further damaged

Memorial to the Murdered Jews of Europe

The Reichstag

at the end of the War, when the Soviets entered Berlin. The picture of a Red Army soldier raising the Soviet flag on the Reichstag is one of the most famous twentieth-century images and symbolized Germany's defeat. The Reichstag was rebuilt between 1958 and 1972, but the central dome and most of the ornamentation were removed. During Berlin's division the West German parliament assembled here once a year as a way to indicate that Bonn was only a temporary capital – and indeed, after reunification, the Bundestag relocated here. The building was renovated again from 1995 to 1999, when the glass dome designed by Sir Norman Foster was added. At first the subject of much controversy, the dome has become one of the city's most recognized landmarks. Since April 1999, the Reichstag is once again the seat of the Bundestag – and also one of the city's largest attractions. Not all the building is open to the public: the most popular (and accessible) part is the glass dome, which features a roof terrace, restaurant and fantastic views over the city. It's currently only open to visitors with a restaurant reservation, who have

registered to attend a sitting or lecture, or who sign up in advance for a guided tour. The audioguides (free) last twenty minutes and give all the facts about the building and the surroundings as you ascend and descend the 230m spiral staircase to the top.

St Hedwig's Cathedral

MAP p.50, POCKET MAP D14
Hinter der Katholischen Kirche 3
Ⓤ Französische Str. Ⓣ 030 20 34 810,
Ⓦ hedwigs-kathedrale.de. Visiting times
(outside services) Mon–Sat 10am–5pm,
Sun 1–5pm. Guided tours available on
request.

The seat of the archbishop of Berlin, St Hedwig's Cathedral was the first Catholic church to be built in Germany after the Protestant Reformation. Consecrated in 1773, it was completely destroyed by Allied bombs in 1943, but reconstruction began in 1952 and was finally completed in 1963. The exterior is striking, but it's also worth popping inside to see the interior of the dome, composed of 84 reinforced concrete segments, and the impressive hanging organ (built in 1978 to replace one destroyed in the War), made by Klais of Bonn.

Shops

Ampelmann Shop

MAP P.50, POCKET MAP C13
Unter den Linden 35 ⓤ Franzözische Str./
Ⓢ Friedrichstr. ☎ 030 42 02 75 56,
ⓦ ampelmann.de. Mon–Sat 9.30am–10pm,
Sun 1pm–6pm.

The very first traffic lights to
feature Karl Peglau's red and
green Ampelmännchen stood on
Unter den Linden. Fitting then,
that this flagship store is here to
pay tribute in the shape of thirty
sets of traffic lights from all over
the world, and a wealth of related
gifts and souvenirs. There's also
a small café selling coffee and
snacks.

Dussmann das KulturKaufhaus

MAP p.50, POCKET MAP C13
Friedrichstr. 90 ⓤ/Ⓢ Friedrichstr. ☎ 030
20 25 11 11. Mon–Fri 9am–midnight, Sat
9am–11.30pm.

This giant store has five levels of
books, CDs, vinyl, DVDs and a
large section of books in English
and ten other foreign languages
across two floors.

Galeries Lafayette

Galeries Lafayette

MAP p.50, POCKET MAP C14
Friedrichstr. 76–78 Ⓢ Stadtmitte ☎ 030 20
94 80. Mon–Sat 10am–8pm.

This elegant branch of the Parisian
store opened in 1996. Housed in
a glass temple designed by Jean
Nouvel, it stocks every super-
exclusive brand you can think of,
from Agent Provocateur to Yves
Saint Laurent. There's also a vast
variety of gourmet foods.

Mall of Berlin

MAP p.50, POCKET MAP B15
Leipziger Platz 12 Ⓢ Potsdamer Platz
☎ 030 20 62 17 70, ⓦ mallofberlin.de.
Mon–Sat 10am–9pm.

Housed on the site of the city's
former Wertheim Department
Store (an architectural and retail
highlight during the Weimar
era), this is Germany's biggest
shopping centre. Housing 270
stores, apartments and a hotel, it's
a modern, elegant space with a
mix of high-street names (Zara,
H&M), independent fashion
boutiques and luxury outlets
(Hugo Boss, Karl Lagerfeld).
There's a third-floor food court.

Quartier 206

MAP p.50, POCKET MAP C14
Friedrichstr. 71 Ⓢ Stadtmitte ☎ 030 20 94
65 00, ⓦ www.q206berlin.de. Mon–Fri
10.30am–7.30pm, Sat 10am–6pm.

Unapologetically posh department
store with flagships for the likes of
Etro, Gant, Wolford and Galerie
Mensing, all set in a lavish, Art
Deco-inspired interior.

Restaurants

Bocca di Bacco

MAP p.50, POCKET MAP C14
Friedrichstr. 167–168 ⓤ Franzözische Str.
☎ 030 20 67 28 28, ⓦ boccadibacco.de.
Mon–Sat noon–midnight, Sun 6pm–
midnight.

Bocca di Bacco blends a down-
to-earth atmosphere with

high-quality cuisine, inspired by Tuscany and other parts of Italy. The menu includes pasta, game, fish and plenty of wonderful desserts. The three-course lunch is a pretty good deal.

Borchardt

MAP p.50, POCKET MAP C14
Französische Str. 47 Ⓤ Französiche Str.
Ⓣ 030 81 88 62 62, Ⓦ www.borchardt-restaurant.de. Daily 11.30am–midnight.
A reincarnation of a nineteenth-century meeting place for high society, *Borchardt* mark two is a tasteful facsimile with marble columns, plush seating and an Art Nouveau mosaic that was discovered during renovations. The place draws politicians, celebrities and tourists, and cuisine is high-quality French-German, though if you're not a regular, service is likely to be offhand at best.

Cookies Cream

MAP p.50, POCKET MAP C13
Behrenstr. 55 Ⓤ Französische Str. Ⓣ 030 27 49 29 40, Ⓦ www.cookiescream.de. Tues–Sat 6–11pm.
Deliberately difficult to find (it's behind the *Westin Grand* on Friedrichstr.; see website for creative directions) this stylish restaurant is worth seeking out. Chef Stephan Hentschel has made this one of the best vegetarian restaurants in the city. At €44 for a three-course menu and €25 for a main, it's pricey but far from prohibitive, and the seasonal, inventive food is worth it.

Crackers

MAP P.50, POCKET MAP C13
Friedrichstr. 158 Ⓤ Französische Str.
Ⓣ 030 68 07 30 488, Ⓦ crackersberlin. com. Daily 7pm–midnight.
Downstairs from *Cookies Cream* (see above), the equally chic *Crackers* offers a European-nouveau menu of meat and fish (and some vegetarian options), a great cocktail bar and hip service.

Ishin

DJ dinner sets on Fri & Sat. Mains €16–33.

Fischers Fritz

MAP p.50, POCKET MAP C14
Regent Berlin, Charlottenstr. 49
Ⓤ Französische Str. Ⓣ 030 20 33 63 63, Ⓦ www.fischersfritzberlin.com. Daily 6.30–11.30am & 6.30–10.30pm.
Fischers Fritz is the domain of Christian Lohse, whose way with fish and seafood has earned him numerous accolades (including two Michelin stars). This is imaginative stuff, bursting with originality in terms of presentation, flavours and ideas. There's a price for Lohse's expertise of course, namely €140 for four courses.

Ishin

MAP p.50, POCKET MAP C13
Mittelstr. 24 Ⓤ/Ⓢ Brandenburger Tor/Friedrichstr. Ⓣ 030 20 67 48 29, Ⓦ ishin.de. Mon–Fri 11.30am–9.30pm, Sat noon–9.30pm.
There are four *Ishin* restaurants in Berlin. The interior of this central one is slightly functional but the decent, fresh sushi, good prices (full menus from €6.50) and quick service make it very popular, especially for lunch. There's a happy hour all day Wednesday and Saturday (plus Mon, Tues, Thurs & Fri till 4pm), plenty of veggie dishes and free green tea.

Käfer Dachgarten

MAP P.50, POCKET MAP A13
Platz der Republik 1 🚇 Bundestag ☎ 030
22 62 990, 🌐 feinkost-kaefer.de/berlin.
Daily 9am–4.30pm & 6.30pm–midnight
(last orders 9.15pm).

Famous for its location on the
roof of the Reichstag and its
180-degree view of eastern
Berlin, this restaurant specializes
in gourmet renditions of
regional German dishes (mains
€17.50–30). A reservation here
also means you get to avoid the
registration process through the
Bundestag.

Lutter & Wegner

MAP p.50, POCKET MAP C14
Charlottenstr. 56 🚇 Französische Str.
☎ 030 20 29 5415, 🌐 www.l-w-berlin.de.
Daily 11am–midnight.

This refined, airy Austro-German
restaurant is the finest of the
Lutter & Wagner mini empire –
it was here the wine merchant
started (in 1811). Prices are
high (set menus around €35,
mains from €15.50) but that's
what happens when The *New
York Times* crowns your Wiener
Schnitzel the best outside Vienna
(though the Sauerbraten is the real
highlight). There's a cheaper bistro
with a shorter menu too.

Cafés and bars

Café Einstein

MAP p.50, POCKET MAP B13
Unter den Linden 42 🚇/Ⓢ Brandenburger
Tor ☎ 030 20 43 632. Daily 7am–10pm.
The younger sibling to the famous
Einstein (see p.138), this branch
doesn't have the same panache,
but it's popular with Berlin's
cultural elite and serves excellent
Austro-Hungarian specialities.
Also good for a coffee and cake.

Café Nö!

MAP p.50, POCKET MAP B14
Glinkastr. 23 🚇 Französische Str. ☎ 030 20

Café Einstein

10 871, 🌐 cafe-noe.de. Mon–Fri
noon–1am, Sat 7pm–1am, kitchen till
midnight.

This wine bar-restaurant serves
good food for good prices. The
menu includes *Flammkuchen*
(from €8.50) and the like, plus
lunch deals (Mon–Fri noon–3pm)
for €10–13.

Newton Bar

MAP p.50, POCKET MAP C14
Charlottenstr. 57 🚇 Stadtmitte ☎ 030 20
29 54 21, 🌐 www.newton-bar.de. Mon–
Wed & Sun 10am–3am, Thurs–Sat
10am–4am.

Dedicated to photographer
Helmut Newton, this classy
cocktail bar, all leather chairs and
oak furnishings, is popular with
a mature, well-heeled crowd.
The large windows look out onto
Gendarmenmarkt, though since
a huge Newton photograph called
Big Nudes covers one wall, you
won't be short on eye candy either
way.

Windhorst

MAP p.50, POCKET MAP C13
Dorotheenstr. 65 🚇/Ⓢ Friedrichstr.
☎ 030 20 45 00 70. Mon–Fri 6pm–late, Sat
9pm–late.

Though it's not in a residential
area, this tucked-away cocktail
haven feels like a neighbourhood

spot. It's a smart, fairly simple place, but the cocktails are above average and go well with the jazz (on vinyl) that they love to play.

Clubs and venues

Komische Oper Berlin

MAP p.50, POCKET MAP C13
Behrenstr. 55–57 ⓤ Französische Str.
☎ 030 47 99 74 00, ⓦ www.komische-oper-berlin.de.

Presenting everything from opera and German operetta to musicals and baroque, the Comic Opera – the smallest of Berlin's three opera houses – was built between 1891 and 1892. Since 2004 it has been operated by the Berliner Opernstiftung.

Konzerthaus Berlin

MAP p.50, POCKET MAP C14
Gendarmenmarkt ⓤ Französische Str.
☎ 030 20 30 92 101 (tickets),
ⓦ konzerthaus.de.

The concert house was built on the ruins of the national theatre by Schinkel in 1821. Since 1984 it has been the home of the Konzerthausorchester Berlin and is numbered amongst the best classical concert venues in the world. Daily tours are available (for example Sat 1pm; 70min, €3).

Maxim Gorki Theater

MAP p.50, POCKET MAP D13
Am Festungsgraben 2 ⓤ/ⓢ Friedrichstr.
☎ 030 20 221 115, ⓦ www.gorki.de.

Named after the Russian socialist-realist author, this large theatre hosts classic dramas by him plus contemporary works by the likes of Fassbinder. All shows except premieres have English surtitles.

Staatsoper

MAP p.50, POCKET MAP D13
Unter den Linden 7 ⓤ Unter den Linden
☎ 030 20 35 45 55, ⓦ staatsoper-berlin.de.

This is one of the world's leading opera houses, its history going back to the eighteenth century and including illustrious conductors like Richard Strauss. Closed for renovation until 2017, performances take place at the Schiller Theater (Bismarckstr. 110; ⓤ Ernst-Reuter-Platz).

Tausend

MAP p.50, POCKET MAP B12
Schiffbauerdamm 11, Albrechtstr. ⓤ/ⓢ Friedrichstr. ☎ 030 27 58 20 70,
ⓦ tausendberlin.com. Tues–Sat from 7.30pm. €10.

Decorated with an enormous eye that emits a golden glow over the tunnel-shaped space, this upmarket bar-club, quite anonymous from the outside, attracts a dapper crowd, so it's advisable to turn up looking the part. Inside you'll find a mix of upbeat disco, jazz and R&B. At the back of the club you'll find a hidden, high-end Ibero-Asian fusion restaurant, *Cantina* – think foie gras risotto, black cod and sashimi salad. Reservations essential.

Komische Oper

Alexanderplatz and the Nikolaiviertel

Alexanderplatz – or Alex, as it's colloquially known – is one of Berlin's ugliest, bleakest and best-known squares. Named in honour of a visit from Russian Tsar Alexander I in 1805, by the start of the twentieth century it had become a commercial centre busy enough to rival Potsdamer Platz. Under the GDR it was a nondescript pedestrianized area and in 1989 was the site of the Peaceful Revolution, the largest demonstration in the history of East Germany. Today its grey, concrete GDR tower blocks, themselves towered over by the needle-like spire of the Fernsehturm (TV Tower), join more recent buildings like the Alexa shopping mall and the Saturn electronics store to create a thoroughly charmless transport hub. More scenic, though touristy, is the adjacent Nikolaiviertel, with its pretty old-town feel and various museums, a reconstruction of the historical heart of the city that dates back to the thirteenth century.

The Berliner Fernsehturm at Christmas

Berliner Fernsehturm

MAP ABOVE, POCKET MAP F12
Panoramastr. 1a Ⓤ/Ⓢ Alexanderplatz
ⓣ 030 24 75 75 875, Ⓦ www.tv-turm.de.
Daily: March–Oct 9am–midnight; Nov–Feb
10am–midnight. €13.

The city's most visible structure, the 368m concrete spike known as the Fernsehturm (television tower), is the building most likely to crop up in all your photographs when you get home – whether you realized you'd been photographing it or not. Built in 1969 as a broadcasting system for East Berlin, and intended as a showpiece structure for the GDR, visible in West Berlin, it has a visitor platform at 203m – a lift zooms you up in forty seconds – and a small photographic exhibition in the lobby where you can see how the tower was built (it took four years). Above the visitor platform, there's also a rotating restaurant, *Sphere*, that serves coffee, snacks and meals while revolving once around the tower's axis every sixty minutes. The tower receives around a million visitors a year and the queues can be long whatever the weather. You don't need a reservation for the tower, but it can be handy for the restaurant (in high season). Another option is to get a Fast Track Ticket (from €17.50 for adults, children aged 4–16 from €10), available on the website in advance, which enables you to dodge the queues and has an option for a table reservation.

If the sun's out when you're out and about, take a look up at the Fernsehturm and see if you can spot the cross that's reflected across the main steel sphere: the religious symbolism caused a great deal of embarrassment for the atheist GDR government.

DDR Museum

MAP p.61, POCKET MAP E13
Karl-Liebknecht-Str. 1 Ⓤ /
Ⓢ Alexanderplatz Ⓣ 030 84 71 23 731
(tickets), Ⓦ www.ddr-museum.de. Mon–
Fri & Sun 10am–8pm, Sat 10am–10pm.
€7 (discounts sometimes offered via
website).

Located opposite the Berliner
Dom (see p.42), this collection of
memorabilia from the Deutsche
Demokratische Republik (DDR/
GDR) makes for a fun, interactive
and informative visit. There are
screens to touch, buttons to press,
drawers to open – even a Trabant
to sit in and a bugged apartment
to listen in on.

Divided into three differently
themed areas ("Public Life", "State
and Ideology", "Life in a Tower
Block"), visitors get to inspect a
reconstruction of a GDR living
room, experience what it's like
to have your phone bugged,
and ponder the East German
penchant for public nudity – little
wonder it's one of the most visited
museums in Berlin.

Though many of the displays
feed on the current penchant for
Ostalgie, there is also an emphasis
on the darker side of GDR life –
Party, State, prison – making this
a much more rounded experience
than it used to be.

Rotes Rathaus

MAP p.61, POCKET MAP E13
Rathausstr. 15 Ⓤ Klosterstr. Ⓤ /
Ⓢ Alexanderplatz Ⓣ 030 90 260. Mon–Fri
9am–6pm. Free (ID required).

This distinctive building gets
its name (which means "red
town hall") from the red
clinker brick of its facade. The
building, inspired by Italian
High Renaissance architecture,
was erected in the 1860s. During
communist times, it was East
Berlin's town hall, when the red
in the name really came into its
own; today it's the office of the
city mayor, and is the political
centre of power in Greater
Berlin. Its neo-Renaissance
clock tower and frieze depicting
Berlin's history until 1879 in
36 terracotta plaques, each 6m

A 1970s sitting room, DDR museum

long, are its most impressive architectural features. At the top of the grand stairwell is a coat-of-arms hall and some exhibits. The building also has a cafeteria with low-price lunches.

Marienkirche

MAP p.61, POCKET MAP E12
Karl-Liebknecht-Str. 8 ⓤ/
Ⓢ Alexanderplatz Ⓦ marienkirche-berlin.
de. Daily: April–Dec 10am–6pm; Jan–April
10am–4pm (no visits during services and
concerts). Free.

Standing somewhat incongruously at the edge of Alexanderplatz and the Marx-Engels-Forum, the Marienkirche (church of St Mary) – one of Berlin's oldest churches – is the last remnant of its time in the area. Built some time in the thirteenth century, its oldest part is the granite base, upon which a hall church (Hallenkirche) stands. The tower was added during the fifteenth century, and the steeple in 1790 by Carl Gotthard Langhan, architect of the Brandenburg Gate. The church escaped heavy damage during World War II and was later fully restored. Visitors today can see *The Dance of Death* (*Totentanz*), a large fresco (2m high, 22m long), dating from about 1485, that was discovered in 1860 under layers of paint and depicts various classes of society dancing with Death. Other notable artworks include a bronze baptismal font from 1437, *The Crucifixion* painted by Michael Ribestein in 1562 and an alabaster pulpit created by Andreas Schlüter in 1703, decorated with reliefs of John the Baptist and personifications of Faith, Hope and Love.

AquaDom and SEA LIFE Center

MAP p.61, POCKET MAP E13
Spandauer Str. 3 Ⓢ Hackescher Markt
ⓣ 0180 666 690 101, Ⓦ visitsealife.com.
Daily 10am–7pm. €17.95.

Rotes Rathaus

The Sea Life Center's chief claim to fame is the AquaDom – the world's largest cylindrical fish aquarium, a 25m-tall acrylic glass aquarium, with built-in transparent elevator, located right in the lobby of the adjacent *Radisson SAS* hotel. Filled with around 900,000 litres of seawater, the aquarium contains around 1500 fish, covering 56 species. The AquaDom can be visited separately, but visitors who want a broader overview of the underwater world can visit the Sea Life Center first, a succession of themed tunnels that illustrate marine life from various habitats including the Spree and the Pacific Ocean. It's insightful enough and a well-laid-out exhibition, though it lacks the comprehensive scope and diversity – not to mention the manatees and sharks – of the Zoo Aquarium (see p.125).

Ephraim Palais

MAP p.61, POCKET MAP E13
Poststr. 16, corner Mühlendamm
Ⓤ Klosterstr. or Ⓤ/Ⓢ Alexanderplatz
☏ 030 24 00 21 62, Ⓦ stadtmuseum.de.
Tues & Thurs–Sun 10am–6pm, Wed
noon–8pm. €5.

This attractive Rococo-style
residential palace, located in
the southern corner of Berlin's
Nikolaiviertel, is a replica of
a 1762 original built by Veitel
Heine Ephraim, a court jeweller.
His original building was torn
down in 1935–36 when the
Mühlendamm was widened, but
a painstaking reconstruction has
produced an exquisite place, with
its elegantly curving, decorated
facade (complete with cherubs),
Tuscan columns, wrought-iron
balconies and an oval staircase
and ornate ceiling crafted by
Schlüter. As well as special
exhibitions on themes relating to
the history and culture of Berlin,
the "Salon Ephraim" and the
Museum Laboratory offer family-
friendly events and workshops.

Märkisches Museum

MAP p.61, POCKET MAP F14
Am Köllnischen Park 5 Ⓤ /
Ⓢ Jannowitzbrücke ☏ 030 24 00 21 62,
Ⓦ www.stadtmuseum.de. Tues & Thurs–
Sun 10am–6pm, Wed noon–8pm. €6.

The red-brick Märkisches
Museum, built at the turn of
the twentieth century, is the
headquarters of Berlin's City
Museum Foundation. The
permanent exhibition "Here
is Berlin" invites you to stroll
through the city's streets
and discover how Berlin has
changed over the centuries. The
museum also hosts a wide array
of art-historic collections in its
atmospheric rooms, with medieval
sculptures, artefacts and paintings
telling the story of Berlin from the
first settlers until now (German
text only). Thoughtfully divided
into sections of the city – Unter
den Linden, Friedrichstrasse

Märkisches Museum

and so on – favourites include
a working mechanical musical
instrument that's shown off every
Sunday (3pm), seven original
graffitied segments of the Berlin
Wall and a Kaiserpanorama:
a stereoscope dating from
around 1900 that produces a
fascinating 3D show of images
from nineteenth-century Berlin.
Note that the museum and its
exhibitions will be undergoing a
comprehensive overhaul in 2018.

Hanf Museum

MAP p.61, POCKET MAP E13
Mühlendamm 5 Ⓤ/Ⓢ Alexanderplatz or
Ⓤ Klosterstr. ☏ 030 24 24 827,
Ⓦ hanfmuseum.de. Tues–Fri 10am–8pm,
Sat & Sun noon–8pm. €4.50.

The Hanf Museum is 300
square metres of space devoted
exclusively to the agricultural,
manufacturing, industrial and
legal aspects of hemp – a plant
most commonly associated
with marijuana. This museum,
while slightly dingy, isn't just
for the stoners: the aim is to
give a broader overview of this
fascinating botanical treasure
and its myriad applications,
from textile and paper to
medicine and cosmetics. Texts
are in German only.

Shops

Apartment

MAP p.61, POCKET MAP F12
Memhardstr. 8 Ⓤ/Ⓢ Alexanderplatz Ⓣ 030
28 04 22 51. Mon–Sat 2–7pm.

You'll have to be careful not to walk right past what looks like an all-white art space: the goods lie downstairs (follow the spiral staircase), where you'll find jeans, jackets, shoes and accessories with a distinctly Berlin twist.

Burg & Schild

MAP p.61, POCKET MAP E12
Rosa-Luxemburg-Str. 3
Ⓤ Rosa-Luxemburg-Platz Ⓣ 030 24 63 05
01. Mon–Sat 11am–7pm.

Visit a long-vanished America by way of brands like Iron Heart, Indigofera, Filson and Buzz Rickson's, all on display alongside vintage motorbikes that generate an authentic odour of oil and tar.

Esther Perbandt

MAP p.61, POCKET MAP E12
Almstadtstr. 3 Ⓤ Weinmeisterstr. Ⓣ 030 88
53 67 91. Mon–Fri 10am–7pm, Sat noon–6pm.

A relative veteran of the Berlin fashion scene, Esther Perbandt sells (priccy) rock and avant-garde styles with an audaciously gender-bending slant. As well as clothing, expect bags, belts and jewellery.

Mykita

MAP p.61, POCKET MAP F12
Rosa-Luxemburg-Str. 6 Ⓤ/
Ⓢ Alexanderplatz Ⓣ 030 67 30 87 15.
Mon–Fri 11am–7pm, Sat noon–6pm.

Sunglasses and spectacles with a stylish twist, sold in a hip, minimal space with large street-facing windows. Berlin-based Mykita opened in 2003, and has achieved international prominence.

Trüffelschwein

MAP p.61, POCKET MAP F11
Rosa-Luxemburg-Str. 21
Ⓤ Rosa-Luxemburg-Platz Ⓣ 030 70 22 12
25. Mon–Fri noon–8pm, Sat noon–7pm.

This pleasant, airy store sells everything from sexy shoes and trendy jumpers to belts and dapper swimwear. Labels include Hannes Roether, La Panoplie, Howlin', Superga and La Paz.

Wood Wood

MAP p.61, POCKET MAP E12
Rochstr. 3–4 Ⓤ/Ⓢ Alexanderplatz Ⓣ 030
28 04 78 77, Ⓦ www.woodwood.com.
Mon–Fri noon–8pm, Sat noon–7pm.

One of the best stops in the area for all things streetwear, this long-serving Berlin branch of Copenhagen-based Wood Wood stocks an incredible sneaker collection plus contemporary fashion items.

ALEXANDERPLATZ AND THE NIKOLAIVIERTEL

Burg & Schild

Restaurants

Emmas

MAP p.61, POCKET MAP E13
Heiligegeistkirchplatz 1 Ⓢ Hackescher
Markt ⓣ 030 24 63 17 32, ⓦ emmas.berlin.
Daily 11.30am–midnight.

Smart bistro specializing in simple
fresh German food of the meat
and potatoes variety, but with the
addition of more fresh veggies
and modern twists to make things
less stodgy. It's a particularly good
choice for inexpensive lunches
(€8.20), such as carrot and ginger
soup followed by a rich goulash.

Lebensmittel in Mitte

MAP p.61, POCKET MAP E12
Rochstr. 2 Ⓤ Weinmeisterstr. ⓣ 030 27 59
61 30. Mon–Fri noon–midnight, Sat 11am–
midnight.

If you're a fan of "slow" home
cooking this unassuming spot
on Rochstrasse is a good choice.
Specializing in German cuisine
(mainly from the south), the
menu features hearty soups,
sausages, sauerkraut and *Spätzle*

(a type of soft egg noodle), as well
as a decent selection of German/
Austrian wines and Bavarian
beer, all served against a homely,
elegant backdrop.

Zille Stube

MAP p.61, POCKET MAP E13
Spreeufer 3 Ⓤ Klosterstr. ⓣ 030 24 25 247,
ⓦ zillestube-nikolaiviertel.de. Daily
11am–10pm; Heinrich Zille show Tues
3–5pm.

A great place to break up a
stroll around the Nikolaiviertel,
the menu here features Berlin
specialities like *Currywurst*
and *Eisbein* (knuckle of pork),
all served in cosy, time-warp
surroundings. Named after the
area's most famous caricaturist,
Heinrich Zille, there's a two-hour
show every Tuesday at 3pm
that transports guests back to
the artist's turn-of-the-century
Berlin.

Zur Letzten Instanz

MAP p.61, POCKET MAP F13
Waisenstr. 14–16 Ⓤ Klosterstr. ⓣ 030 24
25 528, ⓦ www.zurletzteninstanz.de. Mon
6pm–1am, Tues–Sat noon–1am.

Yes it's the oldest restaurant in
Berlin (the building goes right
back to 1561), yes the interior
is textbook Alt Berlin, and yes
it's a tourist haunt, but the food
here – traditional dishes like pork
knuckle, dumplings and Berlin
meatballs – is delicious and care
is taken to source ingredients
from local producers. Portions
are hearty and there's Pilsner on
draught to wash it all down.

Cafés and bars

Dolores

MAP p.61, POCKET MAP E12
Rosa-Luxemburg-Str. 7 Ⓤ /
Ⓢ Alexanderplatz ⓣ 030 28 09 95 97,
ⓦ www.dolores-online.de. Mon–Sat
11.30am–10pm, Sun 1–10pm.

Run by Germans who spent a
considerable time in California,

Dolores

Oliv

Berlin's first burrito shop is a basic but colourful spot that offers preprepared "classics", "make-your-own", customizable burritos and also quesadillas, salads and soups. A good spot for a cheap, filling bite (burritos from €5) or takeaway. There is a second branch in Schöneberg (Bayreuther Str. 36 Ⓤ Wittenbergplatz).

Oliv

MAP p.61, POCKET MAP E12
Münzstr. 8 Ⓤ Weinmeisterstr./
Rosa-Luxemburg-Platz ☎ 030 89 20 65 40,
Ⓦ www.oliv-cafe.de. Mon–Fri
8.30am–7pm, Sat 9.30am–7pm, Sun
10am–6pm.

With a modern interior, great coffee and decent, unpretentious food (sandwiches, quiches, soups, cakes), *Oliv* is a pleasant spot for breakfast or lunch, and very conveniently located if you're seeking respite from boutique bashing. Cash only.

Clubs and venues

Golden Gate

MAP p.61, POCKET MAP J5
Dircksenstr. 77–78 Ⓤ/Ⓢ Jannowitzbrücke
☎ 030 28 29 295, Ⓦ goldengate-berlin.de.
Wed from 10pm, Thurs–Sat from 11pm.
Lurking beneath the tracks near Jannowitzbrücke train station (close to the river Spree), this club consists of two wilfully shabby rooms kitted out in secondhand furniture and is dedicated to two- or three-day-long free-for-alls. The crowds here tend to be a dressed-down, unpretentious lot who arrive well after midnight to try their luck with the difficult bouncers. Music policy is mostly house and techno but there are sometimes surprises.

House of Weekend

MAP p.61, POCKET MAP F12
Alexanderstr. 7 (15th floor and open rooftop) Ⓤ/Ⓢ Alexanderplatz ☎ 0152 24 29 31 40. Summer daily from 7pm; winter Fri–Sun from 11pm. €10–12.
Accessed via a lift that shoots punters up to the top of a Communist-era tower block, this chic, spacious club has attained veteran status in the city thanks to its consistently good house and techno parties. International guests and high-profile residents play most weekends. The wonderful roof terrace – open from 7pm daily in summer – is a must.

Potsdamer Platz and Tiergarten

A major public transport hub and popular entertainment district, Potsdamer Platz was one of the liveliest squares in Europe during the 1920s. Reduced to rubble during the War, afterwards it became – literally – a no-man's land, sandwiched between the different sectors. What little remained was levelled when the Berlin Wall went up in 1961. After the Wall fell, it became the largest construction site in Europe as an ambitious rebuilding programme started. Commercial, even futuristic in tone, the centrepiece today is the Sony Center, surrounded by a new U-Bahn station and a few slabs from the old Berlin Wall. Just to the west is the Kulturforum, a fine collection of cultural institutions, built in the 1960s as West Berlin's response to East Berlin's Museumsinsel, including the Gemäldegalerie, and its important collections of Old Masters. Adjacent to the Platz is the Tiergarten, Berlin's oldest and most beautiful park.

Sony Center

MAP p.70, POCKET MAP A15
Potsdamer Str. 4 ⓤ/Ⓢ Potsdamer Platz
ⓦ www.sonycenter.de. Free.
The striking, ecofriendly, glass-and-steel Sony Center, by Helmut Jahn, opened in 2000 and cost a cool €750 million to build. The centre houses shops for everything from cosmetics and jewellery to, of course, Sony electronics, plus restaurants, a conference centre, art and film museums, cinemas, including an **IMAX**, and a **Legoland** (daily 10am–7pm; ⓦ legolanddiscoverycentre .de; €14–18.50, according to time slots). The "Forum", the semi-enclosed roofed space, is used for occasional cultural and entertainment events. There's

Sony Center

The view from the Panoramapunkt

plenty to do, although the experience is generally soulless and the shopping expensive (though there is free wi-fi).

Film and Television Museum

MAP p.70, POCKET MAP A15
Potsdamer Str. 2 ⓤ / Ⓢ Potsdamer Platz
ⓣ 030 30 09 030, ⓦ deutsche-kinemathek. de. Tues–Sun 10am–6pm, Thurs till 8pm. €7; free Thurs 4–8pm.

One of the must-sees in the Sony Center is the impressively slick **Deutsche Kinemathek** museum, which collects German cinema under one roof. This "journey through film history" explores the pioneering years, silent-film divas, films from the Weimar era, cinema under the Nazis and goes right up to contemporary cinema, with rooms that cover postwar German filmmakers (1946–80) and the present (from 1981). As well as a special exhibit on Germany's biggest star, Marlene Dietrich, there's memorabilia and model film sets from key directors including Fritz Lang and an exhibit that compares East and West German television broadcasts. The museum also organizes the retrospective section of the Berlinale film festival, and hosts special film series, exhibitions and events.

Kollhoff Tower

MAP p.70, POCKET MAP A15
Potsdamer Platz 1 ⓤ / Ⓢ Potsdamer Platz
ⓣ 030 25 93 70 80, ⓦ panoramapunkt.de.
Platform winter: daily 10am–6pm; summer: daily 10am–8pm; last lift 30min before closing. €7.50.

Located on the northern edge of Potsdamer Platz, the 25-storey (103m), dark, peat-fired brick Kollhoff Tower is named after architect Hans Kollhoff, a member of the international team of architects (headed by Renzo Piano) that designed many of the buildings for the new Platz. The ground floor houses a number of restaurants and shops, the upper floors are used for office space and – the real highlight – the **Panoramapunkt** on the top floors, offers an open-air viewing platform, reached via Europe's fastest elevator. From the top you can see the Reichstag, Brandenburg Gate, TV Tower, Sony Center, Tiergarten and Kulturforum. Admission includes entry to the viewing platform, an exhibition on the history of the area and there's also a café.

Daimler Contemporary

MAP BELOW, POCKET MAP A15
Alte Potsdamer Str. 5, in Haus Huth ⓤ/
Ⓢ Potsdamer Platz ☏ 030 25 94 14 20,
ⓦ www.collection.daimler.com. Daily
11am–6pm. Free.

The Daimler art collection was
set up in 1977 as a space for
twentieth-century art, initially
mainly focused on German
artists. The museum expanded
in the 1990s with works by
other European and American
artists, including Andy Warhol
and Jeff Koons, and moved into
the elaborately renovated Haus
Huth in 1999. The collection
includes approximately 1800
works by international artists,
showcased in rotating exhibitions
across this attractive 600-square-
metre space, which used to be a
restaurant and storage area. Much
of the collection is modernist in
nature – geometric, challenging
and abstract – so not one for
traditionalists.

Gemäldegalerie

MAP BELOW, POCKET MAP E6
Matthäikirchplatz 4/6 ⓤ/Ⓢ Potsdamer
Platz ☏ 030 26 62 951, ⓦ smb.museum.
Tues–Sun 10am–6pm (Thurs until 8pm).
€10.

With a history that goes back to
1830, the Gemäldegalerie holds
one of the world's most renowned
collections of classical European
painting. Created from the
treasures of the Prussian royalty
– including that of Frederick the
Great – the collection used to be
part of Museum Island (see p.42).
The museum – and some of the
works – were damaged by Allied
bombing during World War II,
and the artworks were then split
between East and West during
the Cold War. After the Wall
fell the collection came together
again here. Spread across 72

Gemäldegalerie

rooms, divided up by country, with sections on Italian, Flemish and Dutch works, the treasures include many high points of European art by including works by Bruegel, a particularly good selection by Cranach (pictured), Dürer, Raphael, Rubens, Vermeer and many others. The Rembrandt room and Caravaggio's exquisite Cupid, *Love Conquers All*, are both well worth seeking out.

POTSDAMER PLATZ AND TIERGARTEN

Kunstgewerbemuseum

MAP p.70, POCKET MAP E6
Matthäikirchplatz ①/⑤ Potsdamer Platz
☏ 030 26 64 24 242, ⓦ smb.museum.
Tues–Sun 10am–6pm. €8.

Following a major renovation,
Berlin's Museum of Decorative
Arts – one of the oldest in
Germany – reopened in 2014 and
provides a systematic overview
of the key achievements in
European design. Over 7000
square metres of white-walled
space, the museum covers
all major styles and periods,
including jaw-dropping silks,
tapestries, Renaissance bronzes,
contemporary furniture,
Rococo glassware, faïence
work, porcelain, gold and silver.
Newer areas include a Fashion
Gallery – which houses around
130 costumes and accessories
representing 150 years of fashion
history – plus the departments of
Design (think Bauhaus classics
mixed with contemporary
designers like Philippe Starck
and Konstantin Grcic), Jugendstil
and Art Deco. A second
collection can be found at
Schloss Köpenick (Schlossinsel
1 ⑤ Köpenick; April–Sept Tues–
Sun 11am–6pm; Oct–March
Thurs–Sun 11am–5pm; €6),
a Baroque palace located in a
picturesque setting on an island
in the river Dahme. Exhibited
here are over five hundred items
from the sixteenth to eighteenth
centuries, as well as Renaissance,
Baroque and Rococo furniture
and interior decorations.

Kupferstichkabinett

MAP p.70, POCKET MAP E6
Matthäikirchplatz ①/⑤ Potsdamer Platz
☏ 030 26 64 24 242, ⓦ smb.museum/kk.
Tues–Fri 10am–6pm, Sat & Sun
11am–6pm; study room Tues–Fri
9am–4pm. €6.

The Kupferstichkabinett, or
"print room", is the largest
collection of graphic art in
Germany, and one of the four

Berliner Philharmonie

most important museums of its
kind in the world. The museum
houses over 500,000 prints and
110,000 drawings, watercolours,
pastels and oil sketches from
European artists from the
Middle Ages to the present, all
on paper. Major artists such
as Sandro Botticelli, Albrecht
Dürer, Rembrandt, Adolph
von Menzel, Pablo Picasso and
Andy Warhol are represented.
Due to the size and sensitivity
of the collection (being largely
on paper), there's no permanent
display – visitors must check for
special exhibitions, or request
to see specific artworks via the
study room.

Berliner Philharmonie

MAP p.70, POCKET MAP E6
Herbert-von-Karajan-Str. 1 ①/
⑤ Potsdamer Platz ☏ 030 25 48 80,
ⓦ www.berliner-philharmoniker.de.
Built by architect Hans Scharoun
between 1960 and 1963, the
Berliner Philharmonie is one of
the most important concert halls
in Berlin and home to the world-
renowned Berlin Philharmonic.
The asymmetrical, tent-like
building has an equally distinctive

pentagon-shaped concert hall (plus a smaller hall, Kammermusiksaal, which seats 1180) that enables great views from all sides. Guided tours of both the Philharmonic Hall and the Chamber Music Hall are offered daily from 1pm (☎ 030 25 48 81 34; €5/€3).

Musikinstrumenten-Museum

MAP p.70, POCKET MAP E6
Tiergartenstr. 1 (visitors' entrance Ben-Gurion-Str.) Ⓤ/Ⓢ Potsdamer Platz ☎ 030 25 48 11 78, Ⓦ simpk.de. Tues, Wed & Fri 9am–5pm, Thurs 9am–8pm, Sat & Sun 10am–5pm. €6 including audioguide; guided tours Sat (11am) & Thurs (6pm) €3 extra.

The Musikinstrumenten-Museum embraces Germany's glorious musical history, with over three thousand instruments from the sixteenth to the twenty-first centuries, making it one of the country's largest collections. Many are on permanent display here, including a rare Stradivarius violin, Frederick the Great's flutes, a glass harmonica invented by Benjamin Franklin and – the flamboyant centrepiece – a massive Mighty Wurlitzer theatre organ once owned by the Siemens family, which is demonstrated every Saturday at noon. The museum also veers into electronic music with electric guitars, mixing stations and other experimental instruments, including the Mixtur-Trautonium on which composer Oskar Sala created sound effects for Hitchcock's film *The Birds*.

Neue Nationalgalerie

MAP p.70, POCKET MAP E6
Potsdamer Str. 50 Ⓤ/Ⓢ Potsdamer Platz ☎ 030 26 64 23 040, Ⓦ smb.museum/nng. Tues, Wed, & Fri 10am–6pm, Thurs 10am–8pm, Sat & Sun 11am–6pm. €10.
The "temple of light and glass" (as it's modestly known) and its sculpture gardens were famously designed by Bauhaus affiliate Ludwig Mies van der Rohe. Opened in 1968, the museum houses an extensive collection of twentieth-century European paintings, and sculptures from the nineteenth century to the 1960s, including household names like Bacon, Picasso, Klee, Dix and plenty of German art (E.L. Kirchner, Beckmann). The museum displays portions of its permanent collection on a rotating basis, so each visit is different, and a number of special exhibitions also occur throughout the year, during which the permanent collection may not be on view. There's also a café on the ground floor (10.30am–5.45pm). Note, however, that the museum closed at the end of 2014 for refurbishments, with no reopening date specified.

Museum für Kommunikation

MAP p.70, POCKET MAP C15
Leipziger Str. 16 Ⓤ Stadtmitte ☎ 030 20 29 40, Ⓦ www.mfk-berlin.de. Tues 9am–8pm, Wed–Fri 9am–5pm, Sat & Sun 10am–6pm. €5.
Founded in 1872 as the first postal museum of the world, the Museum for Communication experienced a rebirth in 2000, as evidenced by the blue neon writing on the neo-Baroque facade and robots in the lobby. A permanent exhibition showcases the origins, development and future perspectives of the "information society", while highlights of the permanent exhibition are wax seals, postcards and stamps (such as the famous Blue Mauritius), telephones (including some of the first), radios, film, telegraphs and computers. The museum's interactive and lively approach makes it an ideal destination for kids, but adults will appreciate the temporary exhibitions featuring cutting-edge artists.

Haus der Kulturen der Welt

The German Resistance Memorial Center

MAP p.70, POCKET MAP D6
Stauffenbergstr. 13–14 (entrance through the commemorative courtyard); tram M29 to "Gedenkstätte Deutscher Widerstand" ☎ 030 26 99 50 00, ⓦ www.gdw-berlin.de. Mon–Wed & Fri 9am–6pm, Thurs 9am–8pm, Sat & Sun 10am–6pm. Free.

Located in a historic section of the former headquarters of the Nazi army high command, the site of the assassination attempt on Adolf Hitler on July 20, 1944, the **Gedenkstätte Deutscher Widerstand** (German Resistance Memorial Center) documents the action taken against the Nazis between 1933 and 1945. The permanent exhibition has over five thousand photographs and documents spread across eighteen topics that go beyond Nazi dissent to address the wider context of resistance, including the role of Christian beliefs in protest, opposition by young people specifically and general defiance of wartime environments in daily life. The memorial courtyard, meanwhile, is dedicated to the conspiring German army officers who were killed after the assassination attempt. The exhibition is in German and English.

Bauhaus Museum

MAP p.70, POCKET MAP D6
Klingelhöferstr. 14 ⓤ Nollendorfplatz ☎ 030 25 40 020, ⓦ www.bauhaus.de. Daily except Tues 10am–5pm. €8, concessions €5 (includes audio tour).

Germany's Bauhaus ("building house") design school may have only lasted from 1919 to 1933 but it went on to became one of the twentieth century's most influential movements – more famous outside the country than Goethe or Schiller. Founded by Walter Gropius, the movement explored the links between fine art and craftsmanship and – a bit later – art and mass production. The Bauhaus Archive and Museum, housed in a distinctive building designed by Gropius himself, is the best place to explore the breadth and depth of Bauhaus's expansive activities. Here are tubular steel furniture from Marcel Breuer, armchairs and desks from Mies van der Rohe, paintings from Itten, Schlemmer, Feininger, Albers and Klee… even dapper wallpaper and beautiful chess sets. The museum shop stocks an impressive range of high-quality reproductions, and there's an adjoining café.

Haus der Kulturen der Welt

MAP p.70, POCKET MAP E5
John-Foster-Dulles-Allee 10 ⓤ /
ⓈBundestag ⓣ030 39 78 71 75,
ⓦhkw.de. Daily 10am–7pm. Exhibitions:
daily except Tues 11am–7pm; free entry
Mon, varies at other times.

Known as the "pregnant oyster"
because of its distinctively
curvaceous facade, the House
of World Cultures hosts
exhibitions with a focus on
artistic and cultural movements
in contemporary global
societies. Formerly known as the
Kongresshalle conference hall, the
building, designed in 1957 by US
architect Hugh Stubbins Jr, was a
gift from the United States (John
F. Kennedy spoke here during his
1963 visit to West Berlin). In 1980
the roof collapsed, injuring many
people (and killing one) and was
rebuilt in its original style in 1987.
The building's maze of rooms
include two exhibition halls,
auditorium for concerts and
theatre and a congress hall, and
it is an ideal location for the
colourful variety of events held
here throughout the year. The
eclectic and globally minded
spread of events range from
educational programmes to
exhibitions, music, performing
arts, literature festivals and more.

From 2018, the current museum
will be closed for expansion, but
exhibitions will be held in a venue
on the same site.

The Tiergarten

MAP p.70, POCKET MAP D5
Full of paths, forested areas, lakes
and meadows, the luscious and
vast Tiergarten park – bisected by
Strasse des 17. Juni – began its life
as the preferred hunting ground
for the electors of Brandenburg.
Designed in its current form in
1830 by landscape architect Peter
Joseph Lenne, it is now one of the
most relaxing spots in Berlin, and is
dotted with a couple of interesting
attractions, with the Siegessäule its
focal point.

Siegessäule

MAP p.70, POCKET MAP D5
Grosser Stern 1 ⓤHansaplatz. April–Oct
Mon–Fri 9.30am–6.30pm, Sat & Sun
9.30am–7pm; Nov–March Mon–Fri
10am–5pm, Sat & Sun 10am–5.30pm. €3.

You can't miss the huge victory
column at the centre of the
"Grosser Stern" (great star)
roundabout in the Tiergarten. The
cocksure monument is otherwise
known as the-tricky-to-pronounce
Siegessäule, built from 1864 to
1873 after a design by Johann
Heinrich Stack to commemorate
the Prussian victory in the Prusso-
Danish war of 1864. It's 69m (25ft)
tall, weighs 35 tonnes and features
a Goddess of Victory on top,
added later after further Prussian
victories in wars against Austria
and France. At the base you can
see bas-reliefs of battles and at the
top there's an observatory, which
gives great views of the Reichstag,
the Brandenburg Gate and the
Fernschturm, but you have to climb
the 285 steps to access it. There's
also a small café, souvenir shop and
small exhibition connecting the
column with the events in German
history that it represents.

Siegessäule

POTSDAMER PLATZ AND TIERGARTEN

Tiergarten

Schloss Bellevue

MAP p.70, POCKET MAP D5
Spreeweg 1 ⓤ Hansaplatz. Closed to the public.

Situated on an area of 20 hectares (about 50 acres) beside the river Spree, Schloss Bellevue was built for Prince August Ferdinand of Prussia, the younger brother of Frederick II of Prussia. The sparkling white home was designed by architect Philipp Daniel Boumann and has the distinction of being the first Neoclassical building constructed in Germany. It was uninhabited in the nineteenth century and used by various institutions such as a museum of ethnography in the 1930s. In 1938, the building was converted into a guesthouse of the government and the entrance to the palace was redesigned. Severely damaged in World War II, it was renovated during 1954–59 and set up as the official residence of the federal president in Berlin. The main sights include a ballroom designed by Carl Gotthard Langhans, the huge lawn behind the palace and the modern building to the south – known as the "presidential egg" due to its oval shape. The palace is currently closed to visitors.

Buchstabenmuseum

MAP p.65, POCKET MAP C4
Stadtbahnbogen 424 Ⓢ Bellevue/
ⓤ Hansaplatz ☎ 0177 42 01 587, ⓦ www.
buchstabenmuseum.de. Open by appointment only. €6.50.

Buchstaben means "letter" (as in "alphabetic character"), and this unique museum – formerly located near Alexanderplatz before moving to this larger space near the Hansaviertel in 2016 – is dedicated solely to the preservation and protection of artisan-esque examples of lettering in the age of digitalization. Though the museum is still building its permanent collection, the assortment of old and new industrial signs is well worth navigating the slightly eccentric opening hours for. Though the museum collects lettering of any language, the ultimate goal is to honour "local colour", which museum founder Barbara Dechant feels is waning.

Shop

Andreas Murkidis

MAP p.70, pocket map E7
Potsdamer Str. 81 ⓤ Kurfürstenstr. ☎ 030
68 07 98 30, ⓦ andreasmurkudis.com.
Mon–Sat 10am–8pm.

Set in the former *Tagesspiegel*
newspaper building, this vast,
white, bright space designed by
lead architects Gonzales Haase is
almost all used to highlight the
high end (and sometimes pointedly
eccentric) products selected by
Andreas Murkudis, the brother of
fashion designer Kostas Murkudis.
The latter's designs are here, as
are Valextra briefcases and quality
brands like Pringle and Céline.

Restaurants

Angkor Wat

MAP p.70, POCKET MAP D4
Paulstr. 22 ⓤ/ⓢ Hauptbahnhof ☎ 030 39
33 922, ⓦ www.angkorwatrestaurant.de.
Tues–Fri 6–11pm, Sat & Sun noon–11pm.

This cavernous restaurant serves
a mean Cambodian fondue. The
friendly service makes up for the
exotic decor, and if you don't like
frying your own meat, the menu
extends to other Cambodian
classics with plenty of spices and
creamy coconut.

Facil

MAP p.70, POCKET MAP A15
The Mandala Hotel, Potsdamer Str. 3 ⓤ/
ⓢ Potsdamer Platz ☎ 030 59 005 ext 1234,
ⓦ www.facil.de. Mon–Fri noon–3pm &
7–11pm, closed Sat & Sun.

Michael Kempf's restaurant in
The Mandala Hotel not only offers
amazing food but also splendid
views from its fifth-floor dining
room, surrounded by a lush
bamboo garden. Popular with
business types, politicos and
serious foodies, Kempf's Michelin-
starred, fish-heavy menu has
become justly famous. Evening

mains range from €21 to €74; try
a lunch for something slightly
cheaper (€21 for one course, €51
for three; reservations required).

Hugos

MAP p.70, POCKET MAP C6
Hotel InterContinental, Budapester Str. 2
ⓤ Zoologischer Garten ☎ 030 26 02 12 63,
ⓦ www.hugos-restaurant.de. Tues–Sat
6.30–10.30pm, closed mid-July to mid-Aug.

In a gorgeously appointed
room at the top of the *Hotel
InterContinental*, master
chef Eberhard Lange creates
Michelin-starred "New German–
Mediterranean" food that you
can sample – for a price – while
enjoying the restaurant's
panoramic views (menus
€98–142).

Joseph Roth Diele

MAP p.70, POCKET MAP E7
Potsdamer Str. 75 ⓤ Kurfürstenstr. ☎ 030
26 36 98 84, ⓦ www.joseph-roth-diele.de.
Mon–Fri 10am–midnight.

A splash of charm and colour on
nondescript Potsdamer Strasse,
this quirky restaurant pays
homage to interwar Jewish writer
Joseph Roth. The daily specials
are very reasonable (€4.95–9.95),
though the food is far from high
end. Popular with a wide range of
people at lunchtimes.

Joseph Roth Diele

Paris-Moskau

MAP p.70, POCKET MAP E4
Alt-Moabit 141 ⓤ/Ⓢ Hauptbahnhof ☎ 030
39 42 081, ⓦ paris-moskau.de. Daily from
6pm.

This curious mix of old Berlin and contemporary elegance is set in a nineteenth-century rail signalman's house (it's named after the Paris–Moscow line) and serves hearty dishes like deer and rabbit, fish dishes and vegetarian lasagne with beetroot and chestnuts (€39–65). It's all backed up by a fine wine list and a great summer garden with views of the government quarter. Note that it's only open for lunch midweek.

Cafés and bars

Café am Neuen See

MAP p.70, POCKET MAP C6
Lichtensteinallee 2 ⓤ Zoologischer Garten
☎ 30 25 44 930, ⓦ cafeamneuensee.de.
Daily 9am–midnight.

A fine stop-off on any tour of the Tiergarten, this old-school beer

Café Buchwald

garden with modern restaurant (reservations required for larger groups) offers great coffee and draught beers, and a menu including pizza and pasta dishes (€10). It's beautifully set on the Neuen See lake, and there are even rowing boats for rent.

Café Buchwald

MAP p.70, POCKET MAP C4
Bartningallee 29 ⓤ Hansaplatz ☎ 030 39
15 931, ⓦ konditorei-buchwald.de. May–
Sept Mon–Sat 8am–7pm, Sun 9am–7pm;
Oct–April Mon–Sat 8am–6pm, Sun
9am–6pm.

A short stroll down a pleasant path from Schloss Bellevue, *Café Buchwald* has been standing here for over 160 years. Not just standing but selling some of the best cakes in town – former suppliers to the court, they still make such delicious confections as home-made *Baumkuchen*. There are a few seats in the charming little front garden.

Kumpelnest 3000

MAP p.70, POCKET MAP E7
Lützowstr. 23 ⓤ Kurfürstenstr. ☎ 030 26
16 918, ⓦ www.kumpelnest3000.com.
Daily from 7pm.

Hard to believe that this charming den of iniquity is only a few minutes' stroll from Potsdamer Platz. With its deliberately tacky decor, loyal mixed/gay crowd and anything-goes atmosphere, especially at weekends, it's a good place if you're in the area and looking for the lure of the mirrored discoball rather than the commercial glare of the Platz.

Salomon Bagels

MAP p.70, POCKET MAP A15
Alte Potsdamer Str. 7, inside Potsdamer
Platz Arkaden ⓤ/Ⓢ Potsdamer Platz ☎ 030
25 29 76 26, ⓦ www.salomon-bagels.de.
Mon–Sat 10am–9pm, Sun noon–9pm.

Bagels, bagels, bagels. And sandwiches. And excellent cakes, like their New York-style cheesecake. Located in a mall, this shop does takeaways, but there are sofas too – a good spot for a cheap snack (€6–13).

Schleusenkrug

MAP p.70, POCKET MAP B6
Müller-Breslau-Str. corner Unterschleuse
Ⓤ/Ⓢ Zoologischer Garten ☎ 030 31 39 909, Ⓦ www.schleusenkrug.de. Daily: summer 11am–midnight; winter 11am–6pm.

A classic Berlin beer garden, *Schleusenkrug* is a fine place to tuck into a glass of beer and an organic *Wurst*, enjoy a coffee while watching the boats cruise down the canal, or lap up the live music they sometimes have in the summer.

Sushi Express

MAP p.70, POCKET MAP A15
Potsdamer Platz 2 Ⓤ/Ⓢ Potsdamer Platz ☎ 030 26 55 80 55, Ⓦ sushi-expressberlin.de. Mon–Fri 11.30am–10pm, Sat noon–10pm, Sun 2–8pm.

It's a bit of a hassle to find, but *Sushi Express* – located in the Sony Center courtyard in a passage to the S-Bahn – offers a decent range of conveyor-belt sushi, especially when half-price offers are on (daily 11.30am–9pm). Hot dishes and lunchboxes also available, though it's usually packed at lunchtimes. Main courses €5.

Victoria Bar

MAP p.70, POCKET MAP E7
Potsdamer Str. 102 Ⓤ Kurfürstenstr. ☎ 030 25 75 99 77, Ⓦ victoriabar.de. Mon–Thurs & Sun 6.30pm–3am, Fri & Sat 6.30pm–4am.

This much-loved cocktail bar is great for a low-key and decently mixed drink in the week or a livelier atmosphere at weekends. The long bar, subdued lighting and discreet but upbeat music create a decent buzz.

Weilands Wellfood

MAP p.70, POCKET MAP A15
Marlene-Dietrich-Platz 1 Ⓤ/Ⓢ Potsdamer Platz ☎ 030 25 89 97 17, Ⓦ weilands-wellfood.de. Mon–Fri 10am–8.30pm, Sat & Sun noon–8.30pm.

Schleusenkrug

Right by a pond near bustling Potsdamer Platz, this health-conscious, fast-food-style store sells food low in calories and high in vitamins: couscous, salads, curries and sandwiches stacked with fresh ingredients. Popular with local workers at lunchtimes.

Clubs and venues

Meistersaal

MAP p.70, POCKET MAP F6
Köthener Str. 38 Ⓤ/Ⓢ Potsdamer Platz ☎ 030 32 59 99 710, Ⓦ meistersaal-berlin.de.

This hundred-year-old music venue and recording studio has drawn major artists from Kurt Tucholsky and David Bowie to U2 and Herbert Grönemeyer. Built in 1913 in what was once Berlin's music quarter, the building fell into disrepair after World War II. Since then, though, the Meistersaal has become Berlin's version of London's Abbey Road, world-renowned for its excellent acoustics.

Prenzlauer Berg and Wedding

Built in the nineteenth century as a working-class district, Prenzlauer Berg was neglected by the GDR after World War II, becoming a crumbling ghetto for intellectuals, punks and bohemians. Following merciless post-Wall gentrification, wealthy creative types and middle-class families have gravitated here, drawn by the area's handsome, cobbled streets, leafy squares like Helmholtzplatz and Kollwitzplatz, and its distinctive Alt Berlin atmosphere, with lots of independent bars and cafés, Kastanienallee's boutiques and the buzzy Sunday flea market at Mauerpark. While Prenzlauer Berg's nightlife has been reduced to a few late-night bars, just over the famous Bösebrücke – where the Bornholmer Strasse border crossing was first officially breached in November 1989 – lies the former Western district of Wedding. Known for its large immigrant population and edgy charm, this up-and-coming borough is peppered with the kind of underground spaces that were once common in Prenzlauer Berg during the 1990s.

Gedenkstätte Berliner Mauer

MAP p.82, POCKET MAP G2
Bernauer Str. 111–119 ⓤ Bernauer Str./
ⓢ Nordbahnhof ⓣ 030 46 79 86 666,
ⓦ www.berliner-mauer-gedenkstaette.de.

Open-air exhibition and memorial grounds daily 8am–10pm; visitor and documentation centres Tues–Sun 10am–6pm. Free.

Based slightly away from the tourist centre, so avoiding the

Gedenkstätte Berliner Mauer museum

Stall at Mauerpark flea market

crowds that throng Checkpoint Charlie, the Berlin Wall Memorial takes a more academic look at Germany's division. A section of the former border strip is the focus for the **memorial**, while an outdoor exhibition on the former death-strip shows the history of Bernauer Strasse and the Wall itself. Stretching 1.4km up to the Mauerpark, it includes traces of border obstacles that retain the appearance of the Wall as it would have been at the time.

The **museum** opposite, expanded in 2014, now hosts a permanent exhibition ("1961–1989: the Berlin Wall"), which documents the lives of those attempting to escape the dictatorship (the most successful escape tunnels were dug near here) and the resistance efforts – sometimes fatal – organized by those living nearby. There's also a separate exhibition on the division of the U-Bahn and S-Bahn lines displayed in the adjacent **Nordbahnhof** station (open during station opening hours). Prayer services for the victims of the Berlin Wall are held in the **chapel** on weekdays at noon.

Mauerpark Flohmarkt

MAP p.82, POCKET MAP H2
Bernauer Str. 63–65 ⓤ Bernauer Str. ☎ 030 29 77 24 86, ⓦ flohmarktimmauerpark.de. Sun 9am–6pm. Free.

The Mauerpark flea market is a city institution, a popular Sunday stop for hungover students, bargain hunters, families and shade-wearing clubbers who come to scan the international food stalls, clothes shops and nostalgic bric-a-brac that seems to extend forever. You can find everything here from bike parts, 1950s cutlery sets and faded jigsaws to new and vintage clothes, GDR memorabilia, record players and lots of vinyl and CDs. As with most flea markets, there's a decent amount of what might uncharitably be called "junk" but also some genuine antiques. Adjacent to the market you'll find the actual **Mauerpark**, a strip of landscaped green that was once the site of a stretch of Berlin Wall and the associated death-strip, loomed over by the Friedrich-Ludwig-Jahn-Sportpark and the Max-Schmeling-Halle. In warm weather, check out the weekly karaoke session in the "bearpit", which attracts massive crowds from 2.30/3pm.

Prenzlauer Berg

CAFÉS & BARS

Anna Blume	27	Meierei	36
Badfish	4	Metzer Eck	41
Becketts Kopf	5	Morgenrot	28
Bekarei	6	Nalu Diner	10
Bonanza		Prater	20
Coffee Heroes	20	Salt 'N' Bone	8
Café Hilde	42	Saphire Bar	40
Café November	26	Schwarzsauer	22
Dr Pong	15	Scotch & Sofa	37
Elbspeicher	24	Sgaminegg	1
Herman	39	Suicide Sue	18
Kapitalist	25	Vagabund	
Kauf dich Glücklich	21	Brauerei	12
Kiezkind Berlin	13	Wohnzimmer	9
Liebling	14	Zuckerfee	3

ACCOMMODATION

EastSeven	2
Hotel Transit Loft	3
Lette'm Sleep	1
Myer's Hotel	4
Pfefferbett	5

SHOPS

Flagshipstore	5
Goldhahn & Sampson	3
Lunettes Selection	2
Mundo Azul	8
Noodles, Noodles	
& Noodles	7
OYE	4
St George's Bookshop	9
Supalife Kiosk	1
Thatchers	6

SNACKS

Konnopke's Imbiss	16

RESTAURANTS

The Bird	2
Chez Maurice	38
Chutnify	23
Gugelhof	32
Lucky Leek	35
Mao Thai	30
Maria Bonita	17
Marienburgerie	31
Pappa e Ciccia	33
Pasternak	34
Sasaya	7
Weinstein	11
Zula	29

CLUBS & VENUES

Ausland	2
Duncker	1
Panke	3

Kollwitzplatz

MAP p.82, POCKET MAP J2
Kollwitzplatz Ⓤ Eberswalder Str./
Senefelderplatz.

Kollwitzplatz is one of Prenzlauer Berg's best-known and most attractive squares. It was named after artist Käthe Kollwitz (1867–1945), who lived in the area at the turn of the twentieth century (a simple plaque commemorates her former home on Kollwitzstr.) and whose squat, serious-looking **sculpture** is one of the main features of the square. From the appearance of the lavishly restored facades it is hard to tell that Kollwitzplatz was once one of Berlin's poorest areas, but Kollwitz's work (see p.128) reveals the area to have once been home to the city's more impoverished and downtrodden citizens. This was one of the first areas to be gentrified when the Wall fell in 1989 and today symbolizes Prenzlauer Berg's yuppie status as well as its bias towards families (some call this part of the city Pramzlauerberg). It's a lovely place to come for a stroll – three **playgrounds** and a leafy **park** lie within the square and endless restaurants, cafés and smart boutiques are scattered around its perimeter. Saturdays are especially popular thanks to the extensive **farmers' market**, offering everything from organic meat and fish, fruit and veg, sweets and coffee and clothes. A smaller (and less crowded) organic market also takes place on Thursdays. In summer especially the fun carries on till late at night.

Jewish cemetery

MAP p.82, POCKET MAP J2
Schönhauser Allee 23–25
Ⓤ Senefelderplatz ☏ 030 44 19 824. Mon–Thurs 8am–4pm, Fri 7.30am–1pm. Free.

A short hop from the Senefelderplatz U-Bahn, Prenzlauer Berg's small but charming Jewish cemetery (Jüdischer Friedhof) was built to cater for the overspill from the one on Mitte's Grosse Hamburger Strasse. It was mostly used between 1827 and 1880, at a time when the Jewish population in this area was thriving, and holds approximately 22,000 graves and almost a thousand hereditary family plots, including the graves of painter Max Liebermann, the publisher Leopold Ullstein, the composer Giacomo Meyerbeer and German-Jewish banker Joseph Mendelssohn (son of

Table tennis on Kollwitzplatz

the influential philosopher Moses Mendelssohn). Sadly many gravestones, the original cemetery entrance and mourning chapel were destroyed during World War II and subsequent anti-Semitic vandalism – and many graves are still in a dilapidated state, some riddled with bullet holes. The cemetery was rebuilt in the 1960s, and the adjacent lapidarium – on the site of the former mourning hall – was opened in 2004 as a place to preserve and protect sixty of the most valuable stones, as well as to display panels on Jewish culture and Jewish mourning rituals. Note that men are obliged to cover their heads to visit the cemetery: hats can be borrowed from the lapidarium but visitors are urged to bring their own.

Synagoge Rykestrasse

MAP p.82, POCKET MAP J2
Rykestr. 53 ⓤ Senefelderstr. ☏ 030 88 02 80, ⓦ www.synagoge-rykestrasse.de. Open for services only: Fri 6pm (winter), 7pm (summer) & Sat 9.30am.

Built by Johann Hoeniger at the turn of the twentieth century, this gorgeous Neoclassical synagogue (inaugurated in 1904) is one of Germany's largest – and one of Berlin's loveliest. The building survived *Kristallnacht* in 1938 as it was located between "Aryan" apartment buildings, although precious Torah scrolls were damaged and rabbis and congregation members were deported to Sachsenhausen (see p.140). The synagogue was also used as stables during the war, but was finally restored to its former glory by architects Ruth Golan and Kay Zareh in 2007, who used black-and-white photographs and a €6-million budget to lavishly re-create the remarkable original. Outside of service times, the synagogue can only be visited via prior arrangement.

The Wasserturm

MAP p.82, POCKET MAP J2
Corner of Knaackstr. & Rykestr.
ⓤ Eberswalder Str./Senefelderplatz.

Designed by Henry Gill, constructed by the English Waterworks Company and finished in 1877, the 30m-high cylindrical brick water tower, known as "Dicker Hermann", has become one of Prenzlauer Berg's unofficial symbols. Among the oldest of its kind in the city, it was one of the first places to provide running water in the country, and remained in use until the 1950s. Its engine house was used as an unofficial prison by the SA in 1933–45 – 28 bodies were later found in the underground pipe network, and a commemorative plaque stands outside on Knaackstrasse. During GDR times the tower was used to store canned fish, which could apparently be smelled across the whole neighbourhood. The building was then abandoned and became a "playground" for local kids. Today the refurbished tower is home to much-coveted cake-wedge-shaped apartments (formerly belonging to the tower's operators), while the underground reservoir space hosts sporadic cultural events.

Olivin Wellness Lounge

MAP p.82, POCKET MAP J3
Schönhauser Allee 177 ⓤ Senefelderplatz ☏ 030 44 04 25 00, ⓦ www.olivin-berlin.com. Daily: autumn/winter noon–midnight; summer 5pm–midnight. Entrance costs €14 for four hours.

With its exposed brick walls, saunas and an excellent bamboo garden, this Finnish sauna is a great way to unwind whatever the season. Special offers are available in winter and massages start at €18 for twenty minutes. No access to men on Thursdays. Cash only.

Kulturbrauerei

MAP p.82, POCKET MAP J2
Schönhauser Allee 36 (entrance on Sredzkistr.) Ⓤ Eberswalder Str. or trams #20, #50, #53 ☏ 030 44 35 21 70, Ⓦ kulturbrauerei.de. Open 24hr year round. Free for main complex, price varies for specific venues.

This lovely, sprawling, red-and-yellow brick complex dates to 1842, when it was a small brewery and pub. It was expanded to its current size after 1880. Since the late 1990s, it's been one of Prenzlauer Berg's major commercial hubs, with offices, bars, restaurants, clubs and an eight-theatre cinema (Kino in der KulturBrauerei; ☏ 018 05 11 88 11, Ⓦ cinestar. de). As well as the cinema and shops, the weekly Street Food market (every Sunday) and Scandinavian Christmas market (end of November to end of December) are worth a visit, as is the **Museum in der Kulturbrauerei** (Knaackstr. 97; ☏ 030 46 77 77 911; free) – opened 2013 – whose permanent exhibition, "Everyday Life in the GDR", documents East German cultural history. The Kesselhaus concert hall hosts some decent indie rock and pop shows. You can also pick up guided cycle tours (March–Nov; ☏ 030 43 73 99 99, Ⓦ berlinonbike.de).

Museum Pankow

MAP p.82, POCKET MAP J3
Prenzlauer Allee 227–228 Ⓤ Senefelderplatz ☏ 030 90 29 53 917. Tues–Sun 10am–6pm; Sat & Sun 10am–6pm. Free.

Spread across the first floor of a former school, this small but lively museum documents the history of the district and its working-class inhabitants from the nineteenth century to today. The permanent exhibition consists mainly of photos and texts (German only) displayed along corridors, though a couple of large rooms and a separate building across the courtyard occasionally host more modern, multimedia exhibitions on themes such as the evolution of lesbian, gay and transgender life in the area.

Zeiss-Grossplanetarium

MAP p.82, POCKET MAP K1
Prenzlauer Allee 80 Ⓢ Prenzlauer Allee ☏ 030 42 18 45 10. For opening hours and prices see Ⓦ www.planetarium.berlin.

A massive building set back from bustling Prenzlauer Allee, the Zeiss Planetarium was built in 1987. At the time, it was one of Europe's largest and most modern stellar theatres, with a giant, golf-ball-esque silver dome measuring 23m across. Reopened in early 2016, its auditorium still contains a digital projection of Earth's starry skies into the roof, but the program of astronomical, science, film and music events are more cutting edge, as well as entertaining and educational. Many of the new shows are multilingual too (English, Spanish, French).

Kulturbrauerei

Shops

Flagshipstore

MAP p.82, POCKET MAP H2
Oderberger Str. 53 Ⓤ Eberswalder Str.
Ⓣ 030 43 73 53 27, Ⓦ www.flagshipstore-
berlin.de. Mon–Sat noon–8pm.
Representing dozens of Berlin's
fashion labels and international
designers, Flagshipstore offers a
vast range of urban clothing and
accessories for women and men.

Goldhahn & Sampson

MAP p.82, POCKET MAP J1
Dunckerstr. 9 Ⓤ Eberswalder Str. Ⓦ www
.goldhahnundsampson.de. Mon–Fri
8am–8pm, Sat 9am–8pm.
A foodies' paradise that houses
a vast spread of condiments,
spices and other tasty delicacies
from all over the world, plus
cookbooks and utensils. It holds
regular wine tasting and cookery
courses, and there is a second
location at Wilmersdorfer Str. 102
(Ⓤ Wilmersdorfer Str.).

Lunettes Selection

MAP p.82, POCKET MAP K1
Dunckerstr. 18 Ⓤ Eberswalder Str. Ⓣ 030
44 71 80 50, Ⓦ lunettes-selection.de. Mon,
Tues & Fri noon–8pm, Wed 10am–8pm,
Thurs & Sat noon–6pm.
Vintage eyewear fanatics will adore
this small space, which stocks
original frames from brands like
Alain Mikli and Christian Dior,
plus in-house designs by Uta Geyer.

Mundo Azul

MAP p.82, POCKET MAP J2
Choriner Str. 49 Ⓤ Senefelderplatz Ⓣ 030
49 85 38 34. Mon 10am–6pm, Tues–Fri
10am–7pm, Sat 10am–4pm.
"Blue world" is a children's
and illustration bookstore that
stocks beautiful books in French,
Spanish, German and English, and
also runs events and exhibitions.

Noodles, Noodles &
Noodles

MAP p.82, POCKET MAP J2

Mundo Azul

Schönhauser Allee 156 Ⓤ Eberswalder Str.
Ⓣ 030 44 04 54 93. Mon–Fri 10am–7pm,
Sat noon–6pm.
Despite its slightly under-the-
radar location, this store is worth
seeking out for its handsome
furniture, made using old-school
artisanal techniques and high-
quality materials – built to last.

OYE

MAP p.82, POCKET MAP J2
Oderberger Str. 4 Ⓤ Eberswalder Str.
Ⓣ 030 66 64 78 21. Mon–Fri 1–8pm, Sat
noon–8pm.
Originally catering for collectors
of Latin, soul and funk vinyl, OYE
now covers an impressive range
of styles, from Afrobeat to Berlin
club staples house and techno.

St George's Bookshop

MAP p.82, POCKET MAP J2
Wörther Str. 27 Ⓤ Eberswalder Str. or tram
#M2 to Marienburger Ⓣ 030 81 79 83 33.
Mon–Fri 11am–8pm, Sat 11am–7pm.
Founded in 2003 by British twins
Paul and Daniel, this delightful
shop sells a fine selection of
new and used English-language
books. There's a sofa to chill on,
free wi-fi and they'll buy your
used books.

Supalife Kiosk

MAP p.82, POCKET MAP J1
Raumerstr. 40 Ⓤ Eberswalder Str. ☏ 030
44 67 88 26, Ⓦ supalife.de. Mon–Sat
noon–7pm.

This small boutique sells the
wares of Berlin urban artists, from
comics and fanzines to silkscreen
prints and paintings. They're well
connected to some of the city's
best-known artists so expect
special one-offs too.

Thatchers

MAP p.82, POCKET MAP H2
Kastanienallee 21 Ⓤ Eberswalder Str.
☏ 030 24 62 77 51. Mon–Sat 11am–7pm.

Upmarket fashion store for
women who like their dresses,
skirts and shirts classy and sexy
without ever being over the top.
A perfect place to pick up sensual
evening dresses, sophisticated club
wear and also savvy gifts.

Restaurants

The Bird

MAP p.82, POCKET MAP H1
Am Falkplatz 5 Ⓤ/Ⓢ Schönhauser Allee
☏ 030 51 05 32 83, Ⓦ thebirdinberlin.com.

Mon–Fri 5pm–midnight, Sat & Sun noon–
midnight. Cash only.

This no-nonsense New York-style
steakhouse is famed for its large and
tasty burgers, spicy chicken wings
and casual ambience. With the
neon bar, exposed brickwork and
US accents it's a bit like being on the
set of *Cheers*. A great place to fill up
cheaply and sip on a cold beer.

Chez Maurice

MAP p.82, POCKET MAP L3
Bötzowstr. 39 Ⓢ Greifswalder Str. ☏ 030
42 50 506, Ⓦ chez-maurice.com. Daily
from 6pm, Tues–Sat also noon–3.30pm.

One of the finer dining spots in
the quietly upmarket Bötzow-
viertel, *Maurice* is an intimate,
rustic place offering high-quality
seasonal French dishes – they'll
even take requests with enough
notice – and an expansive wine list
(over two hundred from France
alone). The *plat du jour* specials
(noon–3.30pm) are good value:
two courses €12.50, three courses
€17.50.

Chutnify

MAP p.82, POCKET MAP J2
Szredki Str. 43 Ⓤ Eberswalderstr. ☏ 030
44 01 07 95, Ⓦ chutnify.com. Daily
noon–11pm.

Single-handedly challenging
Berlin's dire reputation for
mediocre, spice-avoiding Indian
food, *Chutnify* specializes in
South Indian street food with
an emphasis on delicious *dosas*,
crispy lentil crêpes and spicy
chai teas. Designed by owner
Aparna Aurora, it looks good
too, with colourful furnishings
and outside seating in summer.
A second branch can be found
at Pflügerstr.25 (same opening
times).

Gugelhof

MAP p.82, POCKET MAP J2
Knaackstr. 37, cnr Kollwitzplatz
Ⓤ Senefelderplatz/Eberswalder Str. ☏ 030
44 29 229, Ⓦ www.gugelhof.com. Mon–Fri
from 5pm, Sat & Sun from noon.

Chutnify

Gugelhof

neighbourhood Thai restaurant. Decent service and a tasty range of classics – *tom ka gai*, spring rolls, glass noodle salads – make this a popular place.

Maria Bonita

MAP p.82, POCKET MAP J2
Danziger Str. 33 Ⓤ Eberswalder Str. Ⓦ mariabonita.de. Daily noon–11pm.

Tucked away amidst the slew of *imbisses* and kebab shops that make up much of this part of Danziger Strasse, *Maria Bonita* stands out for its above-average street-style Mexican food. You couldn't swing an enchilada inside, but the burritos, tacos and *quesadillas* – and the guacamole for that matter – are well worth trying.

Marienburgerie

MAP p.82, POCKET MAP K2
Marienburger Str. 47; tram #M2 to Marienburger Str. Ⓣ 030 30 34 05 15, Ⓦ marienburgerie.de. Mon–Fri 11am–11pm, Sat & Sun 1–10pm.

This diminutive but buzzy burger hangout lures locals back again and again with huge, delicious beef, chicken, fish or vegetable burgers (the Marienburger is almost too big to eat in one sitting). Organic options also available.

Pappa e Ciccia

MAP p.82, POCKET MAP H2
Schwedter Str. 18 Ⓤ Senefelderplatz Ⓣ 030 61 62 08 01, Ⓦ pappaeciccia.de. Tues–Fri 6pm–midnight, Sat & Sun 11am–midnight.

Bored of the usual Berlin brunch formula? Check out the weekend brunch at this smart-casual Italian restaurant, where chefs dole out freshly made antipasti and other scrumptious dishes, and diners gather on the long communal tables outside. It's all organic and there are decent vegetarian and vegan options. Ice cream, cakes and more on offer at the adjacent organic deli.

A Kollwitzplatz classic, *Gugelhof* has been serving consistently good Alsatian food since the Wall fell, and counts Bill Clinton among its many dignified diners. It's a surprisingly down-to-earth place, with friendly staff and robust yet refined cuisine that includes *Flammkuchen* (*tarte flambée*) and pork knuckle. Reservations recommended.

Lucky Leek

MAP P.82, POCKET MAP J2
Kollwitzstr. 54 Ⓤ Senefelderplatz Ⓣ 030 66 40 87 10, Ⓦ lucky-leek.com. Wed–Sun 6–10pm.

This high-end vegan spot occupies a smart space inside an old building on one of Prenzlauer Berg's loveliest streets. The menu is inventive and service excellent, but you'll certainly pay above average for the experience. Mains around €18; three-course menu €35.

Mao Thai

MAP p.82, POCKET MAP J2
Wörther Str. 30 Ⓤ Eberswalder Str. Ⓣ 030 44 19 261, Ⓦ maothai.de. Daily noon–11.30pm.

Don't be put off by the beaming Buddhas in the window – there's a refreshing lack of garish decoration inside this reliable

Pasternak

MAP p.82, POCKET MAP J2
Knaackstr. 22–24 ⓤ Senefelderplatz ☎ 030
44 13 399, ⓦ restaurant-pasternak.de.
Daily 9am–1am.

This long-standing Russian/Jewish restaurant, named after the author of *Doctor Zhivago*, is best known for its incredible Sunday brunch (9am–3pm, €13.90): a regal spread of blini, caviar, fish and much more; it's so popular you'll need to get there early (no reservations). The same proprietors run a decent Israeli restaurant over the road (directly opposite the synagogue) called – get it? – *Masel Topf* (☎ 030 443 17 525, ⓦ restaurant-maseltopf.de).

Sasaya

MAP p.82, POCKET MAP J1
Lychener Str. 50 ⓤ / Schönhauser Allee
☎ 030 44 71 77 21. Mon & Thurs–Sun
noon–3pm & 6–11.30pm.

Bucking the trend for catch-all pan-Asian menus, *Sasaya* focuses on serving traditional and innovative Japanese food. The quality and freshness of the ingredients is high, the food is delicious and service is swift – a serious contender for best sushi spot in the city.

Weinstein

MAP p.82, POCKET MAP J1
Lychener Str. 33 ⓤ Eberswalder Str. ☎ 030
44 11 842, ⓦ weinstein.eu. Mon–Sat
5pm–2am, Sun 6pm–2am; kitchen
6–11.30pm.

This intimate wine bar and restaurant, all sturdy wooden tables and wine barrel decoration, is a bit of a local secret. The food has a strong emphasis on local produce and German wines, as well as imported high-quality products like Allgäu cheese and Iberian ham. Mains start at €8.50, and from Monday to Wednesday you can get eight small courses for €48.

Zula

MAP p.82, POCKET MAP J2
Husemann Str. 10 ⓤ Senefelderplatz
☎ 030 41 71 51 00, ⓦ zulaberlin.com.
Daily from 11am.

The humble chickpea dish reaches superlative status at this cosy, Israeli-run hummus spot. Visitors can stick with a traditional hummus plate or try out the *hummus shakshuka* and even *hummus goulash* – all of it is delicious. Home-made pitta bread and a nice wine list seal the deal.

Snacks

Konnopke's Imbiss

MAP p.82, POCKET MAP J1
Below ⓤ Eberswalder Str. ☎ 030 44 27
765, ⓦ www.konnopke-imbiss.de. Mon–Fri
10am–8pm, Sat noon–8pm.

This legendary stand has been serving up Berlin street snacks – *Currywurst, pommes frites, Bratwurst* – since 1930. Incredibly it's been run by the same family all that time – perfect for a quick bite. It's perfect for a quick bite any time of day; if you want to feel like a local, eat your food standing up at one of the tables outside.

Cafés and bars

Anna Blume

MAP p.82, POCKET MAP J2
Kollwitzstr. 83 ⓤ Eberswalder Str. ☎ 030
44 04 87 49, ⓦ www.cafe-anna-blume.de.
Daily 8am–2am.

Part flower shop, part café and part bakery, this Art Deco classic – named after a Kurt Schwitters poem, whose lines are elegantly inscribed on the walls inside – is one of the area's best known cafés. Slide into one of the red leather banquettes and sample one of their superb cakes, or come early at the weekend and try a refined tiered breakfast platter.

Badfish

MAP p.82, POCKET MAP J1
Stargarder Str. 14 ⓤ / ⓢ Schönhauser Allee

030 547 147 88, ⊕ **badfishbarberlin. com.** Daily 5pm–late.

This New York-style neighbourhood bar has become an in-spot for expats and natives alike. Smokey and boisterous (especially at weekends), and with a hip selection of sounds on the jukebox, friendly staff and an excellent array of craft beers, whiskeys and shots, it makes for an almost guaranteed fun night out. "Angry hour" between 5–7pm and free popcorn at all times.

Becketts Kopf

MAP p.82, POCKET MAP J1
Pappelallee 64 ⊕/⑤ Schönhauser Allee ☎ 030 44 03 58 80. Mon–Thurs & Sun 7pm–2am, Fri & Sat 7pm–4am.

It's easy to walk straight past this deliberately clandestine cocktail bar – but you'd be missing out. Look out for the glowering head of Mr Beckett staring at you from the darkness, and enter to find a sophisticated and intimate space with one of the best cocktail lists in town.

Bekarei

MAP p.82, POCKET MAP J1
Dunker Str. 23 ⑤ Prenzlauer Allee ☎ 030 34 62 22 30, ⊕ bekarei.com. Daily 7.30am–6.30pm.

This Greek-Portuguese bakery is a firm local favourite thanks to its freshly baked breads, pretzels, cakes and pastries. The interior is colourfully retro, the staff are friendlier than usual and menu items of note include pancakes, flakey *tiropitakia* and *pastel de nata*. Note that it gets particularly busy with families at weekends.

Bonanza Coffee Heroes

MAP p.82, POCKET MAP H2
Oderberger Str. 35 ⊕ Bernauer Str./ Eberswalder Str. ☎ 030 20 84 88 020, ⊕ bonanzacoffee.de. Mon–Fri 8.30am–6pm, Sat & Sun 10am–6pm.

Coffee connoisseurs flock to *Bonanza* to sample the wares of their famed baristas: perfect lattes and flat whites knocked up on a fancy Slayer Espresso machine. Single origin filter coffees also served, and there is a second location in Kreuzberg (Adalbertstr. 70).

Café Hilde

MAP p.82, POCKET MAP J3
Metzer Str. 22 ⊕ Senefelderplatz ☎ 030 04 05 04 172, ⊕ hilde-berlin.com. Daily 9am–7pm.

This sizeable café on the corner of busy Prenzlauer Allee is a lovely spot to unwind, with books and magazines to read during the day, home-made cakes and lunches, plus film screenings and book readings in the evenings. They also serve up Irish breakfasts and a mean eggs Benedict.

Café November

MAP p.82, POCKET MAP J2
Husemannstr. 15 ⊕ Senefelderplatz/ Eberswalder Str. ☎ 030 44 28 425, ⊕ www. cafe-november.com. Mon–Fri from 2pm, Sat & Sun from 11am.

Café November is an appealing, gay-friendly but mixed café that sells good cakes, soups and mains. There's a breakfast buffet until 3pm on Saturdays and 4pm on Sundays, free wi-fi and the outside patio is great in the summer.

Zula

Dr Pong

MAP p.82, POCKET MAP J2
Eberswalder Str. 21 Ⓤ Eberswalder Str.
Ⓦ www.drpong.net. Mon–Sat 8pm–late,
Sun 7pm–late (from 6pm Oct–April).

Like table tennis? Love beer? Then
Dr Pong is for you. The action
here revolves – literally – around
the central ping-pong table. Rent
a bat and join the crowd as they
move slowly around the table, bats
in one hand, beer bottles in the
other, playing a communal game.
Be warned, though: the bar is on
the tourist beer-crawl route.

Elbspeicher

MAP p.82, POCKET MAP J2
Sredzkistr. 41 Ⓤ Eberswalder Str. ☎ 030
52 68 26 02, Ⓦ www.elbspeicherb.de.
Mon–Fri 9am–7pm, Sat & Sun 10am–7pm.

Specializing in Hamburg
"Elbgold" roasts, this coffee hub
has a battleship-grey espresso bar
downstairs and elegant, spacious
rooms and areas upstairs in which
you can sample the world-class
beans and try the home-made
cookies, cakes and ciabattas.

Herman

MAP p.82, POCKET MAP F10
Schönhauser Allee 173 Ⓤ Senefelderplatz
☎ 30 44312854. Daily 6pm–3am.

Located along the busy section
of Schönhauser Allee that links
Mitte with Prenzlauer Berg, this
Belgian-themed bar – run by
welcoming and knowledgeable
owner Bart Neirynck – has an
incredibly broad selection of
beers. It's a great place to start
the night, but chances are you'll
end up staying for longer than
planned.

Kapitalist

MAP p.82, POCKET MAP J2
Oderberger Str. 2 Ⓤ Eberswalder Str.
☎ 0176 31 02 32 14. Mon–Fri noon–open
end, Sat & Sun 11am–open end.

Kapitalist is a much less anti-
establishment place than its
beaten-up facade suggests – in fact
it's completely harmless, drawing

a friendly, bubbly crowd of locals
who come for coffees and people-
watching in the day and beer and
wine at night.

Kauf Dich Glücklich

MAP p.82, POCKET MAP H2
Oderberger Str. 44 Ⓤ Bernauer Str./
Eberswalder Str. ☎ 030 44 35 21 82,
Ⓦ www.kaufdichgluecklich.de. Mon–Fri
11am–1am, Sat 10am–12.30am, Sun
10am–11pm.

Come here for waffles, ice cream
– and a spot of cutely kitsch
capitalism. "Buy yourself happy"
is an irrepressibly cheerful place
where you can not only get
great coffee and sweet treats, but
also buy any of the secondhand
furniture – tables, chairs, lamps,
sunglasses – you see around you.

Kiezkind Berlin

MAP p.82, POCKET MAP J1
Helmholtzplatz Ⓤ Eberswalderstr. ☎ 030
40 05 78 50, Ⓦ www.mein-kiezkind.de.
Mon–Fri noon–6pm, Sat & Sun 10am–6pm.

Located right on leafy
Helmholtzplatz, this large,
family-oriented café is an ideal
place to take a break with the
little ones. Inside, they can play
with the abundant toys or in the
sandpit, or ride around on the
tricycles outside while you enjoy
a well-made latte and slice of cake
from the counter. Regular family-
friendly flea markets also.

Liebling

MAP p.82, POCKET MAP J1
Raumerstr. 36 Ⓢ Prenzlauer Allee/
Ⓤ Eberswalder Str. ☎ 030 41 19 82 09,
Ⓦ www.cafe-liebling.de. Mon–Fri
9am–2am, Sat & Sun 10am till late.

There's no sign on this café/bar,
but you'll find it right on the
corner of Dunckerstrasse and
Raumerstrasse. Inside is a subtly
cool interior, great cakes and
decent lunch options (soups,
quiches). The good wine and beer,
and the *au courant* music on the
system, makes it popular in the
evenings too.

Meierei

MAP p.82, POCKET MAP J2
Kollwitz Str. 42 ① Senefelderplatz ☎ 030
92 12 95 73, Ⓦ www.meierei.net. Mon–Fri
7.30am–6pm, Sat 9am–6pm, Sun
10am–6pm.

This itsy café-cum-deli in
leafy Kollwitzstrasse offers
a taste of the high life. Styled
around a mountain hut
interior, with Alpine landscapes
painted on the walls, the organic
Swiss and Austrian cuisine –
from *Weisswürst* (veal sausage)
to apple *Strudel* – is best
enjoyed at one of the large
outdoor tables.

Metzer Eck

MAP p.82, POCKET MAP F10
Metzer Str. 33 ① Eberswalder Str.
☎ 030 44 27 656, Ⓦ www.metzer-eck.de.
Mon–Fri 4pm–1am, Sat 6pm–1am.

The oldest inn in Prenzlauer
Berg (1913) inevitably packs
plenty of old-school charm.
It's faded slightly since its days
as a major meeting point for
Prenzlauer Berg's more bohemian
contingent in the GDR, but
still serves a decent Pilsner and
delicious *Bolettes* (meatballs) and
Bockwurst.

Morgenrot

MAP p.82, POCKET MAP H2
Kastanienallee 85 ① Eberswalder Str.
☎ 030 44 31 78 44, Ⓦ cafe-morgenrot.de.
Tues–Thurs noon–1am, Fri & Sat
11am–3am, Sun 11am–1am.

Kastanienallee's best-known
alternative café is located right
next to an immense squat (one of
the last in the area). Despite the
anticapitalist slogans and punk
aura, it's a friendly, open place
that serves up a good weekend
breakfast (vegetarian) for which
you pay between €4 and €7,
depending on your income.

Nalu Diner

MAP p.82, POCKET MAP J1
Dunckerstr. 80a ① Eberswalder Str./
Ⓢ Prenzlauer Allee ☎ 030 79 75 86 33,
Ⓦ www.nalu-diner.com. Wed–Fri
10am–9pm, Sat & Sun 9am–9pm.

Since opening in 2012, *Nalu's*
pancakes (€4–5.50) have become
a firm neighbourhood favourite,
though the menu extends to other
breakfasts (French toast, griddle
combos), lunches and evening
meals (burgers, steak-cheese
sandwiches; €7–13.50). Free coffee
refills and a continuous soundtrack
of 1970s pop seal the deal.

PRENZLAUER BERG AND WEDDING

Kapitalist

Suicide Sue

Prater

MAP p.82, POCKET MAP J2
Kastanienallee 7–9 ⓤ Eberswalder Str.
Ⓣ 030 44 85 688, ⓦ www.pratergarten.de.
Beer garden April–Sept daily from noon;
restaurant year-round Mon–Sat 6–11pm,
Sun noon–11pm.

Dating back to 1837, *Prater* is
the city's oldest beer garden and
remains a fantastic place for a
taste of traditional Berlin boozing,
especially during summer when
people swarm around the long
tables and snack kiosks. During
winter, it's all about feasting on
home-made Berlin cuisine inside
the classic interior.

Salt N Bone

MAP p.82, POCKET MAP J1
Schliemannstr. 3 Ⓢ Schönhauser Allee
Ⓣ 030 91 44 88 85, ⓦ saltnbone.de. Tues–
Fri from 6pm, Sat & Sun from 5pm.

The gastropub scene has well and
truly arrived in Berlin with this
place, where Sunday roasts and
modern bar food are served up
alongside local craft beers, very
good cocktails, and a decent gin
and tonic selection. Friendly staff
and a largely expat clientele.

Saphire Bar

MAP p.82, POCKET MAP L3
Bötzowstr. 31 Ⓢ Greifswalder Str. ⓉⓉ 030
25 56 21 58, ⓦ saphirebar.de. Mon–Thurs
& Sun 8pm–2am, Fri & Sat 8pm–4am.

The *Saphire Bar* mixes together
its whisky and cocktail bar
credentials as well as it mixes

its drinks, with two elegant
lounges to enjoy a cultivated yet
unpretentious evening in.

Schwarzsauer

MAP p.82, POCKET MAP J2
Kastanienallee 13 ⓤ Eberswalder Str.
Ⓣ 030 44 85 633, ⓦ schwarzsauer.com.
Daily 9am–6am.

"Black and Sour" lives up to its
name with its moody service,
average food and smoky, plain
interior. Still, it has a certain
Berlin-esque atmosphere that
makes it decidedly popular.

Scotch & Sofa

MAP p.82, POCKET MAP F10
Kollwitzstr. 18 ⓤ Senefelderplatz Ⓣ 030 68
00 42 03, ⓦ www.scotchandsofa.net. Daily
from 6pm.

This quietly hip neighbourhood
bar is a fine spot for sinking into
a granny-style sofa, sipping on a
cocktail and having a *tête-à-tête*.
They always play interesting
music – everything from Elvis to
rap – and smokers and ping-pong
fans can indulge their passions
downstairs.

Sgaminegg

MAP p.82, POCKET MAP J1
Seelower Str. 2 ⓤ/Ⓢ Schönhauser Allee
Ⓣ 030 44 73 15 25, ⓦ www.sgaminegg.de.
Tues–Fri 8.30am–6pm, Sat 9.30am–6pm.

There are a dearth of decent cafés
north of Stargarderstrasse, but
Sgaminegg is an absolute treasure
thanks to delicious coffees, home-
made lunches – couscous, lentil

and south German dishes – and a little shop that sells local produce.

Suicide Sue

MAP p.82, POCKET MAP J2

Dunckerstr. 2 ⓤ Eberswalder Str. ☎ 030 64 83 47 45, ⓦ suicidesue.com. Mon–Fri 8am–6pm, Sat 9am–7pm, Sun 10am–7pm.

This local fave features crumpled leather armchairs, chunky wooden tables and a street-facing espresso bar. The food is tasty too: breakfast spans croissants and scrambled eggs (served in a tiny frying pan), but the real speciality is the *Stullen* – thick slices of home-made bread with toppings you mix and match yourself.

Vagabund Brauerei

POCKET MAP C1

Antwerpener Str. 3 ⓤ Seestrasse ☎ 030 52 66 76 68, ⓦ www.vagabundbrauerei.com. Mon–Fri from 5pm, Sat & Sun from 1pm.

One of Europe's first crowd-sourced breweries, *Vagabund* is run by three American friends with a highly infectious passion for craft beer. As well as their own excellent brews, they sell classic Belgian ales and lager from family breweries in southern Germany, all in a welcoming, unpretentious atmosphere that draws locals and expats alike.

Wohnzimmer

MAP p.82, POCKET MAP J1

Lettestr. 6 ⓤ Eberswalder Str. ☎ 030 44 55 458, ⓦ www.wohnzimmer-bar.de. Daily 4pm–late.

This retro, elegant "living room" is a local institution. One of the first spots to champion flea-market chic, it serves as both a daytime café and amiable bar later on. At weekends a cocktail bar magically pops up between its two rooms.

Zuckerfee

MAP p.82, POCKET MAP J1

Greifenhagener Str. 15 ⓤ/ⓢ Schönhauser Allee ☎ 030 52 68 61 44, ⓦ zuckerfee-berlin.de. Tues–Sun 10am–6pm.

"Sugar Plum Fairy" is an apt name

for this delightful place, tucked down a quiet street. The interior is dotted with tasteful ornamentation, while the menu features delicious waffles, cakes and uniquely presented breakfasts and lunches (book ahead at weekends).

Clubs and venues

Ausland

MAP p.82, POCKET MAP J1

Lychener Str. 60 ⓢ Prenzlauer Allee ☎ 030 44 77 008, ⓦ ausland-berlin.de.

One for the experimentalists, *Ausland* is a nonprofit club committed to promoting music, performance and related events. You can find anything from free jazz and sound-art gigs to movies and installations, all of which take place in an undecorated bunker in front of an apartment block. Door fees go directly to the artists.

Duncker

MAP p.82, POCKET MAP K1

Dunckerstr. 64 ⓢ Prenzlauer Allee ☎ 030 44 59 509, ⓦ dunckerclub.de. Mon from 10pm, Thurs from 9pm, Fri & Sat from 11pm. Entry fee varies but free Thurs.

Duncker touches the musical parts other Prenzlauer Berg clubs don't reach, thanks to a mix of new wave and indie nights and particularly its weekly "Dark Mondays" – one of the city's few goth/industrial nights. Aptly enough it's located in a striking neo-Gothic church.

Panke

POCKET MAP E1

Gerichtstr. 23 ⓢ Wedding ☎ 0163 831 4755, ⓦ www.pankeculture.com. Wed–Sat from 6pm. Admission varies.

This alternative cultural hub, run by a group of Lithuanian friends, is hidden away in a network of run-down industrial courtyards. Expect underground DJ nights, which veer from hip-hop and soul to world and funk (never techno), plus film and art nights and a decent bar and café.

Friedrichshain

Though part of an ensemble of former East inner-city areas, Friedrichshain has developed a slightly differently mien than that of neighbouring Mitte and Prenzlauer Berg. A magnet for lefties, anarchists and students, it has managed to resist the same levels of gentrification thanks to an organized squatter scene, activist demos and the occasional car-burning frenzy. That said, its defiantly unkempt environs have succumbed to an invasion of bars and cafés around Boxhagener Platz, and an encroaching media presence along the river. It's most popular for bar-hopping, clubbing and cheap midnight snacking, but the area does offer some heavyweight public monuments, the world-famous East Side Gallery and the imposing Karl-Marx-Allee among them. It's also home to – indeed named after – the lovely, sprawling Volkspark Friedrichshain.

Volkspark Friedrichshain

MAP p.98, POCKET MAP K3
Ⓤ Strausberger Platz/Weberweise.

Established 150 years ago to commemorate the centenary of Frederick the Great's accession to the throne, Volkspark Friedrichshain is one of Berlin's oldest parks. Casually straddling the boroughs of Prenzlauer Berg and Friedrichshain, it's a sprawling place featuring lots of recreational

opportunities (tennis courts, volleyball nets and climbing walls) and a wealth of impressive monuments. Highlights include the **Märchenbrunnen**, a neo-Baroque fountain built at the turn of the twentieth century, memorials to Frederick the Great, the German antifascist groups of World War II and a **peace bell** given to East Berlin by Japan. The park's two main hills (the 78m Grosse Bunkerberg and the 48m Kleine Bunkerberg) were constructed with rubble from the war. The park also has a café and a summertime open-air cinema.

East Side Gallery

MAP p.98, POCKET MAP L6
Mühlenstr. 1 Ⓤ Warschauer Str. ☎ 030 25 17 159, Ⓦ eastsidegallery-berlin.com. 24hr.

This 1.3km-long section of the Berlin Wall by the Spree is purportedly the largest open-air gallery in the world and one of the city's best-known landmarks. Painted in 1990 (on the east side) when the Wall fell, the gallery features works from over a hundred artists from all over the world.

East Side Gallery

Café Sybille on Karl-Marx-Allee

Over the years it has fallen victim to vandalism and erosion, hence a controversial decision to repaint it in time for the twentieth-anniversary celebrations in 2009. The East Side Gallery made the news again in 2013 when a section was removed to make way for some luxury apartments; the resulting outcry drew ten thousand protesters and an impromptu appearance by German architect David Hasselhoff. Since 2016 a **museum** close to the Oberbaumbrücke (see p.98) end of the Wall (Mühlenstr. 78-80 ☎030 63 96 26 62, ⓦthewallmuseum .com; daily 10am–7pm; €12.50), tells the story of the Wall years through a multimedia presentation that includes over 100 screens, interactive displays, original newsreel footage and filmed interviews with border guards.

Karl-Marx-Allee

MAP p.98, POCKET MAP L5
ⓤFrankfurter Tor/Strausberger Platz.

The monumental Karl-Marx-Allee, as the name suggests, is a thoroughly Communist phenomenon. Built between 1952 and 1960, the imposing 89m-wide, 2km-long street – book-ended by German architect Hermann Henselmann's tiered "wedding cake" towers at Frankfurter Tor and Strausberger Platz – was originally named Grosse Frankfurter Strasse

and later Stalinallee. The idea was to build luxurious apartments for workers (they were inevitably doled out to party officials) as well as a leisure area featuring shops, restaurants, cafés and the still-standing Kino International. On June 17, 1953, the street was the focus of worker demonstrations; at least 125 people died in the brutal suppression by Soviet forces that followed. Since reunification most of the buildings have been restored and the apartments converted into upmarket flats and offices. The vast dimensions of the street and its run of blocky Soviet architecture make it a fantastic place for a stroll. Stop off at *Café Sybille* (see p.101), which hosts a small but insightful museum on the street's history.

Computerspielemuseum

MAP p.98, POCKET MAP L5
Karl-Marx-Allee 93a ⓤWeberweise ☎030 60 98 85 77, ⓦcomputerspielemuseum.de. Mon–Thurs & Sun 10am–8pm, Fri & Sat 10am–9pm. €8.

The world's first-ever computer games museum is a fun and highly interactive tribute to gaming, featuring pretty much every kind of arcade machine and games console ever made, from the pioneering Nimrod (1951) and legendary PONG (1972), right up to contemporary classics like Tomb Raider. There are plenty of opportunities to punch keyboards and waggle joysticks – and even get a jolly old electric shock via the two-player "Pain Station".

Boxhagener Platz market

MAP p.98, POCKET MAP A17
Boxhagener Platz ⓤSamariterstr. ⓦboxhagenerplatz.org. Farmers' market: Sat 9.30am–3.30pm. Flea market: Sun 10am–6pm.

The Sunday flea market at Boxhagener Platz is a popular place for locals and tourists alike. While not as large as Mauerpark (see p.81), you can find vinyl, vintage fashion, old crockery and more.

Oberbaumbrücke

MAP BELOW, POCKET MAP M7
Ⓤ Warschauer Str.

This attractive, Spree-spanning landmark connects the districts of Friedrichshain and Kreuzberg, today officially part of the same borough but previously divided by the Berlin Wall. The double-decker bridge (and its name) dates back to the eighteenth century when it was originally constructed – from wood – and acted as a gateway to the city. A new version opened in 1896, designed by architect Otto Stahn in brick gothic style. In 1945 the bridge was partly destroyed by the Wehrmacht to stop the Red Army crossing it, and afterwards ended up straddling the American and Soviet sectors. When the Berlin Wall went up in 1961, the bridge became part of East Berlin's border with West Berlin; when it fell in 1989, the bridge was restored to its former appearance with a new steel middle section designed by Spanish architect Santiago Calatrava. Today the bridge stands as a symbol of unity between Friedrichshain and Kreuzberg (and is the site of a friendly "water battle" in summer). Look out for the neon *Stone Paper Scissors* installation by Thorsten Goldberg – a political statement about the apparent arbitrariness of decisions to grant immigration or asylum status.

Stasi Museum

MAP BELOW, POCKET MAP M5
Ruschestr. 103, Haus 1, Lichtenberg
Ⓤ Magdalenenstr. ☎ 030 55 36 854,
Ⓦ www.stasimuseum.de. Mon–Fri
10am–6pm, Sat & Sun 11am–6pm. €6
(reductions for groups).

East Germany's State Security Service – Stasi – struck terror into East Germans, using dark

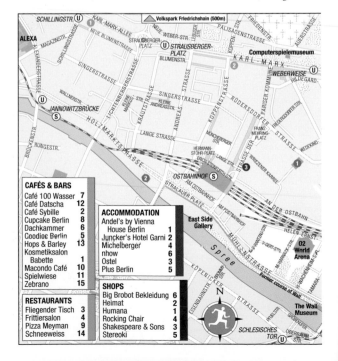

CAFÉS & BARS
Café 100 Wasser 7 / Café Datscha 12 / Café Sybille 2 / Cupcake Berlin 8 / Dachkammer 6 / Coodieg Berlin 5 / Hops & Barley 13 / Kosmetiksalon Babette 1 / Macondo Café 10 / Spielwiese 11 / Zebrano 15

RESTAURANTS
Fliegender Tisch 3 / Frittiersalon 4 / Pizza Meyman 9 / Schneeweiss 14

ACCOMMODATION
Andel's by Vienna House Berlin 1 / Juncker's Hotel Garni 2 / Michelberger 4 / nhow 6 / Ostel 3 / Plus Berlin 5

SHOPS
Big Brobot Bekleidung 6 / Heimat 2 / Humana 1 / Rocking Chair 4 / Shakespeare & Sons 3 / Stereoki 5

and dastardly spying methods to unveil any potential signs of rebellion. This museum – in Lichtenberg, just east of Friedrichshain – used to be the Stasi headquarters: it was stormed and taken over when the Wall fell by an indignant group of people, many of whose lives had been affected by years of abuse, and members of this group still run the museum today. Following extensive renovations, the main building of the campus (Haus 1, which housed the Minister of State Security among others) reopened in 2012 and the exhibition "State Security in the SED Dictatorship" has been on permanent display since 2015. Visitors can see Stasi chief Erich Mielke's ridiculously immense desk (and equally large number of telephones) and the complex filing system that includes samples of body odours. Tours in English, German,

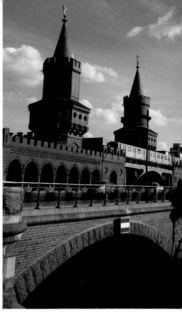

Oberbaumbrücke

Italian and French are available if requested in advance.

Friedrichshain

0 metres 250
0 yards 250

FRIEDRICHSHAIN

Shops

Big Brobot Bekleidung

MAP p.98, POCKET MAP A16
Kopernikusstr. 19 Ⓤ/Ⓢ Warschauerstr.
☏ 030 74 07 83 88. Mon–Fri 11am–8pm,
Sat 11am–6pm.

Friendly and vaguely trashy store where you can browse rare toys, art books and streetwear.

Heimat

MAP p.98, POCKET MAP A16
Niederbarnimstr. 17 Ⓤ Samariterstr. ☏ 030
74 69 99 14. Mon–Fri noon–7pm, Sat
noon–6pm.

Specializes in stylish T-shirts, bags and accessories. Robots, bicycles, strange animals and other hipster designs appear on almost every item.

Humana

MAP p.98, POCKET MAP A16
Frankfurter Tor 3 Ⓤ Frankfurter Tor ☏ 030
422 2018. Mon–Sat 10am–8pm.

This immense five-storey warehouse, part of a grand Soviet "worker palace", brims with secondhand clothes. The top floor has the best vintage gear.

Rocking Chair

MAP p.98, POCKET MAP A17
Gabriel-Max-Str. 13 Ⓤ Samariterstr./
Frankfurter Tor ☏ 030 29 36 42 91. Mon–
Fri noon–7pm, Sat 11am–4pm.

This charming vintage store is a great place for anything from a Hawaiian shirt to a retro handbag. Also open sunny Sundays.

Shakespeare & Sons

MAP p.98, POCKET MAP A16
Warschauerstr. 74 Ⓤ/Ⓢ Warschauerstr.
ⓦ shakesbooks.de. Mon–Sat 9am–0pm,
Sun 10am–8pm.

One of the city's best English-language bookshops, this is a welcoming space filled with literary, sci-fi and academic classics, as well as a great selection of kids' books, French-language titles and Berlin-themed tomes.

Big Brobot Bekleidung

Inside, *Fine Bagels* serves up some of the best bagels in town.

Stereoki

MAP p.98, POCKET MAP A17
Gabriel-Max-Str. 18 Ⓤ/Ⓢ Warschauerstr.
☏ 030 53 79 4667, ⓦ stereoki.com. Mon–
Fri 11.30am–8pm, Sat 11am–7pm.

This slick, white-walled men's fashion store carries shoes, trainers, wallets, bags, hats, tees and more by brands like Adidas and New Balance, Herschel Supply and Element Emerald Collection.

Restaurants

Fliegender Tisch

MAP p.98, POCKET MAP B16
Mainzer Str. 10 Ⓤ Samariterstr. ☏ 030 29
77 64 89, ⓦ fliegender-tisch.de. Daily from
5pm.

"The flying table" is a small, cosy place with just a few wooden tables. It's justly popular thanks to tasty Italian staples like thin-crust pizza and risotto for decent prices (€7–8).

Frittiersalon

MAP p.98, POCKET MAP A16
Boxhagener Str. 104 Ⓤ Samariterstr. ☏ 030
25 93 39 06, ⓦ frittiersalon.de. Tues–Sun
noon–11pm.

With a name that won't appeal to healthy eaters, the "deep fried salon" actually serves delicious organic burgers and *Currywurst*. There's always a burger-of-the-week deal, plus vegetarian and vegan options.

Pizza Meyman

MAP p.98, POCKET MAP A17
Warschauer Str. 80 ⓤ Frankfurter Tor
ⓣ 030 64 49 68 80. Mon–Thurs & Sun noon–2am, Fri & Sat noon–3am.

This unassuming restaurant is great for late-night cravings or for a break between bar hops. Ingredients are fresh, prices are reasonable (€5.50–7.90 for a main), and there's usually a table free. Pasta dishes and salads as well as pizza.

Schneeweiss

MAP p.98, POCKET MAP A17
Simplonstr. 16 ⓤ Warschauer Str. ⓣ 030 29 04 97 04, ⓦ schneeweiss-berlin.de. Mon–Fri 6pm–1am, Sat & Sun 10am–1am (kitchen closes 11pm).

One of Friedrichshain's few upmarket restaurants, "Snow White" is an understated place with a minimalist design and a menu that it describes as "Alpine" – Italian, Austrian and south German recipes such as Schnitzel and pasta. There's a decent weekend brunch (10am–3pm), a fireplace lounge and a low-key bar vibe come evening.

Cafés and bars

Café 100 Wasser

MAP p.98, POCKET MAP A17
Simon-Dach-Str. 39 ⓤ Frankfurter Tor ⓣ 030 29 00 13 56, ⓦ cafe-100-wasser.de. Mon–Thurs & Sun 9am–2am, Fri & Sat 9am–3am.

Named after the Austrian artist Hundertwasser, *100 Wasser* has a fittingly colourful interior of yellow walls and a red-brick bar. It's an unpretentious place, with a hearty menu of burgers, pizza and flans. The weekend all-you-can-eat brunch buffet (€10.50; 9am–4pm) is deservedly popular.

Café Datscha

MAP p.98, POCKET MAP A17
Gabriel-Max-Str. 1 ⓤ Samariterstr. ⓣ 030 70 08 67 35, ⓦ cafe-datscha.de. Mon–Sat 10am–1am, Sun 9am–1am.

Built in the style of a traditional Russian home – wood furniture, tall ceilings – albeit a fairly smart one, *Datscha* offers a rich spread of Russian and Ukrainian dishes like *borscht*, *blini* and *solyanka* (a spicy, sour soup). There's a daily changing lunch menu (€8) and Sunday brunch (10am–3pm; €12.40).

Café Sybille

MAP p.98, POCKET MAP L5
Karl-Marx-Allee 72 ⓤ Strausberger Platz ⓣ 030 29 35 22 03, ⓦ cafe-sibylle.de. Mon 11am–7pm, Tues–Sun 10am–7pm.

It's worth a stop at *Café Sybille* not just for the ice cream, cakes and coffee, but because it also hosts a small museum about the history of Karl-Marx-Allee, with propaganda posters, socialist statues and other exhibits to browse while your drinks are made.

Cupcake Berlin

MAP p.98, POCKET MAP A17
Krossener Str. 12 ⓤ Samariterstr. ⓣ 030 25 76 86 87, ⓦ cupcakeberlin.de. Daily 10am–8pm.

The city's first outlet dedicated to cupcakes, all home-made by American owner, Dawn, for sale in a café that's every bit as sweet and retro as her cakes. Brownies, fantastic New York cheesecake and apple pie are also available (all around €2.80). There's a second *Cupcake Kreuzberg* at Köpenicker Str. 4.

Dachkammer

MAP P.98, POCKET MAP A17
Simon-Dach-Str. 39 Ⓢ/ⓤ Warschauerstr. ⓣ 030 29 04 90 54, ⓦ dachkammer.com. Daily 1pm until late.

The largest and possibly most sociable place on the strip – the combination of rustic bar downstairs and retro bar upstairs has made this a local classic.

Goodies Berlin

MAP p.98, POCKET MAP A17
Warschauer Str. 69 Ⓤ Frankfurter Tor ☏ 030
33 97 6440, Ⓦ goodies-berlin.de. Mon–Fri
7.30am–7pm, Sat & Sun 9am–7pm.

Goodies is a tiny, wholesome café serving home-made baked goods, sandwiches, bagels, daily-changing organic soup, plus salads and vegan options. Free wi-fi and a children's area. Cash only.

Hops & Barley

MAP p.98, POCKET MAP A17
Wühlischstr. 22/23 Ⓤ Samaritenstr. or Ⓢ/
Ⓤ Warschauerstr. ☏ 030 29 36 75 34,
Ⓦ hopsandbarley-berlin.de. Mon–Fri 5pm
till late, Sat & Sun 3pm till late.

This unassuming wood-and-tiles brewpub attracts a diverse crowd that ranges from international hipsters to elderly locals. Five draft beers (three standard and two experimental ones) that are produced on-site, supplemented by simple snacks such as sausages and brewer's grain bread.

Kosmetiksalon Babette

MAP p.98, POCKET MAP K4
Karl-Marx-Allee 36 Ⓤ Schillingstr. ☏ 017
63 83 88 943, Ⓦ www.barbabette.com.
Daily from 6pm.

This glass box, once a GDR cosmetics shop, is now a chic and lively bar. At night, the only identifying marker is the warm glow of the cube's interior lights. The ground floor is sparsely furnished, while the former treatment rooms upstairs occasionally have book readings and performances.

Macondo Café

MAP p.98, POCKET MAP A17
Gärtnerstr. 14 Ⓤ Samariterstr. ☏ 030 54 73
59 43. Mon–Fri noon–late, Sat & Sun from
10am.

Kitted out with fraying vintage furniture, this local chill-out spot offers a good selection of books and board games and a great atmosphere for lounging. Serves brunch at weekends.

Spielwiese

MAP p.98, POCKET MAP A17
Kopernikusstr. 24 Ⓤ Warschauer Str.
☏ 030 28 03 40 88, Ⓦ spielwiese-berlin.
de. Mon & Fri 4pm–midnight, Thurs 7pm–
midnight, Sat 2pm–midnight, Sun 2–8pm.

This café and games publisher stocks over 1800 games, from chess to Risk. For a small fee (€1/ person), you can play games in the café or rent them (€1–3/day) to take home.

Zebrano

MAP p.98, POCKET MAP B17
Sonntagstr. 8 Ⓢ Ostkreuz. ☏ 030 29 36 58
74, Ⓦ zebranobar.de. Mon–Thurs & Sun
10am–1am, Fri & Sat 10am–3am.

Located on the lovely "Sunday Street", *Zebrano* is a fairly hip bar with a good selection of draught beers and cocktails (happy hour daily 7–9pm) plus decent breakfasts (till 5pm; €3.60–9.90).

Clubs and venues

://about blank

MAP p.98, POCKET MAP M7
Markgrafendamm 24c Ⓤ Ostkreuz
Ⓦ aboutparty.net. Club Thurs–Sun
midnight till late; from 7pm for midweek
live shows. €10–14.

Set inside a nondescript concrete

Goodies Berlin

block, this is one of the city's better underground clubs, with two main dancefloors, lots of nooks and crannies, and a garden where DJs spin in the summer. The dominant music policy is house and techno with occasional forays into related electronic genres plus live concerts.

Berghain/Panoramabar

MAP p.98, POCKET MAP L6
Am Wriezener Bahnhof Ⓢ Ostbahnhof
☎ 030 29 36 02 10, Ⓦ berghain.de. Fri &
Sat midnight–late. €12–18.

A strong contender for best club in the city, if not the world, this former power station attracts techno fans from all over the globe for its fantastic sound system, purist music policy and awe-inspiring industrial interior. The best time to arrive is after 5am on Saturday morning; the club runs till Sunday evening. In 2017, the club opened up the ground floor for more experimental sounds.

Insel

MAP p.98, POCKET MAP M7
Alt-Treptow 6, Treptow Ⓢ Plänterwald
☎ 030 20 91 49 90, Ⓦ inselberlin.de. Tues–
Fri noon till late, Sat & Sun 3pm till late.

Reliable venue for thrash/punk gigs and club nights, on a Spree island that's part of Treptower Park. Occasional outdoor raves on the large terrace in summer.

Radialsystem V

MAP p.98, POCKET MAP K6
Holzmarktstr. 33 Ⓢ Ostbahnhof ☎ 030 28
87 88 588, Ⓦ radialsystem.de. Ticket office
Tues–Fri 10am–7pm, Sat noon–7pm. For
evening performances, the box office
opens one hour before the show.

This sprawling space, housed in a former pumping station on the Spree, was retrofitted and reopened as a space for the arts in 2006, with a glass extension added. As well as visual and performing arts exhibitions, it hosts events ranging from opera concerts to relaxed jam sessions.

RAW Gelände

MAP p.98, POCKET MAP A17
Revaler Str. 99 Ⓢ/Ⓤ Warschauerstr.
Ⓦ rawcc.org. Entry prices and opening
times vary.

Sprawling, heavily graffitied ensemble of former train yard buildings, now one of the city's most alternative clubbing and cultural complexes. There are several shabby-chic bars and clubs, including the laidback Crack Bellmer (Ⓦ crackbellmer .de) and the more upbeat electro and techno clubs Cassiopeia (Ⓦ cassiopeia-berlin.de) and Suicide Circus (Ⓦ suicide-berlin .com). Urban Spree (Ⓦ urbanspree .com), a beer garden that often has DJs and live music into the night, is at the Warschauer Strasse side, and there's even a chic outdoor pool with a club and concert space called Haubentauscher (Ⓦ haubentaucher.berlin).

Rosi's

MAP p.98, POCKET MAP B17
Revaler Str. 29 Ⓤ Warschauer Str.
Ⓦ rosis-berlin.de. Thurs–Sat from 11pm.

Nothing more – or less – than a derelict industrial shack, decorated with secondhand furniture, graffiti and ping-pong tables, *Rosi's* puts on some very decent indie, punk and electronic nights. Best in summer when the beer garden is open for barbecues.

Salon zur Wilden Renate

MAP p.98, POCKET MAP M7
Alt-Stralau 70 Ⓢ Treptower Park
Ⓦ renate.cc.

Located near the train tracks that run towards Treptower Park, *Renate* is an artist-run event space in a semi derelict house with three floors, a cocktail bar and flamboyant decor that changes with each party. The music is good and the crowd is mixed. Open-air sister club, *Else*, just across the bridge, hosts open-air parties and has a beer garden open from Wed–Sun.

West Kreuzberg

The western section of Kreuzberg is centred on the main streets of Gneisenaustrasse and Bergmannstrasse, and pretty Viktoriapark. Once one of the poorest areas in Berlin, it's now one of its most bourgeois and bohemian and lies in sharp contrast to the more scruffy, multicultural part of the district to the east. Indeed, walking along café- and boutique-lined streets like Bergmannstrasse you're reminded of the gentrified environs of Prenzlauer Berg. At the end of this street is Viktoriapark, whose Iron Cross monument gives the district its name, and nearby is Chamissoplatz, which hosts a popular organic farmers' market every Saturday morning.

Mauermuseum – Museum Haus am Checkpoint Charlie

MAP OPPOSITE, POCKET MAP C15
Friedrichstr. 43–45 ⊕ Kochstr. ☎ 030 25 37 250, ⓦ mauermuseum.de. Daily 9am–10pm. €14.50.

"Checkpoint C" (or "Checkpoint Charlie" as it was called by the Western Allies) was the best-known Berlin Wall crossing point between East and West Berlin during the Cold War. Today it's one of the key places to learn about life in Berlin during the division. The museum – founded in 1962 by Dr Rainer Hildebrandt – is marked by the well-known "YOU ARE NOW LEAVING THE AMERICAN SECTOR" sign that remains outside the building alongside stone-faced (mock) guards, and a replica of the checkpoint (the original is in the Allied Museum in Dahlem). One of the most visited museums in Berlin, its exhibitions focus mostly on the creative ways East Berliners tried to escape – hot-air balloons, vehicles with special compartments, even a one-man submarine. There are also exhibits on the concept of freedom and nonviolent protest in general, including the Charter 77 typewriter and Mahatma Gandhi's diary.

Checkpoint Charlie

West Kreuzberg

WEST KREUZBERG

| 0 | metres | 250 |
| 0 | yards | 250 |

SHOPS
Ararat 3
été clothing 5
Marheineke
 Markhalle 4
Radio Art 1
Space Hall 2

ACCOMMODATION
Grand Hostel 2
Hotel Transit 5
Johann Hotel 3
Mövenpick Hotel 1
Riehmers Hofgarten 4

RESTAURANTS
Austria 12
Noberlhart &
 Schmutzig 3
Sale e Tabacchi 1

CHEAP EATS
Curry 36 4
Knofi 8,10

CAFÉS & BARS
Barcomi's 11
Molinari & Ko 7
Tomasa 9
westberlin 2
Yorckschlösschen 5
Zyankali Bar 6

CLUBS & VENUES
Gretchen 5
HAU 1 2
HAU 2 3
HAU 3 4
Tempodrom 1

WEST KREUZBERG

Topography of Terror

MAP p.105, POCKET MAP F6
Niederkirchnerstr. 8 Ⓤ/Ⓢ Potsdamer Platz
Ⓣ 030 25 45 09 50, Ⓦ www .topographie.
de. Daily 10am–8pm. Free.

From 1933–1945, the headquarters of the Gestapo, their "house prison" and the Reich Security main office stood on this site, making it one of the most notorious locations of Nazi brutality. It's now called the Topography of Terror (Topographie des Terrors) documentation centre, and though many of the buildings were destroyed in World War II, visitors can walk around the largely open-air museum, where exhibits display the history of the site, and explore the events of the Holocaust. A documentation centre focuses on the central institutions of the SS and police in the Third Reich and their crimes. The displays are graphic, so families with children should exercise caution. An audio-guide is available.

Martin-Gropius-Bau

MAP p.105, POCKET MAP F6
Niederkirchnerstr. 7 Ⓤ/Ⓢ Potsdamer Platz
Ⓣ 030 25 48 60, Ⓦ gropiusbau.de. Prices
vary from €5–10.

Envisioned as an applied arts museum, the stunning Martin-Gropius-Bau has evolved into one of Berlin's major contemporary art venues. The ornate, Renaissance-style building was badly damaged during World War II, and rebuilt 1978–81. It draws big-name international displays on art and history, such as retrospectives of Frida Kahlo and Méret Oppenheim and exhibitions by the likes of Ai Weiwei.

Anhalter Bahnhof

MAP p.105, POCKET MAP F7
Askanischer Platz 6 Ⓤ Mendelssohn-
Bartholdy-Park Ⓣ 030 50 58 68 30. Free.

This haunting landmark is a remnant of the Anhalter Bahnhof, once one of Berlin's busiest railway stations. The terminus opened in 1841, but its notoriety stems from World War II when it was one of the three stations used to deport Jews to Theresienstadt (or Terezín), and from there to the death camps. Nearly ten thousand Jews were deported from here, usually in groups of fifty to a hundred; the last train left on March 27, 1945. Though badly damaged in World War II, it was only closed in 1952. Today, all that remains is a portion of the entrance facade and a commemorative plaque, though an S-Bahn station shares its name.

Deutsches Technikmuseum

Deutsches Technikmuseum

MAP p.105, POCKET MAP F7
Trebbiner Str. 9 Ⓤ Gleisdreieck ☏ 030 90 25 40, Ⓦ www.sdtb.de. Tues–Fri 9am–5.30pm, Sat & Sun 10am–6pm. €8.

Opened in 1982 in the former goods depot of the Anhalter Bahnhof, the German Technology Museum presents a comprehensive (some might say overwhelming) overview of German technology. The vast collection includes trains, planes, computers, radios, cameras and more. There's a strong emphasis on rail, with trains from 1835 to the present day, but there are also maritime and aviation halls and exhibits on the industrial revolution, the computer and space age, and the pharmaceutical and chemical industry. A new exhibition on information and communication networks and the history of mobility is housed in the annexe on Ladestrasse. Much of the museum is based on life-sized reproductions and actual machines, though the Science Center Spectrum annexe at Möckernstrasse 26 is more interactive.

Jewish Museum Berlin

MAP p.105, POCKET MAP G7
Lindenstr. 9–14 Ⓤ Hallesches Tor/Kochstr. ☏ 030 25 99 33 00, Ⓦ www.jmberlin.de. Mon 10am–10pm, Tues–Sun 10am–8pm. €8.

Daniel Libeskind's Jewish Museum (Jüdisches Museum) is a must-see, both historically and architecturally. The stark, zinc-covered building has been thoughtfully designed, with each element symbolizing various aspects of the historical Jewish experience over some two thousand years. The process of moving through the building – which really is a work of art – is an experience in itself, not least thanks to its five vertical voids and walls of dark concrete. Guided tours are available and the restaurant serving traditional Jewish cuisine (though not kosher) is very good.

Memory Void at Jewish Museum Berlin

Berlinische Galerie

MAP p.105, POCKET MAP H7
Alte Jakobstr. 124–128 Ⓤ Hallesches Tor/Kochstr. ☏ 030 78 90 26 00, Ⓦ www .berlinischegalerie.de. Daily except Tues 10am–6pm. €8, €4 first Mon of the month; special exhibition prices vary; combined ticket with Jewish Museum available. Guided tours in English first Mon of month at 3pm.

Founded in 1975 as a private institution, the Berlinische Galerie was once part of the Martin-Gropius-Bau before moving to its current premises in 2004. Its mission is to showcase art made in Berlin, bringing together fine art, photography and architecture. The permanent exhibition includes works from 1870 to the present day, spanning major movements such as the Secessionists, Fluxus, Dada and the Expressionists, with works by Max Liebermann, Otto Dix, Georg Grosz and Hannah Höch. Note that from late 2018, the permanent exhibition will concentrate exclusively on art from 1945 until the present day. A spacious hall also hosts temporary exhibitions and there are tours, occasional lectures and film screenings.

Berlin Story Museum & Hitler Documentation

MAP p.105, POCKET MAP F7
Schöneberger Str. 23a ⓤ Mendelssohn-Bartholdy-Park ⓣ 030 20 45 46 73, ⓦberlinstory.de. Daily 10am–7pm (last admission 6pm). €6 (museum), €12 (Hitler Documentation).

This attraction, set inside a WW2 bunker, features 800 years of Berlin history (free audioguide included) in the Berlin Story Museum, plus a more controversial exhibition about Adolf Hitler's life and WW2 that includes a reconstruction of his living and working rooms from the original "Führerbunker" near Potsdamer Platz.

Viktoriapark

MAP p.105, POCKET MAP F9
Between Kreuzbergstr., Dudenstr., Katzbachstr. and Methfesselstr. ⓤ Yorckstr./Mehringdamm. Open 24hr.
Famous for hosting Berlin's highest peak, "Vikky Park" is one of the most popular in the city. A multitude of pathways winds around and up the hill to give visitors stunning panoramic views, and there are playgrounds, landscaped rose gardens, a tumbling waterfall and even vineyards to enjoy and explore; the well-known *Golgatha* beer garden provides shade and sustenance.

Tempelhofer Park

MAP p.105, POCKET MAP G9

Cyclists in Tempelhofer Park

Columbiadamm 192 ⓤ Südstern ⓦ tempelhofer-park.de. Park daily sunrise to sunset (see website for exact times); free. Airport tours (2hr) Wed, Fri, Sat & Sun 1.30pm. €15. Booking: ⓦ www .thf-berlin.de, ⓣ 030 200 03 7441.

The largest park in continental Europe, Tempelhofer Park is the site of the now defunct Tempelhof airport, an immense building created by the Nazis (the terminal was designed to resemble an eagle) which became famous for the 1948–49 Berlin Airlift. Tours of the airport building, which stages events through the year, relate the story. The huge space surrounding the airport doesn't boast any actual attractions but is still a great place to go cycling, walking, roller-skating – or to enjoy a picnic (which can be purchased on site).

Liquidrom

MAP p.105, POCKET MAP F7
Möckernstr. 10 ⓤ Möckernbrücke ⓣ 030 25 80 07 820, ⓦ liquidrom-berlin.de. Mon–Thurs & Sun 9am–midnight, Fri & Sat 9am–1am.

This designer spa features saunas, slightly cramped chill-out areas and a large, domed flotation pool where you can drift and listen to soft electronic music, sometimes mixed live by DJs, as well as readings and live concerts. A range of massage treatments are also available. A two-hour sauna and thermal bath is €19.50.

Shops

Ararat

MAP p.105, POCKET MAP G9
Bergmannstr. 9 ⓤ Gneisenaustr. ☎ 030 69 49 532. Mon–Sat 10am–8pm.

It's easy to lose yourself in here, surrounded by prints and picture frames; over the road at no. 99, another branch sells postcards and gifts.

été clothing

MAP p.105, POCKET MAP G9
Bergmannstr. 18 ⓤ Gneisenaustr. ☎ 030 32 89 55 43, ⓦ ete-clothing.de. Mon–Sat 11am–8pm.

With shirts and hoodies from trusted brands like RVLT, Volcom and Iriedaily, and a decent range of sneakers, this is a good stop for streetwear in Kreuzberg.

Marheineke Markhalle

MAP p.105, POCKET MAP G9
Marheinekeplatz 15 ⓤ Gneisenaustr. ⓦ meine-markthalle.de. Mon–Fri 8am–8pm, Sat 8am–6pm.

This popular covered market hall is an excellent place for grocery shopping as well as for breakfasts and lunches. Stalls often emphasize organic and regional products. You'll also find crêpes and tapas, as well as regular art exhibitions and events.

Picknweight Concept Store

MAP p.105, POCKET MAP G9
Bergmannstr. 102 ⓤ Mehringdamm ☎ 030 69 43 348, ⓦ picknweight.de. Mon–Sat 11am–7pm.

A retro paradise with secondhand clothes spanning the 1960s to 1980s – particularly good on the 1970s.

Radio Art

MAP p.105, POCKET MAP G8
Zossener Str. 2 ⓤ Mehringdamm ☎ 030 69 39 435. Thurs & Fri noon–6pm, Sat 10am–1pm.

A visually satisfying shop for radio lovers, its shelves brimming with

Radio Art

vintage (and some modern) radio sets and record players.

Space Hall

MAP p.105, POCKET MAP G8
Zossener Str. 33 ⓤ Gneisenaustr. ☎ 030 69 47 664. Mon–Wed & Sat 11am–8pm, Thurs & Fri 11am–10pm.

This excellent two-store, multi-roomed record shop offers a large CD collection at no. 33 (rock, pop, electronic, rap) and DJ-friendly vinyl at no. 35.

Restaurants

Austria

MAP p.105, POCKET MAP G9
Bergmannstr. 30, on Marheineke Platz ⓤ Gneisenaustr. ☎ 030 69 44 440. Mon 6–11pm, Tues–Sun noon–11pm.

Austria serves classic Austrian dishes, using organic ingredients, in a hunting lodge-style interior. The huge Schnitzel is justly famous (mains €13.50–19.80).

Nobelhart & Schmutzig

MAP p.105, POCKET MAP G6
Friedrichstr. 218 ⓤ Kochstr./Checkpoint Charlie ☎ 030 25 94 06 10, ⓦ nobelhartund schmutzig.com. Tues–Sat 6.30–10.30pm.

Founded by sommelier Billy Wagner, formerly of *Weinbar Rutz* (see p.36) and chef Micha Schäfer, this chic spot offers delicious, creative food, fiercely committed to a local and seasonal ethos.

Sale e Tabacchi

MAP p.105, POCKET MAP G6
Rudi-Dutschke-Str. 23 Ⓤ Kochstr. ☎ 030
25 21 155, Ⓦ www.sale-e-tabacchi.de.
Daily 10am–11.30pm.

Located towards the Mitte end
of Kreuzberg, "Salt and Tobacco"
has a more classic feel than most
restaurants in the area. It's known
for its excellent seafood dishes
(tuna €24, sea bass €22.50) and
Italian wines. The interior is
large and airy and there's a garden
out back.

Cheap eats

Curry 36

MAP p.105, POCKET MAP G8
Mehringdamm 36 Ⓤ Mehringdamm ☎ 030
25 17 368. Daily 9am–5pm.

Everyone in Berlin has a favourite
place to eat *Currywurst* – sausage
doused in curry sauce – but *Curry
36* is cited more often than most
(along with *Konnopke's*, see p.90);
its popularity alone guarantees
it's a buzzy place to grab a snack
(around €1.50).

Knofi

MAP p.105, POCKET MAP G9
Bergmannstr. 11 & 98 Ⓤ Gneisenaustr.
☎ 030 69 56 43 59 (no. 11), ☎ 030 69 45
807 (no. 98). Daily 8am–midnight (no. 11);
daily 9am–midnight (no, 98).

There are two *Knofi*s opposite each
other. At no. 11 you'll find a small
deli-style restaurant serving tasty
Turkish food. Over the road is a
Turkish deli.

Cafés and bars

Barcomi's

MAP p.105, POCKET MAP G9
Bergmannstr. 21 Ⓤ Gneisenaustr. ☎ 030 69
48 138, Ⓦ www.barcomis.de. Mon–Fri
8am–9pm, Sat & Sun 9am–9pm.

Not quite as cosy as its Mitte
branch (see p.37), but you can find
excellent quality coffee – *Barcomi's*

roasts its thirteen coffee varieties
here, hence the decorative coffee
sacks and delicious odour – as
well as handmade breads, pastries,
soups and sandwiches.

Molinari & Ko

MAP p.105, POCKET MAP G9
Riemannstr. 13 Ⓤ Gneisenaustr. ☎ 030 69
13 903. Mon–Fri 8am–midnight, Sat & Sun
9am–midnight.

This welcoming Italian café/bar/
restaurant, hidden away on a
residential street, offers a menu of
breakfast and snacks, pasta and
pizza. A decent wine and beer
selection make it a good choice for
evenings, too.

Tomasa

MAP p.105, POCKET MAP F9
Kreuzbergstr. 62 Ⓤ Mehringdamm ☎ 030
81 00 98 85, Ⓦ www.tomasa.de. Daily
9am–1am.

This old-school villa, on the edge
of Viktoriapark, is a particularly
pleasant place for a relaxed
breakfast or lunch. The classic
interior, good seasonal menu
(from tapas to pasta and German
dishes) and friendly service
attract a mixed clientele, families
included. Sunday brunch (€16.50)
is very popular.

Curry 36

Zyankali Bar

MAP p.105, POCKET MAP G8
Gneisenaustr. 17 ⓊGneisenaustr. Ⓣ030 68
83 01 70, Ⓦzyankali.de. Daily from 4pm.
This unique "herbal clinic" bar
has an incredible range of strange
and surprising cocktails (often
with home-made ingredients),
occasional DJs and a "play area"
with football and pinball, and
a beer garden with plenty of
seating. Alcohol-infused ice-cream
(summer only) and snacks like *dim
sum* and Hawaiian toast are also
served.

Clubs and venues

Gretchen

MAP p.105, POCKET MAP G8
Obentrautstr. 19–21 ⓊHallesches Tor
Ⓣ030 25 92 27 02, Ⓦgretchen-club.de.
Opening times and admission varies.
Named after a murderous
character in Goethe's *Faust*, this
alternative club space offers
a handsome interior that's all
columns and vaulted ceilings, and
a mix of electronic sounds (drum
'n' bass, dubstep, trip hop). A
refreshing alternative to the usual
Berlin "techno-shack" formulas.

Hebbel am Ufer

MAP p.105, POCKET MAP G7
HAU1 Stresemannstr. 29; HAU2 Hallesches
Ufer 32; HAU3 Tempelhofer Ufer 10
ⓊHallesches Tor Ⓣ030 25 90 04 27,
Ⓦwww.hebbel-am-ufer.de.
These three neighbouring venues
of HAU Hebbel am Ufer – HAU1,
HAU2 and HAU3 – are *the* places
for ground-breaking theatre, the
occasional concert and more.

Tempodrom

MAP p.105, POCKET MAP F7
Möckernstr. 10 ⓊMöckernbrücke Ⓣ030
74 73 70, Ⓦwww.tempodrom.de.
A giant tent-like arena in the
heart of Berlin, Tempodrom puts
on concerts, shows, plays, galas,
conferences, fashion shows – you
name it, Tempodrom's hosted it.

Tempodrom

westberlin

MAP p.105, POCKET MAP G6
Friedrichstr. 215 ⓊKochstr. Ⓣ030 25 92
27 45, Ⓦwestberlin-bar-shop.de. Mon–Fri
8.30am–7pm, Sat & Sun 10am–7pm.
This handsome haven is part
chic media hangout and part
café. Occupying a grittier part of
Friedrichstrasse that's only just
starting to come to life, you can
sip on a locally roasted flat white
while working away on your
laptop or enjoying a delicious
cake, sandwich or quiche. They
also have a decent selection of
fashion and style magazines as
well as Berlin guides.

Yorckschlösschen

MAP p.105, POCKET MAP F8
Yorckstr. 15 ⓊMehringdamm Ⓣ030 21 58
070, Ⓦwww.yorckschloesschen.de. Mon–
Sat 5pm–3am, Sun 10am–3am.
This place has been a Kreuzberg
institution for over a hundred
years, though it doesn't seem
to have been updated since
the 1970s. The menu is mostly
basic and local – meatballs and
Leberkäse (meatloaf) – and the
service gruff, but the tree-shaded
garden is a very pleasant place to
eat. Live jazz, blues and country
bands play most days (Wed–Sat
9pm, Sun 2pm).

East Kreuzberg

An isolated section of West Berlin throughout the Cold War, Kreuzberg has since grown into one of Berlin's most colourful districts – a magnet for left-wing anarchists, gays, Turkish immigrants (it's sometimes called Little Istanbul) and, increasingly, hipsters and tourists. Despite being a coherent borough (nowadays part of Kreuzberg-Friedrichshain), Kreuzberg is still largely considered two distinct halves roughly coterminous with the former postal codes: SO 36 and SW 61 in the eastern and western sides respectively. Much of the eastern part of Kreuzberg abutted the wall on the West side and was strongly associated with Berlin's squatter and anarchist scenes. Though the area has gentrified somewhat since those heady days, it maintains a grungy, vibrant feel that spreads out from Schlesisches Tor down to Kottbusser Tor and beyond, fuelled by an ever-expanding series of excellent independent bars, clubs and restaurants.

East Kreuzberg

FOOD MARKET

Markthalle Neun	3

RESTAURANTS

Baraka	9
Cocolo	16
Defne	18
Kimchi Princess	12
Long March Canteen	1
RosaCaleta	4

CHEAP EATS

Maroush	6
Musashi	19
Ron Telesky	21
Taka Fish House	10

CAFÉS & BARS

Ankerklause	17
Barbie Deinhoff	11
Club der Visionaere	15
Five Elephant	20
Das Hotel	14
Möbel-Olfe	8
Roses	7
Schwarze Traube	2
Tiki Heart	13
Würgeengel	5

Museum der Dinge

MAP BELOW, POCKET MAP J7
Oranienstr. 25 ⓤ Kottbusser Tor ☏ 030 92
10 63 11, ⓦ www.museumderdinge.de.
Mon & Thurs–Sun noon–7pm. €6.

A museum dedicated to the
somewhat ambiguous culture of
"things" could have gone either way.
In fact it succeeds by presenting
an interesting array of implements
– around 25,000 to be precise.
Everyday houseware, furniture and
knick-knacks are mixed with the
unusual, spanning the nineteenth
century to the present day. Located
on the top floor of a Kreuzberg
apartment block, the museum is a
design-fiend's dream, with exhibits
including Manoli ashtrays, Art
Deco fondue sets and World War
II memorabilia, all inside a room
that's modern and well organized.
One of the latest attractions is
the modular "Frankfurt Kitchen"
designed by Viennese architect

Display in the Museum der Dinge

Margarete Schütte-Lihotzky in 1926
– the model for the fitted kitchen
of today. The exhibition texts are
in German and English, and you'll
also find a colourful and nicely
curated giftshop near the entrance.

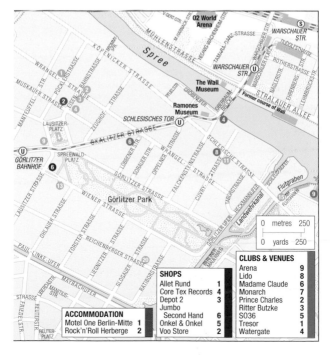

SHOPS	
Allet Rund	1
Core Tex Records	4
Depot 2	3
Jumbo Second Hand	6
Onkel & Onkel	5
Voo Store	2

ACCOMMODATION	
Motel One Berlin-Mitte	1
Rock'n'Roll Herberge	2

CLUBS & VENUES	
Arena	9
Lido	8
Madame Claude	6
Monarch	7
Prince Charles	2
Ritter Butzke	3
SO36	5
Tresor	1
Watergate	4

Ramones Museum

MAP p.112, POCKET MAP L7
Oberbaumstr. 5 ⓤ Schlesisches Tor ☎ 030
75 52 88 89, ⓦ ramonesmuseum.com.
Daily 10am–10pm. €4.50 (concerts vary
but mostly free).

Berlin's own shrine to the
American proto-punks, the
Ramones Museum was started
by music editor Flo Hayler two
decades ago. Back then the
collection amounted to a few
signed posters and some T-shirts,
but today it has expanded to
over three hundred items of
memorabilia. It's certainly an
eclectic assortment, ranging
from childhood photos of the
group to gig set lists and flyers.
The museum also hosts film
screenings, the odd acoustic show
from artists as well known as Fran
Healy from Travis and special
events. There's a decent café
(*Mania*) inside selling coffee, beer
and snacks.

Shops

Allet Rund

MAP p.112, POCKET MAP J7
Dresdener Str. 16 ⓤ Kottbusser Tor ☎ 030
27 01 48 36. Mon–Fri noon–7pm, Sat
noon–5pm.

Joachin Semrau offers fair-trade,
Kreuzberg-made designs for sizes
42 to 60, using European fabrics.

Core Tex Records

MAP p.112, POCKET MAP K7
Oranienstr. 3 ⓤ Görlitzer Bahnhof ☎ 030
61 28 00 50, ⓦ coretexrecords.com. Mon–
Sat 11am–8pm.

Core Tex Records

The best place for punk or hardcore
music, plus T-shirts, accessories,
books and concert tickets.

Depot 2

MAP p.112, POCKET MAP K7
Oranienstr. 9 ⓤ Görlitzer Bahnhof ☎ 030
61 14 655, ⓦ www.depot2.de. Mon–Sat
11am–8pm.

An ice-cool assortment of street-
oriented fashions, including Vans
and other stylish footwear.

Jumbo Second Hand

MAP p.112, POCKET MAP K7
Wiener Str. 63 ⓤ Görlitzer Bahnhof. Mon–
Sat 10am–8pm.

A quantity-over-quality
secondhand clothes and accessories
store. It's worth trying to bargain.

Onkel & Onkel

MAP p.112, POCKET MAP K7
Oranienstr. 195 ⓤ Kottbusser Tor ☎ 033
203 26 90 14. Mon–Sat 10am–6pm.

A magazine shop that specializes
in graphic design, photography
and street-art books, Onkel &
Onkel also publishes its own titles,
all in a library-esque atmosphere.

Voo Store

MAP p.112, POCKET MAP J7
Oranienstr. 24 ⓤ Kottbusser Tor ☎ 030 616
511 12, ⓦ vooberlin.com. Mon–Sat
10am–8pm.

A former locksmiths turned
pop-culture concept shop, Voo
Store's gorgeous interior was created

by Danish designer and architect Sigurd Larsen, while its highly curated stock features both big names and little-known designers.

Food market

Markthalle Neun

MAP p.112, POCKET MAP K7
Eisenbahnstr. 42/43 Ⓤ Görlitzer Bahnhof Ⓦ markthalleneun.com. Basic market Tues–Thurs noon–6pm; farmers' market Fri noon–6pm & Sat 10am–6pm; shops Mon–Sat noon–6pm.

This revitalized nineteenth-century market hall has become Berlin's foodie destination, thanks to a weekly farmers' market (Thurs and Fri) and events focusing on sustainable and local produce and the especially popular weekly Street Food Thursday event (5–10pm).

Restaurants

Baraka

MAP p.112, POCKET MAP K7
Lausitzer Platz 6 Ⓤ Görlitzer Bahnhof ☎ 030 61 26 330, Ⓦ www.baraka-berlin. de. Mon–Thurs & Sun 11am–midnight, Fri & Sat 11am–1am.

North African food fans will adore *Baraka*. The decor is authentic without slipping into kitsch (although the back room comes close) and the food – *tagines*, chicken skewers, *schwarma* – is some of the best in town, and at decent prices (mains €5–12). The mixed plate for two is immense.

Cocolo

MAP p.112, POCKET MAP K8
Paul-Lincke-Ufer 39 Ⓤ Kottbusser Tor ☎ 030 98 33 90 73. Mon–Sat noon–11pm, Sun 6–11pm.

Unarguably Berlin's best dedicated *ramen* spot, *Cocolo* started life with its Mitte branch (Gipstr. 3), expanding to this larger Kreuzberg location in 2014. Enjoy their slurp-a-licious dishes (including sweet

Kimchi Princess

pork belly and *kimchi ramen*) at a shared table inside, or on the canal-facing terrace. Soups start at €9.

Defne

MAP p.112, POCKET MAP J8
Planufer 92c Ⓤ Kottbusser Tor/Schönleinstr. ☎ 030 81 79 71 11, Ⓦ www.defne -restaurant.de. Daily: April–Sept 4pm–1am; Oct–March 5pm–1am (kitchen till midnight all year).

Defne's Turkish and Mediterranean classics include *imam bayildi* (aubergines with pine nuts, peppers and tomato sauce, €9.90) and lamb skewers (€14.50). The interior is simple and spacious; the terrace, overlooking the Landwehrkanal, is lovely in summer.

Kimchi Princess

MAP p.112, POCKET MAP K7
Skalitzer Str. 36 Ⓤ Kottbusser Tor ☎ 0163 45 80 203, Ⓦ kimchiprincess.com. Daily noon–10.30pm.

Part of a trend for cool Korean eateries in Berlin, *Kimchi Princess* offers simple wooden pallets as seating, a spacious interior and cool staff. There's *bibimbap* and more on the menu, but the Korean barbecue is the thing to go for (from €16.90). The owners also run the nearby *Angry Chicken* (Oranienstr. 16), a must for spice fans.

Long March Canteen

MAP p.112, POCKET MAP K7
Wrangelstr. 20 ⓤ Görlitzer Bahnhof ☏ 0178
884 9899, ⓦ longmarchcanteen .com. Daily
6pm–midnight.

Although folk justifiably flock here
for the *dim sum* (€6–10), this trendy
Chinese restaurant also serves up
excellent, tapas-sized portions of
other dishes like *pak choi* salad and
marinated chicken skewers with
water chestnuts. John Malkovich
is just one of the A-listers who has
been spotted here.

RosaCaleta

MAP p.112, POCKET MAP K7
Muskauer Str. 9 ⓤ Görlitzer Bahnhof ☏ 030
69 53 78 59, ⓦ rosacaleta.com. Winter
Tues–Sat 6pm–1am, Sun 2pm–1am;
summer Tues–Fri 11 am–1am, Sat
6pm–1am, Sun 2pm–1am.

This Jamaican/European fusion
restaurant has created quite a
buzz in a city hopelessly devoid of
Caribbean cuisine. There's plenty
of jerk-style food on the menu, but
also dishes like oven-roast pork
fillet, mango-ginger lentil salad
and tofu and vegetable stew (mains
from €10). It also functions as an
art space and hosts DJ parties.

RosaCaleta

Cheap eats

Maroush

MAP p.112, POCKET MAP J7
Adalbertstr. 93 ⓤ Kottbusser Tor ☏ 030 69
53 61 71, ⓦ www.maroush-berlin.de. Daily
11am–2am.

With a cosy dining area, Middle
Eastern decor and tasty sandwiches,
kebabs, falafels and fresh salads, this
small Lebanese restaurant is one
of the better of its type. Vegetarian
options also available.

Musashi

MAP p.112, POCKET MAP J8
Kottbusser Damm 102 ⓤ Schönleinstr.
☏ 030 69 32 042. Mon–Sat noon–10.30pm,
Sun 2–8pm.

This tiny spot serves up decent
sushi in a refreshingly designer-
free space, decorated with posters
of sumo wrestlers and populated
with just a few bar tables. The
Japanese chefs prepare fresh, tasty
makis and inside-out rolls for very
good prices (€6.50 for a set menu).

Ron Telesky

MAP p.112, POCKET MAP J8
Dieffenbachstr. 62 ⓤ Schönleinstr. ☏ 030
61 62 11 11. Mon–Fri 12.30–10pm, Sat &
Sun 1.30–10pm.

Canadian pizza served from a
canoe – how can you say no?
Especially when the pizza toppings
include sweet potato, mango, feta
and maple syrup. Aside from the
canoe (outside) the interior features
national emblems like a moose
head. Vegan options available.

Taka Fish House

MAP p.112, POCKET MAP J7
Adalbertstr. 97 ⓤ Kottbusser Tor ☏ 0157
74 24 62 19. Mon–Thurs 9am–11pm, Fri–
Sun 9am–2am.

Tucked away on bustling Kottbusser
Tor and surrounded by kebab and
falafel shops, this unassuming
Turkish *Imbiss* has just a handful of
tables inside and out, but serves up
some of the most delicious, freshly
grilled fish sandwiches in the city.

Cafés and bars

Ankerklause

MAP p.112, POCKET MAP J8
Kottbusser Damm 104 Ⓤ Kottbusser Tor
Ⓣ 030 69 35 649, Ⓦ www.ankerklause.de.
Mon 4pm–4am, Tues–Sun 10am–4am.

Situated by Maybachufer, next to the Turkish market (Tues & Fri; see p.121), *Ankerklause* is a popular café during the day, with a decent range of snacks (and seats out front and a terrace overlooking the water out back). Later, there's something of the alternative scene about it when the jukebox plays rock 'n' roll classics.

Barbie Deinhoff

MAP p.112, POCKET MAP L7
Schlesische Str. 16 Ⓤ Schlesisches Tor.
Tues–Sat 6pm–late.

This colourful dive bar is a lot of fun, attracting a heady mix of transvestites, gay men and curious onlookers. The decor runs from deliberately kitsch to the colourfully futuristic and there are regular DJs and happenings. A fun place to get comprehensively trashed (two-for-one happy hour Tues 7pm–midnight), though there are also often cultural events early evening.

Club der Visionaere

MAP p.112, POCKET MAP M8
Am Flutgraben 1 Ⓤ Schlesisches Tor Ⓣ 030
69 51 89 42, Ⓦ www.clubdervisionaere.
com. May–Sept: Mon–Fri 2pm–late, Sat &
Sun noon–late. Admission €1–5.

Just beyond the Kreuzberg/Treptow border, this legendary summer-only techno bar enjoys a unique setting on the intersection of the Spree and Flutgraben canal. The bar and DJ booth is in an old ceramic-tiled boathouse, and punters stand (and dance) on the floating docks outside. It's minimal techno all the way and a fantastically upbeat place.

Five Elephant

MAP p.112, POCKET MAP L8
Reichenberger Str. 101 Ⓤ Görlitzer
Bahnhof Ⓣ 030 96 08 15 27, Ⓦ www
.fiveelephant.com. Mon–Fri 8.30am–7pm,
Sat & Sun 10am–7pm.

Opened by American and Austrian team Kris Shackman and Sophie Weigensamer in 2010, this highly regarded café not only brews (and roasts) some of the best "third wave" coffee in town, but also has a much talked about cheesecake selection. There's a second location at Alte Schönhauser Str. 14, in Mitte.

Das Hotel

MAP p.112, POCKET MAP J8
Mariannenstr. 26a Ⓤ Kottbusser Tor Ⓣ 030
84 11 84 33. Daily noon–open end.

Located on a residential street near the Paul-Linke-Ufer, *Das Hotel* is a combination bar, club and bistro that serves burritos and coffee. The candlelit bar is charming but get there early at weekends or you won't get a seat. The downstairs club plays music from the 1940s onwards, with a "no hits and no techno" policy.

Möbel-Olfe

MAP p.112, POCKET MAP J7
Reichenberger Str. 177 Ⓤ Kottbusser Tor
Ⓣ 030 23 27 46 90, Ⓦ moebel-olfe.de.
Tues–Sun 6pm–late.

Sandwiched between a string of Turkish snack bars in a run-down building behind Kottbusser Tor, this unusual, smoky, local bar attracts gays, hipsters, ageing drunks and more. There are regular DJ nights but it's more about experiencing the diversity of the Kreuzberg crowds.

Roses

MAP p.112, POCKET MAP K7
Oranienstr. 187 Ⓤ Kottbusser Tor/Görlitzer
Bahnhof Ⓣ 030 61 56 570. Daily 10pm–6am.

A legendary gay hangout, *Roses* provides a welcoming bosom for all manner of sexual orientations to crowd around. The kitsch decor mirrors the clientele and the fun vibe well. Sunday is the main day – and the "gayest" – but women are welcome anytime.

Schwarze Traube

MAP p.112, POCKET MAP K7
Wrangelstr. 24 ⓤ Görlitzer Bahnhof ☎ 030 23 13 55 69. Daily 7pm till late.

Like many of Berlin's best drinking spots, this cocktail bar looks fairly nondescript from the outside. Knock on the door and – if it's not full – you'll be ushered into a cosy, dimly lit bar with rickety furnishings and award-winning drinks.

Tiki Heart

MAP p.112, POCKET MAP K8
Wiener Str. 20 ⓤ Görlitzer Bahnhof ☎ 030 61 07 47 03, ⓦ tikiheart.de. Summer Mon–Fri noon–open end, Sat & Sun 10am–open end; winter Mon–Fri 4pm–open end, Sat & Sun 10am–open end.

Berlin's only Hawaiian rockabilly-themed joint is renowned for its unapologetically kitsch interior and innovative menu. The breakfasts, served till 5pm, feature items like the "Oi-Fast" – a heady mix of scrambled eggs and chorizo. There are veggie burgers and – one for the serious rockers – a Lemmy burger grilled in whisky. Strong cocktails are served and the Wild at Heart club next door (ⓦ wildatheartberlin.de) roars into action with regular rock, punk, metal and surf nights.

Roses

Würgeengel

MAP p.112, POCKET MAP J7
Dresdener Str. 122 ⓤ Kottbusser Tor ☎ 030 61 55 560. Daily 7pm–late.

One of the best cocktail bars in Kreuzberg, "the exterminating angel" has red walls, great tapas, decadent decor and an extensive cocktail and wine list. The feel is timeless, though with a trendy clientele.

Clubs and venues

Arena

MAP p.112, POCKET MAP M8
Eichenstr. 4 ⓤ Treptower Park ☎ 030 53 32030, ⓦ arena-berlin.de. Badeschiff entrance: €6 (open May–Sept 8am–midnight); other venues vary (often free).

This huge area next to the Spree encompasses the *Arena Club*, *Glashaus*, the actual Arena, the *Badeschiff* and the *Hoppetosse*. There are frequent electronic open-air parties and live acts at *Arena Club*, sometimes the *Hoppetosse* café (on a boat) can turn into a club, and at Arena itself you can catch rock and metal shows, as well as events and festivals.

Lido

MAP p.112, POCKET MAP L7
Cuvrystr. 7 ⓤ Schlesisches Tor ☎ 030 69 56 68 40, ⓦ www.lido-berlin.de. Times and prices vary according to event.

An old-school club in a former theatre that's been going for nearly ten years, *Lido* is known for championing new music, and is home to a younger indie crowd, with the occasional techno or house event. The club also has a courtyard with canopy that makes it suitable for winter throw-downs.

Madame Claude

MAP p.112, POCKET MAP L7
Lübbener Str. 19 ⓤ Görlitzer Bahnhof ☎ 030 84 11 08 59, ⓦ madameclaude.de. Daily 7pm–late.

This quirky hangout has live music six days a week, ranging from indie-rock and experimental to folk. Be prepared to feel slightly unsettled by the decor, which is upside down and on the ceiling. Pay what you want for entrance.

Monarch

MAP p.112, POCKET MAP J7
Skalitzer Str. 134 Ⓤ Kottbusser Tor ☏ 030 61 65 60 03, Ⓦ kottimonarch.de. Tues–Sat 9pm till late. Entry varies; often as low as €3.

Unpretentious and slightly ragged place that attracts a hip crowd who groove to a wide range of tunes – swing, rockabilly, folk, punk, indie (no techno) – and enjoy views over Kottbusser Tor from huge windows. Entrance is via an unmarked door and stairwell opposite the *Misir Casisi* kebab shop.

Prince Charles

MAP p.112, POCKET MAP K7
Prinzenstr. 85f Ⓤ Moritzplatz Ⓦ princecharlesberlin.com. Opening times vary according to event; club nights usually Thurs–Sat 11pm–open end. Admission varies.

Hidden away in a basement near Moritzplatz that once housed a swimming pool, this square-shaped, fairly upscale club has a penchant for bass-heavy parties that transcend techno tropes in favour of house, jazzy beats and hip hop spun by a mix of local and international DJs.

Ritter Butzke

MAP p.112, POCKET MAP H7
Ritter Str. 24 Ⓤ Moritzplatz Ⓦ club .ritterbutzke.de. Fri & Sat from noon. Admission €8–15.

This former factory now comprises two main club rooms and an outside space, generally used only in summer. The music is usually electronic (house, electro, techno) and the crowd a considered but dedicated bunch.

SO36

MAP p.112, POCKET MAP K7
Oranienstr. 190 Ⓤ Görlitzer Bahnhof ☏ 030 61 40 13 06, Ⓦ www.so36.de. Opening times and admission vary.

One of the city's most legendary clubs, *SO36* has its roots in punk, post-punk and alternative music – musical heroes who've played here include Iggy Pop, David Bowie and Einstürzende Neubauten. Nowadays it hosts alternative and electronic shows, including monthly parties like Gayhane, a Turkish "homoriental" party, and "Ich bin ein Berliner", where you can catch an array of Berlin-based artists playing everything from garage to synth-pop.

Tresor

POCKET MAP J6
Köpenicker Str. 70 Ⓤ/Ⓢ Heinrich-Heine-Str./Jannowitzbrücke. Mon, Wed, Fri & Sat midnight–late. Admission varies.

Housed in what was the main central-heating power station for East Berlin, the colossal location of the third incarnation of this ground-breaking club is breathtaking. Only a tiny portion of its 28,000 square metres is in use, but the club is sizeable enough with three different rooms dedicated to cutting-edge, muscular techno played by a rotating roster of international DJs.

Watergate

MAP p.112, POCKET MAP L7
Falckensteinstr. 49 Ⓤ Schlesisches Tor ☏ 030 61 28 03 94. Wed, Fri & Sat midnight–late, occasional Tues & Thurs events. €10–20.

This slick, split-level club right on the Spree enjoys a killer combination of panoramic windows, excellent sound system and constant flow of renowned DJs. Music is electro, house and minimal techno. Expect to see residents like Sven Väth and Solomun too.

EAST KREUZBERG

Neukölln

Neukölln, with its strings of bars, galleries, shops and cafés, is one of the city's most overtly hip districts. Once upon a time it was Rixdorf, a tiny village outside Berlin studded with windmills and boasting fantastic views from its impressive hillsides. In came the Industrial Revolution and away went the hills (used for buildings as the city expanded), and Rixdorf developed into a district of entertainment and revelry – so much so that in 1912 it was renamed Neukölln in an effort to change its riotous image. Postwar Neukölln became home to many Turkish, Aran and Kurdish communities, who still give the area its character, along with the more recent influx of expats and artists priced out of Berlin's other inner-city districts. Indeed, the resultant clash of working-class residents and middle-class creatives – reflected in intensely rising rents and odd juxtapositions of gaudy video arcades and hipster hangouts around Weserstrasse and bustling Hermannplatz – forms the heart of Berlin's gentrification debate and lends Neukölln its somewhat edgy reputation.

Alt-Rixdorf

MAP OPPOSITE
Ⓤ Karl-Marx-Str.

The most obvious reminders of Neukölln's medieval origins lie between the main arteries of Karl-Marx-Strasse and Sonnenallee, an area known as Alt-Rixdorf. A wander around the cobbled streets – centred on historical **Richardplatz** – reveals a centuries-old blacksmith's business, attractive churches and the remains of the district's eighteenth-century Bohemian village – founded for Protestant refugees fleeing persecution – with its cute houses and attractive gardens.

Körnerpark

MAP OPPOSITE
Schierker Str. 8 Ⓢ Berlin-Neukölln ☏ 030 90 23 92 876, Ⓦ www.körnerpark.de. Park Tues–Sun 10am–6pm; café till 8pm. Free.

Refined Körnerpark might not be the biggest park in Neukölln, but it is easily the prettiest – a stark contrast to the vast, featureless expanse of nearby Tempelhofer Park (see p.108). With its manicured hedges,

Hermannplatz

Neukölln

SHOPS	
Sing Blackbird	1
Vin Aqua Vin	2

CAFÉS & BARS	
Ä Wirtschaft	5
The California Breakfast Slam	3
Geist im Glas	2
Das Gift	6
Klunkerkranich	7

RESTAURANTS	
Berlin Burger International	4
Lavanderia Vecchia	8

SNACKS	
Fräulein Frost	1

elegant promenades and marble fountains, it provides an ideal setting for wedding photos and summertime events such as galas, fairs and concerts. The charming, ivy-covered **Orangerie** – unique among Berlin's parks – is a highlight, and contains the elegant covered *Café im Körnerpark*, which has a popular outdoor terrace in the warmer months.

Volkspark Hasenheide

MAP ABOVE, POCKET MAP J9
Entrances on Hasenheide, Columbiadamm and Karlsgartenstr. ⓤ Hermannplatz. Open 24hr.

Originally used as a hunting ground for the Grand Elector in the seventeenth century, then as parade grounds for the Prussian military, this green expanse in the heart of Neukölln is today the domain of local sun-worshippers and picnickers. The long rows of trees are reminders of the former shooting ranges but little else of the park's past remains; instead, the main draws are a popular petting zoo, restaurant and a (summer-only) open-air stage for music, films and theatre. A popular funfair is also held in the southern part of the park each May.

Türkenmarkt

MAP ABOVE, POCKET MAP K8
Maybachufer Str. ⓤ Schönleinstr. ⓦ tuerkenmarkt.de. Tues & Fri 11am–6.30pm.

Located on the border between Neukölln and Kreuzberg (Kreuzkölln as it's widely known), the twice-weekly Turkish Market has become an institution for Berlin's significant Turkish population as well as families, hipsters and tourists. It's colourfully chaotic, complete with yelling vendors peddling the usual arrays of fruit and vegetables, fabric and shoe stalls, stands selling tasty snacks and, occasionally, live music.

Shops

Sing Blackbird

MAP p.121, POCKET MAP K8
Sanderstr. 11 ⓤ Schönleinstr. ☎ 030 54 84
50 51, ⓦ www.singblackbird.tumblr.com.
Daily 1–7pm.

Housed in a former phone-sex HQ, Sing Blackbird has the edge over other secondhand clothes stores thanks to a savvy selection that favours vintage garments from the 1970s, 1980s and 1990s. They also host occasional flea markets.

Vin Aqua Vin

MAP p.121, POCKET MAP K9
Weserstr. 204 ⓤ Hermannplatz ☎ 030 94
05 28 86, ⓦ www.vinaquavin.de. Mon–
Wed 4–9pm, Thurs & Fri 3–9pm, Sat
2–9pm.

This sophisticated wine shop and bar has introduced a new level of sophistication to this famously hipster street. In addition to a fine selection of international wines (many available by the glass), there's a roaring fireplace for the colder months, chesterfield armchairs and a dining table out back for tastings and private dinner events.

Restaurants

Berlin Burger International

MAP p.121, POCKET MAP K9
Pannierstr. 5 ⓤ Hermannplatz ☎ 016 04 82
65 05, ⓦ berlinburgerinternational .com.
Mon–Thurs noon–midnight, Fri & Sat
noon–1am, Sun noon–10pm.

There can never be enough burger joints in Berlin, it seems. This tiny space – just a long food bar and a smattering of outdoor picnic tables – lures punters in with fresh ingredients and generous portions: the BBI burger is enormous. Burgers from €4.90.

Lavanderia Vecchia

MAP p.121, POCKET MAP K9
Flughafenstr. 46 ⓤ Boddinstrasse ☎ 030
627 22 152, ⓦ lavanderiavecchia
.wordpress.com. Mon–Sat noon–2.30pm &
7.30–11pm.

This Italian spot reached cult status pretty quickly after opening in 2013, chiefly for its evening set menus, which consist of *antipasti*, *primi*, *secondi* and *dolci* (€60 per person). The delicious and abundant food is worth every penny, while the lighter lunch deals are much cheaper (three

California Breakfast Slam

courses from €11). Evening reservations essential. Small courtyard garden at the back.

Snacks

Fräulein Frost

MAP p.121, POCKET MAP K6
Friedelstr. 39 Ⓤ Schönleinstr. ☎ 030 95 59 55 21. Daily noon–8pm.

One of the district's best-loved ice-cream shops, the Frosty Fräulein serves up delicious cones and tubs of *bio-eis*, as well as sweet and savoury waffles. In summer, the outdoor patio provides a meeting point for hipsters, romantic couples and local families alike.

Cafés and bars

Ä Wirtschaft

MAP p.121, POCKET MAP L9
Weserstr. 40 Ⓤ Rathaus Neukölln ☎ 0177 406 38 37, Ⓦ ae-neukoelln.de. Daily 5pm–late.

One of the first of many informal bars to open up on boho Weserstrasse, the *Ä Bar* still holds its own as a meeting point for young creative types, expats and locals. Flea-market decor, dim lighting and table football give it a classic Berlin dive-bar atmosphere, matched to a soundtrack of indie and electro and occasional acoustic gigs from international bands.

The California Breakfast Slam (Cabslam)

MAP p.121, POCKET MAP K8
Innstr. 47 Ⓤ Rathaus Neukölln ☎ 030 68 69 624. Daily 10am–5pm.

Created by a Californian musician longing for an escape from the typical German breakfast of cold cuts and *Brötchen* (rolls), this Neukölln hipster haven is big on portions as well as flavour, with fluffy pancakes and dozens of different egg dishes,

all prepared from scratch with fresh ingredients. All-day brunch served till 4pm weekdays and 5pm weekends and holidays.

Geist im Glas

MAP p.121, POCKET MAP K9
Lenaustr. 27 Ⓤ Hermannplatz ☎ 017 655 330 450, Ⓦ www.geistimglas.com. Daily from 7pm (open end).

This trendy bar prides itself on its large selection of infused spirits that are skilfully mixed into Prohibition-era-inspired cocktails. Saturday and Sunday, there's a "Southern American" brunch (10am–4pm) with *huevos rancheros*, fluffy pancakes loaded with *dulce de leche* and lots of caramelized bacon.

Das Gift

MAP p.121, POCKET MAP L9
Donaustr. 19 Ⓤ Hermannplatz Ⓦ dasgift. de. Mon–Fri 5pm–late, Sat & Sun noon–late.

Founded by Barry Burns, of Scottish post-rock band Mogwai, and his wife Rachel, this corner pub has quickly become a local in-spot. Its charm lies in its simplicity: just a regular wood interior with a long bar and an artisan drink menu that includes Scottish ales, German brews and lots of whisky and cocktails. The kitchen offers fabulous haggis, mac 'n' cheese and an all-day breakfast at weekends. There's also a pub quiz, DJ sets and an exhibition space (Das Giftraum) that regularly hosts work by local artists.

Klunkerkranich

MAP p.121, POCKET MAP L9
Karl-Marx-Str. 66 Ⓤ Rathaus Neukölln Ⓦ klunkerkranich.org. Mon–Sat 10am–1.30pm, Sun noon–1.30am.

This shabby-chic rooftop hangout is hidden on top of a distinctly unglamorous shopping centre. The urban bar vibe is complemented by a sandy floor, great views over the city and occasional concerts and film screenings.

Charlottenburg

Part of the four boroughs that make up City West (along with Wilmersdorf, Schöneberg and Tiergarten) Charlottenburg has long been the beating heart of West Berlin and remains so today. Known for its wealthy residents and expensive shops, it's generally dismissed by the more boho east, and has much more in common with cities like London, Paris or Milan. The area's main artery, Kurfürstendamm (Ku'damm as it's colloquially known), which takes its name from the former Kurfürsten (Electors) of the Holy Roman Empire, is one of the most famous avenues in the city. It's often described as the city's Champs-Élysées, but the abundance of shops and relative dearth of impressive architecture makes it feel more like London's Oxford Street. However, many of the streets that run between Ku'damm and Kantstrasse have a charm of their own, with a wealth of independent cafés, bars, restaurants, bookstores and boutiques. The area is also home to some of the city's major sights such as Berlin's zoo and aquarium, Schloss Charlottenburg, the Kaiser Wilhelm Memorial Church and the Käthe Kollwitz Museum.

Berlin Zoo

Berlin Zoo

MAP p.126, POCKET MAP B6
Hardenbergplatz 8 ⓤ/Ⓢ Zoologischer
Garten ☎ 030 25 40 10, ⓦ zoo-berlin.de.
Daily: Jan, Feb, Nov &
Dec 9am–4.30pm, March & Oct 9am–6pm,
April–Sept 9am–6.30pm. €14.50, zoo &
aquarium €20. Family tickets available.

Berlin's zoo is Germany's oldest and one of the world's most popular, attracting (along with the adjacent aquarium) more than three million visitors in 2016. It opened in 1844 with animals donated by the royal family but was decimated during World War II, leaving only 91 surviving animals. It now houses over nineteen thousand animals spanning 1300 species. The hippo house is a highlight, while famous residents include the world's second-oldest gorilla: 60-year-old Fatou.

Museum für Fotografie

Berlin Aquarium

MAP p.126, POCKET MAP C6
Budapester Str. 32 Ⓤ/Ⓢ Zoologischer
Garten ☎ 030 25 40 10,
Ⓦ aquarium-berlin.de. Daily 9am–6pm.
€14.50, zoo & aquarium €20. Family
tickets available.

Situated next to the zoo, the city's
impressive aquarium holds the
title for world's most biodiverse
collection. From jellyfish to
crocodiles and other reptiles and
tropical fish, the aquarium has
over fourteen thousand creatures
on three floors. Built in 1913,
the aquarium has retained its
old-fashioned appearance albeit
incorporating modern elements.

Museum für Fotografie

MAP p.126, POCKET MAP B6
Jebensstr. 2 Ⓤ/Ⓢ Zoologischer Garten
☎ 030 26 64 24 242, Ⓦ smb.museum/mf.
Daily 11am–7pm (until 8pm Thurs). €10.

The Museum of Photography
opened in 2004 in a former casino
building, and has quickly risen in
popularity, drawing about 120,000
visitors a year. The city's largest
museum dedicated to the art
form, it covers 2000 square metres
and houses a thousand images
by famous *Vogue* photographer
Helmut Newton, whose
provocative black-and-white
photographs made him famous in
the world of fashion photography
and beyond; his work is shown
on a rotating basis in addition to
exhibits of other photographers.
In the large Kaisersaal, on the
second floor, you'll find the
Kunstbibliothek's collection, which
explores all kinds of photography
ranging from the nineteenth to
twenty-first centuries.

C/O Berlin (Amerika Haus)

MAP p.126, POCKET MAP B6
Hardenbergstr. 22–24 Ⓤ Zoologischer
Garten ☎ 030 28 44 41 60, Ⓦ co-berlin
.org. Daily 11am–8pm. €10.

Since its foundation back in 2000,
C/O Berlin has hosted some of the
city's best photography exhibitions,
with shows featuring international
heavyweights such as Martin
Parr, Annie Leibovitz, Rene Burri
and Karl Lagerfeld. In 2014, C/O
Berlin moved from Mitte to West
Berlin's Amerika Haus, where it
hosted open-air exhibitions until
the venue's reopening later that
year. Visitors can expect a high
standard of curation and big-name
retrospectives, as well as continued
promotion of young and new
local talent.

Charlottenburg

CHEAP EATS

Ashoka	5
Bier's Ku'damm 195	25
Dao	11
Lon-Men's Noodle House	8

CAFÉS & BARS

Café im Literaturhaus	23
Café Savigny	3
Diener	20
Einhorn	22
Gainsbourg	19
Monkey Bar	12
Paper & Tea	7
Schwarzes Café	14
Zwiebelfisch	6

RESTAURANTS

12 Apostel	17
Alt Luxemburg	2
Dressler	24
Engelbecken	1
Glass	4
Good Friends	9
Kuchi	10
Jules Verne Restaurant	13
Marjellchen	21
Ottenthal	16
Paris Bar	15
Restaurant Brel	18

CLUBS & VENUES

A Trane	1
Puro Sky Lounge	3
Quasimodo	2

ACCOMMODATION

25Hours Hotel Bikini Berlin	5
Am Savignyplatz	3
Am Steinplatz	2
Art Hotel Charlottenburger Hof	4
Hotel Otto	1
Hotel Q!	8
Hotel Zoo	6
Swissôtel	7

SHOPS

Bikini Berlin	5
Bücherbogen	6
Budapester Schuhe	11
Emma & Co.	7
English Scent	1
Firma London	4
Harvey's	12
Leysieffer	9
Marga Schoeller	8
Rio Modeschmuck-Design	2
Stilwerk	3
Solebox	10

Kaiser-Wilhelm-Gedächtnis-Kirche

Kaiser-Wilhelm-Gedächtnis-Kirche

MAP p.126, POCKET MAP B7
Breitscheidplatz Ⓤ Kurfürstendamm ☎ 030
21 85 023, ⓦ gedaechtniskirche-berlin.de.
Church: daily 9am–7pm. Hall of
Remembrance: Mon–Fri 10am–6pm, Sat
10am–5.30pm, Sun noon–5.30pm. Guided
tours: see website.

The Kaiser Wilhelm Memorial
Church, built between 1891 and
1895 in neo-Romanesque style
by architect Franz Schwechten,
was commissioned by Kaiser
Wilhelm II and served as a
symbol of Prussian unity.
Nearly destroyed during a
World War II air raid, all that
remains are the ruins of the
spire and entrance hall. A new
structure was built in 1961, and
the stunning, blue stained-glass
windows fitted in concrete bricks
contrast memorably with the
haunting skeleton of the old. The
base of the old spire and entrance
hall is now a memorial hall,
with exhibits documenting the
old church through photos and
artefacts that survived
the bombing.

Käthe Kollwitz Museum

MAP p.126, POCKET MAP B7
Fasanenstr. 24 Ⓤ Uhlandstr. ☎ 030 88 25
210, ⓦ www.kaethe-kollwitz.de. Daily
11am–6pm. €7.

German artist Käthe Kollwitz's
work was greatly influenced by the
loss of her son in World War I and
her grandson in World War II. She
was a pacifist who lived in Berlin
for fifty years, and was the first
woman elected to the Prussian
Academy of the Arts but resigned
her post in 1933 in protest at
Hitler's rise to power. Kollwitz's
works were banned by the Nazis.
Many of her pieces are powerful
reminders of some of the most
painful aspects of her life. Works
on display here include dour
self-portraits, plaintively titled
sketches, woodcuts, lithographs,
war protest posters and sculptures.
The building itself is the oldest
private home on Fasanenstrasse,
built in 1871 and restored in the
1980s.

Story of Berlin

MAP p.126, POCKET MAP A7
Kurfürstendamm 207–208 Ⓤ Uhlandstr.
☎ 030 88 72 01 00, ⓦ story-of-berlin.de.
Daily 10am–8pm, last admission 6pm;
bunker tours in English at noon, 2pm, 4pm
& 6pm €12.

The Story of Berlin aims to
transport visitors to each of the
eight centuries of Berlin's history
through multimedia displays
that include photos, films and
interactive exhibits. It follows
the history of the city from its
founding in 1237, to the Thirty
Years' War, Frederick the Great's
reign, the 1920s, World War II,
the Cold War and the fall of the
Wall. Also included is a guided
tour of an atomic bomb shelter on
the site.

Schloss Charlottenburg

MAP p.126, POCKET MAP A4
Spandauer Damm 10–22 Ⓤ Sophie-
Charlotte-Platz/Richard-Wagner-Platz
☎ 033 19 69 40, ⓦ www.spsg.de. Old

Palace Tues–Sun: Jan–March noon–4pm; April–Oct 10am–6pm; €12. New Wing daily except Tues: April–Oct 10am–6pm; Nov–March 10am–5pm; €8. Belvedere April–Oct Tues–Sun 10am–6pm; closed Nov–March; €3. Mausoleum April–Oct Tues–Sun 10am–6pm; €2. New Pavilion Tues–Sun: April–Oct 10am–6pm; Nov–March 10am–5pm; €4. Combined ticket €17.

As you walk through Schloss Charlottenburg, you'll be in no doubt as to why its builder, Frederick I, was known as an extravagant spender who nearly bankrupted the state. The former Elector of Brandenburg, who named himself king of Prussia in 1701, had this ornate Baroque palace built as a summer home for his wife, Sophie Charlotte, in 1695. It started as a relatively modest dwelling but ballooned to its present palatial status with additions throughout the 1700s. Majestic rooms, art and plenty of porcelain characterize the interiors. In fact, the art in the palace constitutes the largest collection of eighteenth-century French paintings outside of France. There's a separate entrance fee for each of the three main buildings; The **Old Palace** features Baroque rooms, royal apartments, Chinese and Japanese porcelain and silverware chambers; the **New Wing** is more Rococo with an array of refined furniture in apartments built by Frederick the Great; and the Schinkel-built **New Pavilion** features a collection of arts and crafts. Visitors can also visit the **Mausoleum**, which contains the graves of, and memorials to, members of the Hohenzollern family, and the **Belvedere**, which displays a collection of Berlin porcelain. The reconstructed **Orangerie** is also open for concerts and the gardens are open and free. Guided tours are offered of the historic apartments and chapel.

Olympic Stadium

MAP p.126, POCKET MAP A5
Olympischer Platz 3 ⓢ Olympiastadion
ⓣ 030 30 68 81 00, ⓦ olympiastadion-berlin.de. Daily: April–Oct 9am–7pm; Nov–March 10am–4pm; Aug 9am–8pm. €8. Guided tours available.

Berlin's Olympic stadium, built for the 1936 Summer Olympics (immortalized in the film *Olympia* by Leni Riefenstahl), is one of the last surviving remnants of Nazi architecture in Berlin. Occupied by the British military following the war and used by them until 1994, the stadium is now used for concerts and events and also as the official ground of Hertha BSC, Berlin's most famous football club. It was renovated for the 2006 World Cup and now has the highest all-seated capacity in Germany (74,228). The stadium remains an impressive place to visit.

Schloss Charlottenburg

Shops

Bikini Berlin

MAP p.126, POCKET MAP B6
Budapester Str. 38–50 Ⓤ/Ⓢ Zoologischer
Garten Ⓣ 030 55 49 64 55,
Ⓦ www.bikiniberlin.de. Mon–Sat
10am–8pm.

This trendy concept mall in
a 1950s building place was,
arguably, the place that put
West Berlin back on the map.
Spanning offices and a cinema,
as well as the *25hours* hotel
and bar (see p.152 and p.135),
the lower three floors of the
Bikinihaus offer chic retail and
gastronomy.

Bücherbogen

MAP p.126, POCKET MAP A7
Stadtbahnbogen 593 Ⓢ Savignyplatz
Ⓣ 030 31 86 59 11. Mon–Fri 10am–8pm,
Sat 10am–7pm.

You could spend hours in this
famed art book store, located
beneath Savignyplatz S-Bahn.
You'll find plenty of English-
language books in the design,
photography, art and theatre
sections, though nothing in the
literature section, sadly.

Budapester Schuhe

MAP p.126, POCKET MAP A7
Kurfürstendamm 199 Ⓤ Uhlandstr. Ⓣ 030
88 11 707. Mon–Fri 10am–7pm, Sat
10am–6pm.

A spacious and well-stocked shoe
shop whose wares run the gamut
from reasonably priced leather
classics to designer models from
Prada and Tod's.

Emma & Co

MAP p.126, POCKET MAP A7
Niebuhrstr. 2 Ⓢ Savignyplatz Ⓣ 030 88 67
67 87. Mon–Fri 11am–7pm, Sat
11am–4pm.

Lovingly decorated store with
attentive staff. They carry
alternative wooden toys, as well
as the classic brands for children,
and babywear.

Bücherbogen

English Scent

MAP p.126, POCKET MAP A6
Goethestr. 15 Ⓢ Deutsche Oper Ⓣ 030 32
44 655. Tues & Fri 10am–2pm, Sat
10am–3pm.

Located in a suitably evocative
old building, English Scent offers
a range of fragrances, skincare
products, shaving supplies, and
even toothpastes.

Firma London

MAP p.126, POCKET MAP A6
Bleibtreustr. 50 Ⓢ Savignyplatz Ⓣ 030 83
21 08 93. Tues–Fri noon–7pm, Sat
noon–5pm.

Run by former Stella McCartney
designer Sandra Tietje and
gallerist Florian von Holstein, this
is not for the financially faint-
hearted, but it does stock some
gorgeous vintage furniture and
accessories. There is also a large
warehouse in Lise-Meitner-Strasse
7 that's open Saturdays from
noon–pm or by appointment.

Harvey's

MAP p.126, POCKET MAP A7
Kurfürstendamm 56 Ⓤ Adenauerplatz
Ⓣ 030 88 33 803. Mon–Sat 11am–8pm.

A wonderland of men's designer
clothes from designers such as
Comme des Garçons and Yohji
Yamamoto.

Leysieffer

MAP p.126, POCKET MAP B7
Kurfürstendamm 218 ⓤ Uhlandstr. ⓣ 030
88 57 480. Mon–Sat 9am–7pm, Sun
10am–5pm (closed Sun from June–Aug).

This Ku'damm branch of the
famed German chocolateria does
a brisk trade. Aside from the
usual sweet goodies, there's also
a small coffee bar, useful if you're
looking for a break from all the
shopping.

Marga Schoeller

MAP p.126, POCKET MAP A7
Knesebeckstr. 33 ⓤ Uhlandstr. ⓣ 030 88
11 112, ⓦ margaschoeller.de. Mon–Wed
9.30am–7pm, Thurs & Fri 9.30am–8pm,
Sat 9.30am–6pm.

Opened in 1929 by the
eponymous Frau Schoeller, this
bookstore, one of the longest
running in Europe, was a focal
point for West Berlin's postwar
literary scene. Originally located
on Kurfürstendamm, the shop
moved to Knesebeckstr. in 1974
and continues to sell a fantastic
range of German- and English-
language books on poetry, theatre
and philosophy as well as fiction,
history and plenty of tomes about
Berlin and Germany.

Rio Modeschmuck-Design

MAP p.126, POCKET MAP A6
Bleibtreustr. 52 Ⓢ Savignyplatz ⓣ 030 31
33 152. Mon–Wed & Fri 11am–6.30pm,
Thurs 11am–7pm, Sat 11am–6pm.

Designer Barbara Kranz opened
her jewellery store back in
1984 – she calls her creations
"after 5pm" jewellery due to
their natural evening-wear
flamboyance.

Stilwerk

MAP p.126, POCKET MAP A6
Kantstr. 17 Ⓢ Savignyplatz ⓣ 030 31 51
50. Mon–Sat 10am–7pm.

Swanky designer mall, located
near Zoologischer Garten,
comprising shops dedicated
to home decoration, jewellery
and fashion. Expect high-end
stores like Bang & Olufsen, with
one or two cheaper options as
well. There's a café and even a
babysitting service for those who
want to dump the kids.

Solebox

MAP p.126, POCKET MAP C7
Nürnbergerstr. 14 ⓤ Wittenbergplatz
ⓣ 030 23 60 71 21. Mon–Sat 11am–8pm.

A spacious shrine to streetwear,
stocking Reebok, Converse,
Ellesse and Adidas sneakers plus
T-shirts and hoodies.

Restaurants

12 Apostel

MAP p.126, POCKET MAP A6
Bleibtreustr. 49 Ⓢ Savignyplatz ⓣ 030 31
21 433, ⓦ 12-apostel.de. Mon–Thurs
11am–midnight, Fri & Sat 11am–1am, Sun
noon–midnight.

A smart, Baroque-style interior
(check the kitsch religious
frescoes) and generously sized
thin pizzas mark this place out.
They're slightly on the expensive
side – around €12 – but specials
on the Mon–Fri lunch menu
start at €6.95. The Sunday brunch
buffet (10am–3pm) is €22.50 but
comes with a glass of sparkling
wine and a hot drink.

Stilwerk

Alt Luxemburg

MAP p.126, POCKET MAP A6
Windscheidstr. 31 ⓤ Sophie-
Charlotte-Platz ⓣ 030 32 38 730, ⓦ www
.alt-luxemburg.de. Mon–Sat 5pm–late.

Located in a renovated customs
house, *Alt Luxemburg* boasts
antique furnishings, attentive
service and a great menu of
traditional German cuisine, plus a
good wine list. There are four- or
five-course fixed-price menus (€74
and €79) and a daily happy hour
(5–7pm) with a fifteen percent
reduction.

Dressler

MAP p.126, POCKET MAP A7
Kurfürstendamm 206–208 ⓤ Uhlandstr.
ⓣ 030 88 33 530, ⓦ restaurant-dressler.
de. Daily 8am–1am, (kitchen till midnight).

This German take on a French
brasserie enjoys something
of a time warp ambience thanks
to its Art Nouveau interior, formal
but friendly service and very good
seasonal food. The main dining
area might be a bit stiff for some,
but the small front bar is perfect
for a quick coffee or lunch if you're
on Ku'damm.

Engelbecken

MAP p.126, POCKET MAP A6
Witzlebenstr. 31 ⓤ Sophie-Charlotte-Platz
ⓣ 030 61 52 810, ⓦ engelbecken.de. Mon–
Fri 5pm–1am, Sat 4pm–1am, Sun
noon–1am.

A high-quality restaurant that
serves Bavarian and Alpine
cuisine – *schnitzel*, goulash –
with an emphasis on organic
products and home-made sauces.
Vegetarian and vegan options
are available, and the park-facing
terrace is nice in the summer.

Glass

MAP p.126, POCKET MAP B6
Uhlandstr. 195 ⓤ Uhlandstrasse ⓣ 030 54
71 08 61, ⓦ glassberlin.de. Tues–Sat
6–11pm.

Run by talented young Israeli chef
Gal Ben Moshe, this restaurant
blends a stylish but low-key
interior with high-end, innovative
Middle East-themed cuisine that
can be enjoyed a la carte or as a
five-, seven- or nine-course tasting
menu (€50–109). Excellent wine
list too.

Good Friends

MAP p.126, POCKET MAP A6
Kantstr. 30 ⓢ Savignyplatz ⓣ 030 31 32
659, ⓦ goodfriends-berlin.de. Daily
noon–2am.

One of Berlin's few really authentic
Cantonese restaurants, with
plain decor and a full range of
classics (mains €11–19.70). It's
always busy; evening bookings
recommended.

Jules Verne Restaurant

MAP p.126, POCKET MAP A6
Schlüterstr. 61 ⓢ Savignyplatz ⓣ 030 31
80 94 10, ⓦ jules-verne-berlin.de. Daily
9am–1am, kitchen till 11.45pm.

The interior feels classic French
but the menu is aptly global,
ranging from *Flammen* (*tarte
flambée*) and *schnitzel* to *couscous*
and *satay*. Lunchtime deals change
daily.

Kuchi

MAP p.126, POCKET MAP A6
Kantstr. 30 ⓢ Savignyplatz ⓣ 030 31 50
78 15, ⓦ kuchi.de. Daily noon–midnight.

With a sister restaurant in Mitte,
this place sells the same range of
innovative sushi, *sashimi*, *yakitori*,
as well as some Thai, Chinese and
Korean recipes. Busy at peak
times so it's best to reserve a table.
Happy hour from 5pm includes
noodle soups for €6 and sushi
for €7.

Marjellchen

MAP p.126, POCKET MAP A7
Mommsenstr. 9 ⓢ Savignyplatz ⓣ 030 88
32 676, ⓦ marjellchen-berlin.de. Daily
5pm–midnight.

It's obvious from the window
displays – books, photos and
other paraphernalia – that this is
a time warp kind of place. Indeed,
Marjellchen specializes in cuisine

Restaurant Brel

MAP p.126, POCKET MAP A6
Savignyplatz 1 Ⓢ Savignyplatz ☎ 030 31 80 00 20, Ⓦ cafebrel.berlin. Daily 10am–1am.
This well-established bistro has a comfortable, friendly but sophisticated feel, with a long wooden bar, black-and-white photos and grand piano. It's matched by excellent French food and wines.

Cheap eats

Ashoka

MAP p.126, POCKET MAP A6
Grolmanstr. 51 Ⓢ Savignyplatz ☎ 030 31 01 58 06. Daily 11am–midnight.
Ashok Sharma opened this restaurant in 1975 as he was missing the food from his home in Punjab. It offers well-priced, decent quality food in a small *Imbiss*-style place. Vegetarian options and friendly staff.

Bier's Kudamm 195

MAP p.126, POCKET MAP A7
Kurfürstendamm 195 Ⓤ Uhlandstr. ☎ 030 88 18 942. Mon–Thurs 11am–5am, Fri & Sat 11am–6pm, Sun noon–5pm.
One of several spots claimed as the "best in Berlin" for *Currywurst*. It also serves meat skewers and meatballs, and is generally busy all night; if you feel like splashing out ask for champagne with your *Wurst*.

Dao

MAP p.126, POCKET MAP A6
Kantstr. 133 Ⓢ Savignyplatz ☎ 030 37 59 14 14, Ⓦ dao-restaurant.de. Daily noon–11pm.
Opened by a Berliner and his Thai wife Dao in the 1970s, this Thai spot serves dishes brimful of flavour. Alongside *pad Thai* (€9.90) and fish and duck dishes (up to €20) there are specials like "Bloodnoodlesoup".

from East Prussia, Pomerania and Silesia, all served up in a cosy, traditional atmosphere. Portions are generous and service is friendly (mains €11.80–20.50).

Ottenthal

MAP p.126, POCKET MAP B6
Kantstr. 153 Ⓢ Savignyplatz ☎ 030 31 33 162, Ⓦ ottenthal.com. Daily 5pm–1am.
White-clothed tables and relatively sparse white walls lend this place an unfussy, classic feel that ties in well with the Austrian cuisine – which is simple yet some of the best in the area. Organic ingredients feature on the menu, which includes fish dishes, risotto and a famed *Wiener schnitzel*. Good Austrian wine list too.

Paris Bar

MAP p.126, POCKET MAP B6
Kantstr. 152 Ⓢ/Ⓤ Zoologischer Garten ☎ 030 31 38 052, Ⓦ parisbar.net. Daily noon–2am.
There's still something tangibly bohemian about the *Paris Bar*, once one of the centres of West Berlin's art scene until the Wall fell and the East took over. Interesting artworks vie for your attention and the somewhat pricey food takes second place to the social networking action. Lunch €15–28, dinner mains €28–40.

Dressler

Lon-Men's Noodle House

MAP p.126, POCKET MAP A6
Kantstr. 33 ⑤ Savignyplatz ☏ 030 31 51 96
78. Daily noon–11pm.

Tiny Taiwanese noodle shop run
by a friendly family who make
excellent dumplings and noodle
soups (small and large portions
available).

Cafés and bars

Café im Literaturhaus

MAP p.126, POCKET MAP B7
Fasanenstr. 23 Ⓤ Uhlandstr. ☏ 030 88 25
414, Ⓦ www.literaturhaus-berlin.de. Daily
9am–midnight.

This place is every bit as classic
and elegant as its name suggests.
The spacious interior or beautiful
summer garden are great spots
for coffee and cake, lunch or
dinner: the largely organic
menu changes regularly and has
vegetarian options.

Café im Literaturhaus

Café Savigny

MAP p.126, POCKET MAP A6
Grolmanstr. 53 ⑤ Savignyplatz ☏ 0157 52
00 48 10. Daily 9am–midnight.

A small, classic spot that's been
serving great breakfasts and coffee
for over a decade. Lunches start at
€6 (soups) with hearty Burgundy
stew for €13.50. Service is good and
it's also nice for an evening drink.

Diener

MAP p.126, POCKET MAP A6
Grolmanstr. 47 ⑤ Savignyplatz ☏ 030 88
15 329, Ⓦ www.diener-berlin.de. Daily
6pm–3am.

This Berlin ale house is a local
institution – not only because it was
opened in 1954 by former German
heavyweight boxer Franz Diener,
but because it serves dishes like
Königsberger Klopse (meatballs in
white sauce with capers, €10.50)
and has an atmosphere as old
school as the menu.

Einhorn

MAP p.126, POCKET MAP A7
Mommsenstr. 2 ⑤ Savignyplatz ☏ 030 88
14 241, Ⓦ einhorn-catering.de. Daily Mon–
Fri 10am–5pm.

A great place if you're seeking a
tasty veggie lunch. There's a buffet
selection including antipasti and
and dishes like lentils with goat's
cheese. Mostly priced by weight
(€1.50/100g).

Gainsbourg

MAP p.126, POCKET MAP A6
Jeanne-Mammen-Bogen 576–577
⑤ Savignyplatz ☏ 030 313 74 64. Daily
5pm until late.

The name may pay homage to the
master of risqué *chanson*, but the
cocktails (€8–10) and food are
more mainstream. Nevertheless,
the drinks are some of the best in
the neighbourhood.

Monkey Bar

MAP p.126, POCKET MAP B6
Budapesterstr. 40 Ⓤ/⑤ Zoologischer
Garten ☏ 030 12 02 21 210,
Ⓦ monkeybarberlin.de. Daily noon–2am.

Schwarzes Café

Part of the buzz for the new *25hours* hotel (see p.152) has been that there's finally a decent rooftop bar in West Berlin. The floor-to-ceiling windows make for great sundowner vibes.

Paper & Tea (P & T)

MAP p.126, POCKET MAP A6
Bleibtreustr. 4 Ⓢ Savignyplatz ☎ 030 55 57 98 080, Ⓦ paperandtea.com. Mon–Sat 11am–8pm.

A Zen-style breath of fresh air in a city obsessed with coffee, this minimal and chic teahouse feels as much like a museum as a shop, with its gorgeously curated goods laid out on trays with detailed notes. Related accessories and gifts also available.

Schwarzes Café

MAP p.126, POCKET MAP A6
Kantstr. 148 Ⓢ Savignyplatz ☎ 030 31 38 038, Ⓦ schwarzescafe-berlin.de. Daily 24hr.

The slightly ragged charm of the "Black Café" makes it feel like it would be better placed in the east. The downstairs is small and intimate, but upstairs the large, airy room has a relaxed, convivial vibe. Food is served 24 hours, including breakfasts (from €4.50) – but this is a night-owl place really.

Zwiebelfisch

MAP p.126, POCKET MAP A6
Savignyplatz 7 SSavignyplatz, ☎ 030 312 73 63, Ⓦ zwiebelfisch-berlin.de. Daily noon–6am.

Corner bar and 1970s throwback for would-be arty and intellectual types. Jazz, earnest debate and good cheap grub (€8–12.50), including goulash and Swabian Maultaschen, served until 1am.

Clubs and venues

A-Trane

MAP p.126, POCKET MAP A6
Bleibtreustr. 1 Ⓢ Savignyplatz ☎ 030 31 32 550, Ⓦ www.a-trane.de. Daily from 8pm, music from around 10pm.

Good jazz and decent cocktails in a classic jazz-style interior (small and smoky). Often hosts major international acts.

Puro Sky Lounge

MAP p.126, POCKET MAP C7
Tauentzienstr. 9–11 Ⓤ Kurfürstendamm ☎ 030 26 36 78 75, Ⓦ www.puro-berlin.de. Thurs 10pm–6am, Sat 11pm–6am

Ensconced on the twentieth floor of the ugly Europa Center, the *Puro Sky Lounge* is filled with eye candy thanks to the beautiful people who flock here for the jaw-dropping views. What it lacks in musical edge – think 1980s classics– it makes up for with an upbeat crowd.

Quasimodo

MAP p.126, POCKET MAP B6
Kantstr. 12A Ⓤ Savignyplatz ☎ 030 31 80 45 60, Ⓦ www.quasimodo.de.

A classic jazz bar, *Quasimodo* (underneath the Delphi Cinema) features black-and-white photos, low ceilings and intimate tables. Aside from jazz there's funk, blues and Latin and the odd international star.

Schöneberg

Famous during the 1920s as the centre of Berlin's decadent nightlife scene and again in the 1970s when it was home to David Bowie during his dissipated sojourn in the city, Schöneberg's star waned in the 1990s as the cool kids moved east. But while East Berlin has become increasingly slick and unaffordable, this part of town has – as they say – kept it real. Nowadays the hipsters are heading back, attracted by the still-low rents and the burgeoning gallery scene in Potsdamer Strasse, and it maintains its reputation as the pinkest borough in Berlin, especially around Nollendorfplatz. It's also long-been a popular spot for writers – Christopher Isherwood had his digs in Nollendorfstrasse back in the day, and a new generation of writers including Helen DeWitt and Ida Hattemer-Higgins have called the neighbourhood home. Though it lacks any major sights, the charming Winterfeldtplatz hosts a highly popular farmers' market (Sat 8am–4pm).

Schöneberg

0 metres 250
0 yards 250

ACCOMMODATION	
Hotel de Ela	2
Jugendhotel Berlincity	3
Tom's Hotel	1

CAFÉS & BARS	
Café Einstein Stammhaus	2
Felsenkeller	15
Green Door	3
Kneipe Leuchtturm	10
Mamsell	7
Sorgenfrei	6
Winterfeldt Schokoladen	5

RESTAURANTS	
Aroma	9
Garda Pizza	12
Ixthys	4
Renger-Patzsch	11
Taverna Ousies	8

CHEAP EATS	
Café BilderBuch	13
Ebbes	14
Witty's	1

CLUBS & VENUES	
Havanna	2
Heile Welt	1

SHOPS	
Herz + Stöhr	3
KaDeWe	1
Mr Dead & Mrs Free	2

Shops

Herz + Stöhr

MAP OPPOSITE, POCKET MAP D8
Winterfeldtstr. 52 ⓤ Nollendorfplatz ☎ 030
21 64 425. Tues–Fri noon–7.30pm, Sat
noon–6pm.

Intelligent, elegant designs from
this German fashion duo – the
dresses and suits are grown-up but
not dowdy, and everything can be
altered to fit.

KaDeWe

MAP OPPOSITE, POCKET MAP C7
Tauentzienstr. 21–24 ⓤ Wittenbergplatz
☎ 030 21 210, ⓦ kadewe.de. Mon–Thurs
10am–8pm, Fri 10am–9pm, Sat
9.30am–8pm.

If you're tired of Berlin's austere
side, check out KaDeWe
(Kaufhaus Des Westerns),
a temple to conspicuous
consumption. The largest
department store in continental
Europe, it sports designer gear
alongside some surprisingly
affordable accessories and
homewares. The legendary sixth-
floor food hall will leave all but the
most jaded of foodies starry-eyed.

Mr Dead & Mrs Free

MAP OPPOSITE, POCKET MAP D7
Bülowstr. 5 ⓤ Nollendorfplatz ☎ 030 21 51
449, ⓦ deadandfree.com. Mon–Fri
noon–7pm, Sat 11am–4pm.

A dusty little legend of a music
shop crammed full of everything
from the latest imports to rare
vintage albums.

Restaurants

Aroma

MAP OPPOSITE, POCKET MAP E9
Hochkirchstr. 8 Ⓢ/ⓤ Yorckstr. ☎ 030 78
25 821, ⓦ cafe-aroma.de. Mon–Fri from
5pm, Sat from noon, Sun brunch
11am–2pm, from 2pm à la carte.

Tucked into a sleepy residential
street, this rustic Italian gem is
the unofficial headquarters for

Berlin's slow food movement. The
antipasti spread at Sunday brunch
(€14.50) is legendary, while classic
pastas (€9–12), pizzas (€6–9)
and changing seasonal specials
(€15–20) satisfy the dinner crowd.
The terrace is a peaceful haven.

Garda Pizza

MAP OPPOSITE, POCKET MAP D9
Crellestr. 48 Ⓢ Julius-Leber-Brücke ☎ 030
78 09 79 70. Mon–Sat 11am–9pm.

Locals flock to *Garda Pizza* for
their trays of thin-crust Roman-
style *focaccia*. Their most popular
slice (€2) combines fresh aubergine,
mushroom, sheep's salami and
artichokes. A tray (€15) will feed
a hungry group of four. Join the
crowd on the pavement, or mosey
down a few metres and let your
children burn off the calories in the
neighbouring playground.

Ixthys

MAP OPPOSITE, POCKET MAP D8
Pallasstr. 21 ⓤ Nollendorfplatz ☎ 030 81
47 47 69. Mon–Sat noon–10pm.

A tiny café run by two Korean
widows (who've festooned the
walls with biblical slogans), this
places is all about great home-style
cooking. Guests squeeze in to
enjoy the home-made noodles
with vegetables (€5) or seafood
(€8.50) and the fiery, sizzling
bibimbap (€7.50).

KaDeWe

SCHÖNEBERG

Renger-Patzsch

MAP p.136, POCKET MAP D9
Wartburgstr. 54 Ⓤ Eisenacher Str. ☎ 030
78 42 059, Ⓦ www.renger-patzsch.com.
Mon–Sat 6–11.30pm.

An interior of dark wood and white tablecloths forms the backdrop to an expertly prepared selection of German dishes (starters €6–11; mains €16–21.50; *tartes flambées* €8–11). In spring, look for the dandelion salad with lardons; in winter, the braised ox cheeks with bacon-wrapped plums, turnips and mashed potatoes.

Taverna Ousies

MAP p.136, POCKET MAP D9
Grunewaldstr. 16 Ⓤ Eisenacher Str. ☎ 030
21 67 957, Ⓦ www.taverna-ousies.de.
Daily from 5pm.

This kitschy, raucous Greek taverna is a perennial favourite. There are no real duds, so go wild with the meze menu (€4–7) and be entertained by the jolly staff. Reservations essential at weekends.

Cheap eats

Café BilderBuch

MAP P.136, POCKET MAP D9
Akazienstr. 28 Ⓢ Julius-Leber-Brücke T030
78 70 60 57, Wcafe-bilderbuch.de. Mon–Sat 9am–midnight, Sun 10am–midnight.

Lovely rambling café in the Viennese tradition. It doesn't look particularly special from outside, but the comfortable back parlour may well hold you captive for hours. Great breakfasts (€5.40–7.90), lovely cakes, elegant coffees and courtyard seating, too.

Ebbes

MAP p.136, POCKET MAP D9
Crellestr. 5 Ⓢ Julius-Leber-Brücke ☎ 030
70 09 48 13. Mon–Fri 10am–7.30pm, Sat 9am–4pm.

This quirky Swabian deli is crowded with rings of venison salami and trays of fresh *spätzle* (noodles). Owner Wolfgang

Steppes finds his suppliers on trips to southern Germany. Buy a picnic and wander north to Kleistpark, or grab a stool outside and try one of the daily specials (€2.50–5), such as *Maultaschen* (ravioli) in broth.

Witty's

MAP p.136, POCKET MAP C7
Wittenbergplatz 5 Ⓤ Wittenbergplatz
☎ 030 21 19 496, Ⓦ www.wittys-berlin.de.
Mon–Sat 11am–10.30pm, Sun noon–9.30pm.

One of the city's first and finest organic sausage stands, *Witty's* has customers lined up along the square for their *Currywurst* and crispy fries.

Cafés and bars

Café Einstein Stammhaus

MAP p.136, POCKET MAP D7
Kurfürstenstr. 58 Ⓤ Nollendorfplatz ☎ 030
26 39 19 18, Ⓦ www.cafeeinstein.com.
Daily 8am–1am.

Set in a beautiful historic villa, this classic coffeehouse and restaurant offers fantastic breakfasts, *schnitzels* and cakes. On sunny days make a beeline for the spacious garden and sip bellinis while the shadows lengthen.

Felsenkeller

MAP p.136, POCKET MAP D9
Akazienstr. 2 Ⓢ Julius-Leber-Brücke
☎ 030 78 13 447. Mon–Sat 4pm–midnight.

The perfect destination when you're nostalgic for old Berlin. Founded in 1923, this bar is famous for its eight beers on tap; they're drawn the old-fashioned way, so be prepared to wait. There's hearty, simple food (dishes from €5), such as lentil soup and swede stew. No music, but plenty of atmosphere.

Green Door

MAP p.136, POCKET MAP D8
Winterfeldtstr. 50 Ⓤ Nollendorfplatz ☎ 030
21 52 515, Ⓦ greendoor.de. Mon–Thurs & Sun 6pm–3am, Fri & Sat 6pm–4am.

Green Door

Ring the bell and enter one of Berlin's best-loved cocktail bars. The expert but unpretentious staff will recommend the perfect drink. An older crowd fills the cosy room.

Kneipe Leuchtturm

MAP p.136, POCKET MAP D9
Crellestr. 41 ⓤ Kleistpark ☎ 030 78 18 519, ⓦ leuchtturm-kneipe.de. Mon–Fri 6pm-late, Sat from 6.30pm, Sun from 7.30pm.
If you think beer just isn't the same without a cigarette, head for the "Lighthouse", with its unpretentious, welcoming atmosphere favoured by former hippies and locals. The wines can be middling so go for one of the beers on tap.

Mamsell

MAP p.136, POCKET MAP D8
Goltzstr. 48 ⓤ Eisenacher Str. ☎ 030 92 12 29 00. Mon–Fri 10am–7pm, Sat 10am–5pm, Sun 2–6pm.
Those with a penchant for pink will be delighted by this sweet café/shop. The addictive real hot chocolate is served with a dusting of freshly grated ginger.

Sorgenfrei

MAP p.136, POCKET MAP D8
Goltzstr. 18 ⓤ Nollendorfplatz ☎ 030 30 10 40 71, ⓦ www.sorgenfrei-in-berlin.de.

Tues–Fri noon–7pm, Sat 10am–6pm, Sun 1–6pm.
This gay-friendly café will take you straight back to the 1950s. There's Hawaiian-style toast on the menu and Bing Crosby on the speakers. The Bakelite radios and kidney-shaped tables aren't just for decoration – most of the items are for sale.

Winterfeldt Schokoladen

MAP p.136, POCKET MAP D8
Goltzstr. 23 ⓤ Nollendorfplatz ☎ 030 23 62 32 56. Mon–Fri 9am–8pm, Sat 9am–6pm, Sun noon–7pm.
Once an apothecary, this café-chocolate shop serves a lovely selection of pastries to cure all your ills. Scones with clotted cream and jam and warm chocolate fondant cake are popular.

Clubs and venues

Havanna

MAP p.136, POCKET MAP D9
Hauptstr. 30 Ⓢ Julius-Leber-Brücke ☎ 030 78 48 565, ⓦ www.havanna-berlin.de. Wed from 9pm, Fri & Sat from 10pm.
With four floors and seven bars, this magnet for Latin American music fans draws a diverse clientele. Serious salsa and tango fans will find like-minded devotees to shake it on the dancefloor.

Heile Welt

MAP p.136, POCKET MAP D7
Motzstr. 5 ⓤ Nollendorfplatz ☎ 030 21 91 75 07. Daily from 8pm.
A much-beloved destination for gay men and the women who love them. Music runs the gamut from soul and dance to house and home-brewed "Schlager". During the week, enjoy one of the friendly bar staff's famously strong cocktails and settle into a comfortable sofa. The action picks up at the weekend, when it gets too crowded for some, and just right for others.

Day-trips from Berlin

There's so much to do in Berlin that it's easy to forget there's a world outside the city. Berlin's surroundings are surprisingly sparse and beautiful – a bucolic swathe of lakes, forests and small villages. Amidst the vast landscape lie some of the city's highlights, many of them less than an hour from the centre. Easily accessible by public transport, areas such as Dahlem, Potsdam and Wannsee make for enjoyable and edifying visits (as well as memorials to the darker side of the city's past). The most popular day-trip is Potsdam, which includes Schloss Sanssouci and Babelsberg film studios as well as a town centre distinct from anything in Berlin. The Wannsee area offers lakeside beaches as well as historical villas and the magical Pfaueninsel, while Dahlem has botanical gardens and the Museum of European Cultures. History buffs will find journeys to Sachsenhausen concentration camp, Villa Wannsee and Hohenschönhausen Stasi prison both chilling and instructive.

Sachsenhausen

Str. der Nationen 22, Oranienburg Ⓢ Oranienburg (RE5 or S1 from Alexanderplatz, then follow signs for Gedenkstätte Sachsenhausen) ☎ 033 01 20 00, Ⓦ stiftung-bg.de. Daily: March 15–Oct 14 8.30am–6pm; Oct 15–March 14 8.30am–4.30pm. During the winter season, the museums are closed Mon, but the Visitor Information Centre, the open-air exhibition, "Murder and Mass Murder in Sachsenhausen Concentration Camp" and the site of commemoration "Station Z", are open to the public every day. Free. Guided tours available for groups (€15–25) in a range of different languages.

Located in Oranienburg, 35km north of the city, Sachsenhausen ranks among Berlin's most emotionally wrenching wartime memorials – which is saying a lot for a city like this. Established in 1936, it was first used as a prison for political opponents. It became a training ground for SS officers, and from 1938 to 1945 the central administration for all concentration camps was located here. After the war started, prisoners from all over Europe were brought here. In 1943 a small gas chamber was added. By 1945 some 200,000 people had passed through the prison, with tens of thousands dying of starvation, disease, mistreatment or murdered systematically by

Sachsenhausen

the SS. In April 1945 more than 33,000 prisoners were sent on the notorious death marches, during which more than a thousand died – those who collapsed en route were routinely shot. When the camp was liberated by Russian soldiers on April 22, 1945 only three thousand prisoners remained, many of whom who died in the days afterwards. The camp became a Soviet-run prison named "Special Camp No. 7" (renamed in 1948 to "Special Camp No. 1"). Sixty thousand people were interned here over five years, including six thousand German officers transferred from Western Allied POW camps. By the time the camp closed in the spring of 1950, twelve thousand had died of malnutrition and disease. In 1961, the GDR turned the site into a memorial, removing many of the original buildings and constructing an obelisk, statue and meeting area. Today the memorial is a place of commemoration as well as a museum that includes a wealth of information on the camp, artwork by inmates, models, pictures and more. Following the discovery in 1990 of mass graves from the Soviet period, a separate museum was opened about the Soviet-era history.

Potsdam

Direct line to Wannsee, then change on S7 (20–30min; ticket for zones A,B and C); or regional trains (RE1) to Potsdam and Dabelsburg. You can cover most of Potsdam by foot, though the Berlin and Potsdam WelcomeCard (see p.158), available from the tourist centre at the train station, includes transport and gives discounts on over two hundred attractions. Visit Ⓦpotsdam-tourism.com.

Located 24km southwest of Berlin, Potsdam makes for an easy and pleasant day-trip, with plenty to see and do, from the wonderful Schloss Sanssouci and its gardens to the Babelsberg film studios (see p.146). There are two quaint historic quarters in the city itself that are worth

Potsdam

seeking out. The **Russian Colony Alexandrowka** (Alexandrowka 2; ☎0331 817 02 03, Ⓦalexandrowka .de; Tues–Sun 10am–6pm, June–Sept Fri till 9pm; €3.50), created in 1826–27 on the request of Friedrich Wilhelm III in memory of his friend Tsar Alexander I, is an artist's village with twelve picturesque wooden houses and a small Russian Orthodox chapel (1829) on Kapellenberg hill to the north. Check out the Russian tearoom in the warden's house. The **Holländisches Viertel**, or Dutch quarter (Ⓦwww.hollaendisches-viertel.net), consists of around 150 three-storey redbrick houses, and was built between 1734 and 1742 for Dutch craftsmen invited to Potsdam by Friedrich Wilhelm I. The houses are built in the classic Dutch style with shuttered windows and slanted roofs; at Mittelstrasse 8 the **Jan Bouman Haus** preserves a typical house of the era (☎0331 28 03 773; Mon–Fri 1–6pm, Sat & Sun 11am–6pm; €2), while the **Potsdam Museum** at Alter Markt 9 (☎0331 289 68 03; daily 10am–6pm; €3) displays historic paintings and photos of the city.

Museum Barberini

Humboldtstr. 5–6 ☎ 033 12 36 01 44 99, ⓦ museum-barberini.com. Mon & Wed–Sun 10am–7pm (closes 9pm every first Thurs of the month). €14.

In January 2017, the **Museum Barberini** opened inside Frederick the Great's former Barberini Palace on the Alter Markt. As well as exhibiting a permanent collection of works from the former GDR, the museum also hosts three temporary exhibitions per year, ranging in aesthetic scope from Old Masters to contemporary art.

Schloss Sanssouci and park

Park Sanssouci ⓢ Potsdam. Around 5km from Potsdam train station; bus #695 goes from the train station, with stops at Schloss Sanssouci, the Orangerie and Neues Palais (among others). ☎ 033 19 69 42 00, ⓦ spsg.de. Palace Tues–Sun: April–Oct 10am–6pm; Nov–March 10am–5pm, timed guided tours only (tickets at ⓦ tickets.spsg.de). Park daily 9am–dusk. Admission to palace €12; other attractions individually priced, or €19 day ticket for all buildings. Park: free.

The highlight of any trip to Potsdam, Schloss Sanssouci was built for Frederick the Great by the magnificently titled Georg Wenzeslaus von Knobelsdorff between 1745 and 1747. It was his summer residence – the place he came for some peace and quiet and to be with his beloved dogs (*Sans Souci* means "without worries" in French); parts of the park, buildings and palaces dotted around it were added to by later Prussian kings. Having survived unscathed from the War, the palace is considered one of the most significant examples of Rococo architecture – much of the original artworks were moved to Rheinsberg during the War or were transferred as booty to the Soviet Union, though Frederick's library and 36

Schloss Sanssouci

oil paintings were returned and can be viewed today alongside furnishings and decorations from the original rooms. The adjacent **picture gallery** exhibits works by Rubens, van Dyck, Caravaggio and other renowned artists, and the historic windmill – built in the Dutch style and rebuilt in 1993 – is worth a visit, as is the **Chinese House** (same times as Sanssouci; €3) and the **New Palace** (Neues Palais; Mon & Wed–Sun 10am–5/6pm; €8), a larger Baroque-style palace intended to display Frederick's power to the world. Best of all is the surrounding **park**, an inspiring display of terraced vineyards, flamboyant flower beds, hedges and abundant fruit trees. Note that the palaces are highly popular in summer and tours inside the main palace are limited, so arrive early or book ahead.

Filmpark Babelsberg

Grossbeerenstr. 200 Ⓢ Babelsburg, then bus #601, #619, #690 to Filmpark or RE1 to Medienstadt ☏ 033 17 21 27 50, Ⓦ filmpark-babelsberg.de. Daily: April–Sept 10am–6pm; Oct & Nov 10am–5pm. €22.

Some of Germany's most famous films were created at Studio Babelsberg, including masterpieces such as *Metropolis* (1927) and *The Blue Angel* (1930), starring Marlene Dietrich – in its heyday the studios were Europe's version of Hollywood. This associated theme park allows visitors to roam sets from old films, witness stuntmen in action and marvel at the special effects. It's especially good (if not better) for kids, who will enjoy the Jungle Playground and the Animal Farm.

Museum Europäischer Kulturen (MEK)

Arnimallee 25, a short signposted walk down Iltisstrasse directly opposite Ⓤ Dahlem-Dorf ☏ 030 266 42 42 42, Ⓦ smb.museum/mek • Tues–Fri 10am–5pm, Sat & Sun 11am–6pm • €8 •

The one museum that will remain in Dahlem after 2017 is the **Museum Europäischer Kulturen** (Museum of European Cultures), which is devoted to the life worlds of people in Europe. With around 280,000 cultural historical objects, its collection provides a unique insight into European everyday culture and popular art. The permanent exhibition "Cultural Contacts. Living in Europe" provides a cross-section of the rich collection of the MEK and deals with discussions on social movements and national boundaries in Europe.

Domäne Dahlem

Königin-Luise-Str. 49 (just west of and over the road from Ⓤ Dahlemdorf) ☏ 030 66 63 000, Ⓦ domaene-dahlem.de. Daily 8am–7pm; museum Tues–Sun 10am–5pm. €4 (free for under 18s).

A working farm and handicrafts centre, **Domäne Dahlem** attempts to show off the lifestyle and skills of the pre-industrial age. The old estate house has a few odds and ends, most intriguing of which are the thirteenth-century swastikas, but the collection of agricultural instruments in an outbuilding is more comprehensive. Elsewhere there are ponies, turkeys, pigs, sheep and cows in the grounds, and demonstrations of woodcarving, wool- and cotton-spinning and various other farm crafts. At weekends some of the old agricultural machinery is fired up and the animals are paraded. The complex also now features the **Culinarium**: a kid-friendly, interactive cultural history of food – from farm to fork – complete with locally produced goods to buy. A visit out here is best combined with a visit to the nearby **Museum Europäischer Kulturen** and/or the city's **Botanical Garden**.

Dahlem Botanic Garden and Botanical Museum

Königin-Luise-Str. 6–8 ⓤ/Ⓢ Rathaus
Steglitz, and 15min walk or bus #X83 to
Königin-Luise-Str./Botanischer Garten.
☎ 030 83 85 01 00, ⓦ bgbm.org. Daily:
Jan, Nov & Dec 9am–4pm; Feb 9am–5pm;
March 9am–6pm, April–Oct 9am–8pm.
Gardens (inc. museum) €6.

Founded as an extension to
the kitchen garden of the
Berlin palace by the Elector of
Brandenburg, by 1815 the royal
herbarium had developed hugely
thanks to extensive botanical
research by C.L. Willdenow. The
collection was moved to Dahlem
1897–1910 and today hosts 20,000
species of plants over 43 hectares,
making it one of the largest and
most diverse botanical gardens
in the world. The sixteen green-
houses (Gewächshäuser) feature
an array of specialist areas such as
desert and rainforest. The garden
resembles a planted map with
"Prairie", "Himalaya" and "Alps"
sections topped by aquatic and
marsh plants, an aroma and touch
garden and medicinal plants.
The attached museum features
sections of preserved fossils and
plant formations on artificially
constructed landscapes.

Pfaueninsel

Ⓢ Wannsee, then bus #208 to the
passenger ferry (€4 inc. entry to the
island). Castle: April–Oct Tues–Sun
10am–5.30pm (€6). Island: daily April–
June 9am–7pm; July & Aug 9am–8pm; Oct
9am–6pm (€4 inc. ferry).

Formerly known as
Kaninchenwerder ("Rabbit
Island"), Peacock Island features
a castle built by Prussian king
Frederick William II in 1793 for
him and his mistress Wilhelmine
Enke. His successor Frederick
William III turned the island
into a model farm and from 1816
had the park redesigned by Peter
Joseph Lenné. Karl Friedrich
Schinkel also planned a few of the
buildings, for example the former
Palm House and Llama House,
and also the Cavalier House in the
middle of the island. The king also
laid out a menagerie modelled
on the Ménagerie du Jardin des
Plantes in Paris, in which exotic
animals and birds including
peacocks were housed. In addition
to several free-ranging peacocks,
chickens and pheasants can be
found in captivity, complemented
by a rich variety of flora. The
entire island is designated as a
nature reserve.

House of the Wannsee Conference

Ⓢ Wannsee, then bus #114 (direction
"Krankenhaus Heckeshorn") to Haus der
Wannsee-Konferenz ☎ 030 80 50 010,
ⓦ ghwk.de. Daily 10am–6pm. Free (guided
tour €3, German only).

It's hard to imagine that this
handsome villa at Wannsee lake
has an iniquitous history, but it
was here that the "Final Solution
of the Jewish Question" was
discussed by fifteen high-ranking
Nazi officials, who agreed to
exterminate the entire Jewish
population of Europe. Since 1992
it has served as a memorial and

Strandbad Wannsee

documentation centre, with a permanent exhibit that draws on detailed historical research to profile the conference and the process of deporting Jews to the ghettoes and camps. A library on the second floor (named after Joseph Wulf, an Auschwitz survivor and campaigner for this memorial) holds thousands of books on Nazism, anti-Semitism, the Holocaust, as well as Nazi-era documents such as children's books promoting Nazism. However, the most spine-tingling experience is simply standing in the room where the plans were made for the murder of millions.

Strandbad Wannsee

Wannseebadeweg 25 Ⓢ Wannsee/ Nikolaisee Ⓦ berlinerbaeder.de. Daily April–Sept; check website for exact times. €5.50.

Strandbad Wannsee's impressive 1275m long (and 80m wide) sweep of sandy beach has long been a venerable summer destination for Berliners. Officially the largest lido in Europe, it's located on the eastern side of the Wannsee, just a twenty-minute train ride from the city centre. Its current "look" was formulated by architects Martin Wagner and Richard Ermisch. Today the "Mother of all Lidos" attracts up to 230,000 visitors per year and has been designated a cultural heritage site. Between 2004 and 2007, it underwent a €12.5 million refurbishment for its centenary celebrations.

Max Liebermann Villa

Colomierstr. 3 Ⓢ Wannsee then either bus #114 toward Heckeshorn to Liebermann-Villa (5min) or 20min walk Ⓣ 030 80 58 59 00, Ⓦ liebermann-villa .de. April–Sept Mon, Wed, Fri & Sat 10am–6pm, Thurs & Sun till 7pm; Oct–March daily except Tues 11am–5pm. Winter €6, summer €8.

German Impressionist Max Liebermann's "castle by the sea", built in 1909, and particularly its expansive, 7000-square-metre garden, was the subject of more than two hundred of his paintings. An exhibition documents Liebermann's life here, with prints and photographs. On the upper floor are around forty paintings, pastels and prints that revolve around his Wannsee works – pictures of the flower terrace, perennial garden, birch grove and the lawn leading down to the lake – plus portraits of family and personalities. The garden has been reconstructed today as it was originally planned by Liebermann, and brims with rare and diverse species.

Gedenkstätte Berlin-Hohenschönhausen

Genslerstr. 66 Ⓜ M5 from Ⓢ Freienwalder Str. (then 10min walk) or Ⓜ M6 from Hackescher Markt Genslerstr. (then 10min walk) Ⓣ 030 98 60 82 30, Ⓦ stiftung-hsh. de. Daily 9am–6pm, English tours 11.30am & 2.30pm €6.

With its intact buildings, equipment and furniture, the Stasi prison at Hohenschönhausen provides a particularly authentic – and grisly – portrait of public persecution during GDR times. The Stasi used it to detain and physically and psychologically torture dissenters. The prison, which remained largely a secret until the Wall fell in 1989, was turned into a memorial in 1994, and since 2000 has been an independent foundation that researches the history of the prison and produces exhibitions, events and publications. The only way to see the memorial is via a guided tour, available in German, English and other languages; tours with former inmates are also available, though mostly in German. The tour includes a survey of the older and newer prison blocks and detailed descriptions of daily life in the prison.

ACCOMMODATION

Accommodation

Berlin's accommodation options run the gamut from cheap and cheerful hostels to corporate hotels, super-deluxe five stars and intimate boutique and "art" hotels. Prices quoted usually include taxes and service charges, though breakfast and parking are sometimes extra – it's worth double-checking when booking. While there are many rooms in the city, there are also a lot of visitors; booking ahead in the warmer, more popular months is recommended, especially during large events such as the film festival (see p.161).

Spandauer Vorstadt

CIRCUS HOSTEL MAP P.28, POCKET MAP D11. Weinbergsweg 1a Ⓤ Rosenthaler Platz ☏ 030 20 00 39 39, Ⓦ circus-berlin .de. One of the most popular hostels in the city, *Circus* offers pleasant, clean dorms, private rooms – even penthouse apartments – and a convivial, upbeat vibe right on buzzing Rosenthaler Platz. Bicycles for rent, free walking tours and their own microbrewery add to the appeal. Buffet breakfast €5. **Dorms from €19, doubles from €85**

CIRCUS HOTEL MAP P.28, POCKET MAP E10. Rosenthalerstr. 1 Ⓤ Rosenthaler Platz ☏ 030 20 00 39 39, Ⓦ circus-berlin .de. The sister establishment of the *Circus* hostel (located just over the road) is a more upmarket and more ecofriendly place. Sixty rooms include junior suites and apartments, decorated in striking colours with wooden floors and a mix of antique and modern furniture. Buffet breakfast €12. Doubles from €95

HEART OF GOLD MAP P.28, POCKET MAP C12. Johannisstr. 11 Ⓢ Oranienburg ☏ 030 29 00 33 00, Ⓦ heartofgold-hostel.de. Good-value and friendly hostel near one of the busiest strips in Mitte. Dorms and rooms are basic but clean, and staff go the extra mile to make staying here fun. Expect lots of space-themed decorative touches. Buffet breakfast €5. **Dorms from €9.50, rooms from €45**

KASTANIENHOF MAP P.28, POCKET MAP H2. Kastanienallee 65 Ⓤ Senefelderplatz ☏ 030 44 30 50, Ⓦ kastanienhof.berlin. This recently renovated hotel has 44 rooms in an elegant house, with decor that nods to Berlin's fascinating history, including photos, illustrations and maps. Great location for Prenzlauer Berg and Mitte. Breakfast (€9) not included. **Doubles from €87**

Apartment rentals

Private apartments are a popular, and often good-value choice for many travellers to Berlin. The best apartments offer value for money, are well located and usually stylish or interestingly decorated. Although Airbnb was banned from renting out complete apartments in the city in 2016 (rooms within a house are still possible), that seems to have done little to diminish offerings on the site. Also check out Ⓦ bed-and-breakfast-berlin.de, Ⓦ brilliant-apartments.de, Ⓦ ferienwohnungen-berlin.de and Ⓦ oh-berlin.com, which all offer a good spread of apartments, rooms and regular special deals.

SOHO HOUSE MAP P.28, POCKET MAP
F11. Torstr. 1 ⓤ Rosa–Luxemburg–Platz
☎ 030 40 50 440, ⓦ sohohouseberlin
.com. Private members' club in a restored
Bauhaus building with forty swanky
apartments, four huge lofts and forty
hotel rooms that range from tiny to extra
large. Decor is quirky and fun, and hints
at the faded glamour of the late 1920s.
There's also a lovely spa, gym, rooftop
pool, restaurant, bars, screening room and
private dining area. **From €270**

WEINMEISTER MAP P.28, POCKET MAP
E11. Weinmeisterstr. 2 ⓤ Weinmeisterstr.
☎ 030 75 56 670, ⓦ the-weinmeister
.com. This swish hotel features 84 spacious
rooms with large beds and a stylish design
ethic. There's also a decent bar and lounge,
a rooftop bar and a sixth-floor beauty spa.
Breakfast €18. **Doubles from €129**

Unter den Linden and the government quarter

ADLON KEMPINSKI MAP P.50, POCKET
MAP B14. Unter den Linden 77 ⓤ /
Ⓢ Brandenburger Tor ☎ 030 22 610,
ⓦ hotel-adlon.de. Probably the most
famous hotel in the city, and definitely
one of the most luxurious, the *Hotel
Adlon Kempinski* matches a wealth of
history (previous guests include Emperor
Wilhelm II, Albert Einstein and Michael
Jackson, who famously dangled a baby
from one of the hotel balconies) with
serious five-star swagger and an enviable
location overlooking the Brandenburg Gate
on Pariser Platz. Breakfast €42. **Doubles
from €260**

ARCOTEL JOHN F MAP P.50, POCKET
MAP D14. Werderscher Markt 11
ⓤ Hausvogteiplatz ☎ 030 40 50
460, ⓦ arcotelhotels.com. Close to
Gendarmenmarkt, this 190-room hotel
is a slightly cheaper option than the
neighbouring big guns, but has all the
facilities you'll need – gym, sauna, meeting
rooms, restaurant, bar. Breakfast not
included. **Doubles from €117**

ARTE LUISE KUNSTHOTEL MAP P.50,
POCKET MAP B12. Luisenstr. 19 ⓤ /
Ⓢ Friedrichstr. ☎ 030 28 44 80,
ⓦ luise-berlin.com. Within walking
distance of the Reichstag and Unter den
Linden, this art hotel has fifty charmingly
appointed and highly individual rooms,
Dutch sculptures in the large lobby and
an in-house restaurant serving German-
Mediterranean cuisine. Breakfast €11.
Doubles from €99

HOTEL DE ROME MAP P.50,
POCKET MAP C14. Behrenstr. 37
ⓤ Französische Str. ☎ 030 46 06 090,
ⓦ roccofortecollection .com. Occupying
a nineteenth-century former Dresdner
Bank building, this high-class hotel
mixes history with a swanky interior,
luxurious rooms, an expansive spa and
a fantastic restaurant (*La Banca*) and
rooftop terrace. Breakfast €35. **Doubles
from €295**

WESTIN GRAND MAP P.50, POCKET MAP
C13. Friedrichstr. 158–164 ⓤ Französische
Str. ☎ 030 20 270, ⓦ westingrandberlin
.com. Built during the GDR, this large
hotel, well positioned on Friedrichstrasse
and close to the Brandenburg Gate, has
been refurbished to feature a refined *belle
époque* interior and beautifully appointed
rooms and suites. Breakfast €32. **Doubles
from €169**

Alexanderplatz and the Nikolaiviertel

ART'OTEL MAP P.61, POCKET MAP F14.
Wallstr. 70–73 ⓤ Märkisches Museum
☎ 030 24 06 20, ⓦ artotelberlinmitte
.com. With its impressive range of
paintings by Georg Baselitz (and others),
this design hotel has reasonable rates,
good in-house food and drink options and
friendly staff. Breakfast €17.50. **Doubles
from €99**

CITYSTAY HOSTEL MAP P.61, POCKET
MAP E12. Rosenstr. 16 Ⓢ Hackescher
Markt ☎ 030 23 62 40 31, ⓦ citystay
.de. Close to Hackescher Markt, the
Citystay is a big, loft-style space in a
nineteenth-century building with dorms
and private rooms. No leisure facilities
but the bar serves craft beer, coffee and
snacks, and there's a nice courtyard (until
10pm). Breakfast buffet (partly organic) is
€5.50. **Dorms from €10 (bedding €2.50),
doubles from €40**

LUX 11 MAP P.61, POCKET MAP
F12. Rosa-Luxemburg-Str. 9–13
ⓤ Rosa-Luxemburg-Platz ⓣ 030 93 62
800, ⓦ lux-eleven.com. This designer
apartment-hotel oozes style and has
big, comfy rooms (with kitchenettes and
spacious, open bathrooms), a decent
restaurant–bar (*Prince*) and a concept
store with a milk bar. Breakfast buffet €18.
Doubles from €109

NIKOLAI RESIDENCE HOTEL MAP P.61,
POCKET MAP E13. Am Nussbaum 5
ⓤ Klosterstr. ⓣ 03 04 00 44 59 00,
ⓦ nikolai-residence.com. Cute and
well-run 3-star in the heart of the
Nikolaivertel. Decor is fairly modern
and dotted with paintings and photos
by German artists, and the 21 rooms are
simple, reasonably stylish and comfortable.
No breakfast. **Doubles from €90.**

PARK INN MAP P.61, POCKET MAP F12.
Alexanderplatz 7 ⓤ/ⓢ Alexanderplatz
ⓣ 030 23 890, ⓦ parkinn-berlin.de.
This towering 37-floor GDR-era building
looks better on the inside than the out.
Unexciting but comfortable rooms feature
cosy beds, marble bathrooms and, past the
twentieth floor, panoramic views across
Berlin. Gym, sauna and a rooftop terrace,
too. Breakfast not included. **Doubles from
€79**

Potsdamer Platz and Tiergarten

BERLIN MARRIOTT HOTEL MAP P.70,
POCKET MAP A15. Inge-Beisheim-Platz
1 ⓣ 030 22 00 00, ⓦ berlinmarriott
.de. This business hotel is a surprisingly
dynamic spot for leisure travellers too.
Located right on Potsdamer Platz, it boasts
a slick "fashion bar" designed by local star
Michael Michalsky (with DJs at weekends),
an excellent restaurant (*Midtown Grill*),
plus a pool and comprehensive fitness
centre. **Doubles from €129**

**HOTEL ALTBERLIN AT POTSDAMER
PLATZ** MAP P.70, POCKET MAP E7.
Potsdamer Str. 67 ⓤ/ⓢ Potsdamer
Platz ⓣ 030 26 06 70, ⓦ altberlin
.de. A turn-of-the-twentieth-century,
Wilhelminian-era hotel with "grandma"
style rooms, old-world decor and
long-forgotten Berlin specialities served at

its restaurant, *Rike's*. Breakfast included.
Rooms from €83

HOTEL HANSABLICK MAP P.70, POCKET
MAP B5. Flotowstr. 6 ⓤ Tiergarten
ⓣ 030 39 04 800, ⓦ hansablick.de. The
Hansablick, located right on the water, has
rooms with balconies and/or river views
and a traditional interior that features
artworks by the likes of Otmar Alt and
Heinrich Zille. Rates include breakfast,
wi-fi and parking. **Doubles from €79**

RITZ CARLTON MAP P.70, POCKET MAP
A15. Potsdamer Platz 3 ⓢ/ⓤ Potsdamer
Platz ⓣ 030 33 77 77, ⓦ ritzcarlton.com.
This distinctive skyscraper hotel has 303
rooms with expensive cherry-wood closets
and watercolour paintings. There are
also bars, a tea lounge, a great brasserie,
and fantastic five-star service. Breakfast
included. **Doubles from €220**

**SHERATON BERLIN GRAND HOTEL
ESPLANADE** MAP P.70, POCKET MAP D6.
Lützowufer 15 ⓤ Nollendorfplatz ⓣ 030
25 47 80, ⓦ esplanadeberlin.com. Smack
between Ku'damm and Potsdamer Platz,
this large, fancy hotel has two restaurants,
a New York-style cocktail bar and spa.
Breakfast €22. **Doubles from €99**

Prenzlauer Berg

EASTSEVEN MAP P.82, POCKET MAP F10.
Schwedter Str. 7 ⓤ Senefelderplatz
ⓣ 030 93 62 22 40, ⓦ eastseven.de.
Laid-back hostel located on the border of
Mitte and Prenzlauer Berg. Rooms (singles,
doubles, twins, dorms) and public areas
are clean and functional, furnishings are
decent quality and there's a lounge area
with books and board games. No stag or
hen groups. Breakfast €3. **Dorms from €14,
doubles from €68.**

HOTEL TRANSIT LOFT MAP P.82, POCKET
MAP K3. Immanuelkirchstr. 14a ⓤ/
ⓢ Alexanderplatz ⓣ 030 48 49 37 73,
ⓦ transit-loft.de. A modern hotel set in a
nineteenth-century, yellow-brick factory
and well located for Kollwitzplatz (see
p.84). The 47 rooms (dorms included) are
airy and well lit with basic furnishings
and en-suite showers. The same owners
run *Hotel Transit* in Kreuzberg (see p.152).
Breakfast included. **Dorms from €21,
doubles from €59**

LETTE'M SLEEP MAP P.82, POCKET MAP J3. Lettestr. 7 ⑤ Prenzlauer Allee ☎ 030 44 73 36 23, ⓌⓌ backpackers.de. Located directly on Helmholtzplatz, this vaguely hip backpacker hostel has basic but clean dorms (four- to seven-bed) as well as twins and private apartments. There's a common room, kitchen (but no breakfast), free wi-fi and a beer garden in summer. **Dorms from €15, doubles from €49**

MYER'S HOTEL MAP P.82, POCKET MAP J3. Metzer Str. 26 Ⓤ Senefelderplatz ☎ 030 44 01 40, Ⓦ myershotel.de. Set in a nineteenth-century Neoclassical building, this tasteful hotel has 51 rooms in a range of shapes and sizes, a glass-roofed courtyard with lounge and gallery with changing exhibitions. There's also a garden with terrace. Breakfast not included. **Doubles from €87**

PFEFFERBETT MAP P.82, POCKET MAP F10. Christinenstr. 18–19 Ⓤ Senefelderplatz ☎ 030 93 93 58 58, Ⓦ pfefferbett.de. This welcoming hostel has clean, smart rooms and dorms, a buzzy lobby and a lovely courtyard garden that doubles as a beer garden. Bicycle hire (€12 per day), free guided tours and laundry services available. Breakfast €6.70. **Dorms from €12, doubles from €32.50**

Friedrichshain

ANDEL'S BY VIENNA HOUSE BERLIN MAP P.98, POCKET MAP M3. Landsberger Allee 106 ⑤ Landsberger Allee ☎ 030 45 30 5300, Ⓦ andelsberlin.com. This sprawling design hotel has 557 small and retro-ish rooms with full amenities and spacious bathrooms. The top-floor *Skykitchen* and *Skybar* have great city views and there's a 550-square-metre spa. Breakfast included. **Doubles from €99**

JUNCKER'S HOTEL GARNI MAP P.98, POCKET MAP A16. Grünberger Str. 21 Ⓤ Frankfurter Tor ☎ 030 29 33 550, Ⓦ junckershotel.de. A small, family-run hotel with medium-size but good-quality rooms, friendly staff and a quiet atmosphere. Breakfast €8. **Doubles from €59**

MICHELBERGER MAP P.98, POCKET MAP M7. Warschauer Str. 39–40 Ⓤ Warschauer Str. ☎ 030 29 77 85 90,

Ⓦ michelbergerhotel.com. Creative, welcoming and trendy, the rooms here are imaginatively and individually designed, the stylish lounge area has regular gigs and the drinks and food are good. Recent additions include a sauna, a renovated kitchen and several self-contained apartments. **Doubles from €70**

NHOW MAP P.98, POCKET MAP M7. Stralauer Allee 3 ⑤ Warschauer Str. ☎ 030 29 02 990, Ⓦ nhow-berlin.com. This four-star concept hotel merges a music theme with designer hotel rooms. Recreational amenities include a health club, sauna and fitness facility and some rooms have great views over the river. Breakfast included. **Doubles from €139**

OSTEL MAP P.98, POCKET MAP L6. Wriezener Karree 5 Ⓤ Ostbahnhof ☎ 030 25 76 86 60, Ⓦ ostel.eu. This shrine to *Ostalgie* – nostalgia for the old Communist GDR – is kitted out with a wealth of GDR memorabilia like brown floral wallpaper, 1970s radio clocks and photographs of GDR leaders. Prices will satisfy contemporary communists too. **Doubles from €39**

PLUS BERLIN MAP P.98, POCKET MAP M7. Warschauer Platz 6 Ⓤ / ⑤ Warschauer Str. ☎ 030 31 16 98 820, Ⓦ plushostels.com. Upscale and vibrant backpacker hostel located inside a striking red-brick building with stylish, high-ceilinged rooms, a lively bar and restaurant, and even a pool, sauna and large garden area. Breakfast €6.50. **Dorms from €8, doubles from €120**

West Kreuzberg

GRAND HOSTEL MAP P.105, POCKET MAP F7. Tempelhofer Ufer 14 Ⓤ Möckernbrück ☎ 030 200 95 450, Ⓦ grandhostel-berlin .de. Set inside a listed historic building near the Landwehr Canal, this award-winning hostel ups the ante in terms of elegance and space. There's a bar and library room on site, furnishings are design-savvy and the bright, stylish rooms and dorms don't have bunks. Bed linen service €3.60, breakfast €6.50. **Dorms €12, doubles €48**

HOTEL TRANSIT MAP P.105, POCKET MAP F8. Hagelberger Str. 53 Ⓤ Mehringdamm ☎ 030 78 90 470, Ⓦ hotel-transit.de. This bright, breezy hostel occupies a former factory building and has basic but decently sized rooms and an upbeat atmosphere. Breakfast included. **Doubles from €59**

JOHANN HOTEL MAP P.105, POCKET MAP H8. Johanniterstr. 8 ⓤ Prinzenstr. ⓣ 030 22 50 740, Ⓦ hotel-johann-berlin.de. Close to Bergmannstrasse. and the Jewish Museum, the *Johann* is a fairly nondescript but friendly hotel, with spacious rooms and a peaceful garden. Breakfast included. **Doubles from €105**

MÖVENPICK HOTEL MAP P.105, POCKET MAP F7. Schöneberger Str. 3 Ⓢ Anhalter Bahnhof ⓣ 030 23 00 60, Ⓦ moevenpick-hotels.com. This former Siemens office has a unique mix of contemporary and industrial decor: Philippe Starck pieces in the rooms, wood and glass in abundance and a pleasant courtyard restaurant (*Hof zwei*) and bar. Breakfast €22. **Doubles from €99**

RIEHMERS HOFGARTEN MAP P.105, POCKET MAP F8. Yorckstr. 83 ⓤ Mehringdamm ⓣ 030 78 09 88 00, Ⓦ riehmers-hofgarten.com. There's a low-key, residential atmosphere at this hotel in a historically protected building. The 22 rooms and apartments have a correspondingly nineteenth-century feel and there's a delightful living room for relaxation. **Doubles from €131**

East Kreuzberg

MOTEL ONE BERLIN-MITTE MAP P.112, POCKET MAP J7. Prinzenstr. 40 ⓤ Moritzplatz ⓣ 030 69 56 71 740, Ⓦ motel-one.com. Well located for Alexanderplatz and the Oranienstrasse scene, this functional hotel has comfortable enough rooms with all necessary conveniences, a bar for snacks and drinks and free wi-fi. Breakfast €9.50. **Doubles from €77**

ROCK'N'ROLL HERBERGE MAP P.112, POCKET MAP K7. Muskauer Str. 11 ⓤ Görlitzer Bahnhof ⓣ 030 61 62 31 00, Ⓦ rnrherberge.de. With six rooms designed by local artists, billiards and table football and vegan and non-vegan breakfasts and snacks, this budget hangout is especially set up for musicians and music lovers – as the graffiti of Falco and Joe Strummer testify to. Rooms for up to

five people (not dorms) are available (from €34 per person). **Doubles from €52**

Charlottenburg

25HOURS HOTEL BIKINI BERLIN MAP P.126, POCKET MAP B6. Budapester Str. 40 ⓤ / Ⓢ Zoologischer Garten ⓣ 030 12 02 210, Ⓦ 25hours-hotels.com. The hotel that single-handedly funked up West Berlin, the *25hours* comes with a playfully cool design aesthetic, quirky bedrooms and a fabulous rooftop restaurant and bar (see p.134). The Kaiser Wilhelm Church (see p.128) is right across the street. **Doubles from €170**

AM SAVIGNYPLATZ HOTEL MAP P.126, POCKET MAP A6. Kantstr. 22 Ⓢ Savignyplatz ⓣ 030 50 18 17 36, Ⓦ am-savignyplatz-hotel.de. A beautiful old building that has been thoroughly modernized, the *Am Savignyplatz* is surprisingly stylish – its eleven rooms are spacious and modern, and one of them even has a small garden. **Doubles from €69**

AM STEINPLATZ MAP P.126, POCKET MAP B6. Steinplatz 4 Ⓢ Zoologischer Garten ⓣ 030 55 44 440, Ⓦ marriott .com. Sumptuous boutique set inside a heritage-listed building that was once the haunt of the more well-heeled and intellectual Weimar set. Rooms are richly appointed with a mix of vintage and modern furnishings and there's a top-notch restaurant and classy bar with craft beer and occasional DJs. Breakfast €25–35. **Doubles from €190.**

ART HOTEL CHARLOTTENBURGER HOF MAP P.126, POCKET MAP A6. Stuttgarter Platz 14 Ⓢ Charlottenburg ⓣ 030 32 90 70, Ⓦ charlottenburger-hof.de. Bright contemporary hotel, replete with modern art, Bauhaus design and multicoloured furniture. Perks include an on-site café-restaurant with terrace and courtyard. Rates can often be slashed by booking specials online. **Doubles from €63**

HOTEL OTTO MAP P.126, POCKET MAP A6. Knesebeckstr. 10 ⓤ Ernst-Reuter-Platz ⓣ 030 54 71 00 80, Ⓦ hotelotto.com. *Otto* eschews the traditional for a cheery, modern experience that's all blues, magentas and greens. The 46 rooms are chic and individually designed and the organic food at the restaurant is good too. Breakfast €18. **Doubles from €100**

HOTEL Q! MAP P.126, POCKET MAP A6. **Knesebeckstr. 67** Ⓤ **Uhlandstr.** ☎ **030 81 00 660,** Ⓦ **loock-hotels.com.** One of west Berlin's swankiest hotels, the *Q!* has bathtubs built into bed frames, elegantly minimal rooms, chocolate massages and the *Fox Bar*, plus a lounge and garden. **Doubles from €110**

HOTEL ZOO MAP P.126, POCKET MAP B6. **Kurfürstendamm 25** Ⓤ **Kurfürstendamm** ☎ **030 88 43 70,** Ⓦ **hotelzoo.de.** This historic hotel reopened to great fanfare in 2014. Its 144 rooms are sumptuously appointed with tasteful fashion photographs and high-quality wooden floors and furnishings. There's a restaurant and lounge, and two sixth-floor penthouse suites if you feel like splashing. **Doubles from €150.**

SWISSÔTEL MAP P.126, POCKET MAP B7. **Augsburger Str. 44** Ⓤ **Kurfürstendamm** ☎ **030 22 01 00,** Ⓦ **swissotel.com.** A short stroll from the Kaiser-Wilhelm-Gedächtnis-Kirche (see p.128) and Berlin Zoo (see p.124), this ecofriendly corporate hotel has 316 rooms, restaurant and a bar/lounge, sauna and fitness facilities. **Doubles from €125**

Schöneberg

HOTEL DE ELA MAP P.136, POCKET MAP C8. **Landshuter Str. 1** Ⓤ **Viktoria-Luise-Platz** ☎ **030 23 63 39 60,** Ⓦ **hotel-de-ela.de.** A mix of twenty-first-century design in a nineteenth-century Victorian building, *De Ela* has large, comfortable rooms with a classic feel for decent prices. Family friendly too. Breakfast and wi-fi included. **Doubles from €40**

JUGENDHOTEL BERLINCITY MAP P.136, POCKET MAP E9. **Crellestr. 22** Ⓤ **Kleistpark** ☎ **030 78 70 21 30,** Ⓦ **jugendhotel-berlin. de.** With 170 plain but comfy beds in a renovated factory building, this is a good option for budget-conscious travellers. Pool tables, decent rooms and a convivial bar. **Dorms from €21, doubles from €65**

TOM'S HOTEL MAP P.136, POCKET MAP C7. **Motzstr. 19** Ⓤ **Nollendorfplatz** ☎ **030 21 96 66 04,** Ⓦ **toms-hotel.de.** This friendly gay hangout has a great bar (*Tom's*), a vibrant café and is close to the gay scene of Nollendorfplatz. Rooms are comfortable and artistically decorated and apartments feature a flat-screen TV and free wi-fi. Breakfast €6.50. **Doubles from €79**

ESSENTIALS

Bar on the River Spree

Arrival

By air

Flying is, predictably, the cheapest and most convenient way to get to Germany from overseas, as well as from many other European countries thanks to the proliferation of discount airlines.

Both Berlin's airports (ⓦ berlin-airport.de) are within Berlin public transport's zone ABC (Tegel is within AB). An ABC ticket costs €3.40 while an AB costs €2.80. From Berlin's **Schönefeld airport** (SXF) S-Bahn lines S9 and S45 run regularly (every 10–20min) to main stations like Alexanderplatz (38min), the Hauptbahnhof (44min) and Bahnhof Zoo (50min). There are also regional trains like RE7 that head to the centre. Bus #X7 (N7 at night) runs every 20min to nearby U-Bahn Rudow. From **Tegel airport** (TXL) the frequent #TXL express bus runs to the Hauptbahnhof and Alexanderplatz, while #X9 express or local #109 and #128 buses run to Bahnhof Zoo. **Taxis** from Tegel tend to cost €20–35, depending on which part of the city you want to get to; from Schönefeld expect to pay more like €30–50.

In 2019/2020, Tegel is due to close and Schönefeld extended into **Berlin Brandenburg International** airport.

By train

Germany is well connected by train with destinations throughout continental Europe. Check Deutsche Bahn's excellent website (ⓦ www .bahn.de) for international routes. From the UK, a slow but comfortable option is via Paris, with the overnight sleeper departing weekly in summer only from Paris Est (total travel time from London around 16hr); a quicker daytime route is via Brussels and Cologne (from 10hr 30min).

The huge **Hauptbahnhof** northeast of the Brandenburg Gate is well connected to the rest of the city by S- and U-Bahn. Many long-distance routes also stop at Ostbahnhof, convenient for Friedrichshain, or Bahnhof Zoo, for Charlottenburg. All are well connected by S-Bahn.

By bus

Several private bus companies, such as Flixbus (ⓦ flixbus.com) and Eurolines (ⓦ eurolines.com/en) run routes from as far afield as Barcelona and Bucharest.

Most international buses stop at the bus station (ZOB), linked to the centre by express buses #X34 and #X49, as well as regular buses #104, #139, #218, #349 and #M49; U-Bahn #2, from Kaiserdamm station; and S-Bahn from Messe-Nord/ICC.

Getting around

U- and S-Bahn

BVG (ⓦ bvg.de) operate an efficient, integrated system of U- and S-Bahn train lines, buses and trams. U- and S-Bahn trains run daily 4.30am–12.30am (Fri & Sat all night).

Buses and trams

The city bus network – and the tram system mainly in eastern Berlin – covers most of the gaps left by the U-Bahn; several useful **tram** routes centre on Hackescher Markt, including the M1 to Prenzlauer Berg.

A night-time network of buses and trams operates, with buses (around every 30min) often following U-Bahn line routes; free maps are available at most stations.

Buses #100 and **#200** drive past many famous Berlin sights en

City tours

Original Berlin Walks ☎ 030 30 19 194, ⓦ berlinwalks.de. Offers a range of walking tours of between three and six hours, many of which cover the main sights and beyond. Prices vary according to tour.

Trabi Safaris ⓦ trabi-safari.de. Drive around the city (slowly) in a Trabant, the car of choice for the GDR (with guides and without) with live information delivered to you via radio. Day and night "safaris" available. Around €60 depending on numbers (maximum four in a car).

Slow Travel Berlin ⓦ slowtravelberlin.com. English-speaking cultural/historical walking tours (2hr), mostly run by long-term residents. €20

Alternative Berlin ☎ 0162 81 98 264, ⓦ alternativeberlin.com. Street art tours, pub crawls and other "alternative culture" trawls.

Berlin Music Tours ☎ 030 30 87 56 33, ⓦ musictours-berlin.com. Follow the musical trails of Bowie, Iggy Pop, Depeche Mode and U2.

route from Zoologischer Garten to Alexanderplatz, providing a cheap alternative to a sightseeing tour.

Tickets and passes

Tickets are available from machines at U-Bahn stations, on trams (machines on trams only take coins) or from bus drivers. Zone AB **single tickets** cost €2.80; zone ABC single €3.40; **short-trip tickets** (*Kurzstreckentarif*) are available for three train or six bus/tram stops for €1.80; zone AB **day-tickets** cost €7. Validate single tickets in the yellow machines on platforms before travelling.

For two, three or five days the **WelcomeCard** (see p.158) is good value.

Bike rental and tours

Cycling in Berlin is very easy, safe and very popular. Not only is the city (mostly) as flat as a pancake, there are dedicated cycle lanes throughout.

There are also numerous rental places, including: Fat Tire (daily: March–Nov 9.30am–6pm; mid-April to Sept till 8pm; call or email out of season ☎ 030 24 04 79 91, ⓦ fattirebiketours.com/berlin), beneath the TV tower at Alexanderplatz. They also offer half-day **bike tours** (4hr 30min; €28). Nearly all hostels rent bikes for around €14/day.

Taxis

Taxi fares are €3.90 flag-fall plus €2/km for the first 7km, then €1.50/km thereafter; if you hail a taxi on the street – rather than at a stand or by phone – you can ask for a short-trip price (*Kurzstreckentarif*) before the trip starts and pay €5 for a 2km ride. Taxi firms include: Taxi Funk ☎ 030 44 33 22 and Funk Taxi ☎ 030 26 10 26.

Directory A–Z

Addresses

If you are looking for an address in the former East, bear in mind house numbers run in different directions on each side of the street, as opposed to the usual odd/even system.

Children

Berlin is a surprisingly child-friendly city. There are public playgrounds all over the city (many created from transforming bombed-out areas), plenty of green areas to play in such as Tiergarten, Volkspark Friedrichshain and Viktoriapark, and, in the colder months, kindercafés (see *Kiezkind*, p.92) where parents can enjoy a frothy coffee while their kids enjoy the toys.

Cinema

Movies in English play at Babylon Kreuzberg (ⓦ yorck.de), Cinemaxx Colosseum (ⓦ cinemaxx.de), Cinestar Originals (ⓦ cinestar.de) and in the Sony Center (ⓦ sonycenter.de).

Crime and emergencies

Serious crime is relatively low in Berlin, though petty crime such as bike theft can be rife. You can get help at any police station where English is usually spoken. Reporting thefts at local police stations is straightforward, but inevitably there'll be a great deal of bureaucracy to wade through. **Emergency numbers** are: police ☏ 110; fire and ambulance ☏ 112.

Discount passes

The **WelcomeCard** (Berlin AB: 48hr €19.90, 72hr €27.90, 5-day €36.50; Berlin and Potsdam ABC: 48hr €21.90, 72hr €29.90, 5-day €41; ⓦ berlin-welcomecard.de) includes public transport and up to fifty percent off at many of the major tourist sights. Though the standard card doesn't cover the Museum Island, a version that does include these museums is available. Many of the discounts are the same as student prices.

Electricity

230 V, 50 Hz. The Continental two-round-pin plug is standard.

Embassies and consulates

Australia, Wallstr. 76–79 ☏ 030 88 00 880; Canada, Leipziger Platz 17 ☏ 030 20 31 20; Ireland, Jaegerstr. 51 ☏ 030 22 07 20; New Zealand, Friedrichstr. 60 ☏ 030 20 62 10; South Africa, Tiergartenstr.18 ☏ 030 22 07 30; UK, Wilhelmstr. 70–71 ☏ 030 20 45 70; US, Pariser Platz 2 (postal address Clayallee 170) ☏ 030 83 050.

Gay and lesbian Berlin

Berlin's diverse gay scene is spread across the city, but with a focus of sorts in Schöneberg, especially around Nollendorfplatz. The magazine *Siegessäule* (ⓦ siegessaeule .de) has listings and can be picked up in many cafés and shops. Club nights by GMF (ⓦ gmf-berlin.de) at various venues, including Sundays at *House of Weekend* (see p.67), are always worth checking out. The Christopher Street Day Gay Pride festival takes place every year in June (see p.161; ⓦ csd-berlin.de).

Health

Emergency room at Campus Charité Mitte (entrance Luisenstr. 65/66), ☏ 030 450 531 000. Most doctors speak English. Pharmacies (Apotheken) can deal with minor complaints; all display local pharmacies open 24hr, including Apotheke Hauptbahnhof, at the Hauptbahnhof.

Internet

Free wi-fi at the Sony Center and at other public malls and spaces, and in most hotels and hostels. Internet cafés charge around €1.50/30min.

Listings and websites

ExBerliner is a monthly English-language magazine focusing on arts and music listings in Berlin (ⓦ www .exberliner.com). The two main listings magazines in German are *Tip* (ⓦ tip-berlin.de) and *Zitty* (ⓦ zitty.de); all are widely available in cafés and bars. For adverts and classifications also check Craig's List Berlin (ⓦ berlin.de.craigslist.de). Useful English-language websites include ⓦ iheartberlin.de and ⓦ slowtravelberlin.com.

Lost property

Allegedly only 25 percent of lost items in Berlin turn up again, but it's worth contacting Zentrales Fundbüro, Platz der Luftbrücke 6 (ⓣ 030 75 60 31 01), who will help you with the search (there are six such offices around the city). Left or lost luggage can also be reclaimed at both airports and at the Lost & Found section at the Deutsche Bahn. Look for the "Fundbüro" at Hauptbahnhof if you lost something in the subway or tram, or contact BVG-Fundbüro, Potsdamer Str. 180–182 (BVG-Callcenter ⓣ 030 19 449).

Money and banks

The German currency is the euro (€). Exchange facilities are available in most banks, post offices and commercial exchange shops called **Wechselstuben**. The Reisebank has branches in most main train stations (generally open daily, often till 10/11pm) and ATMs are widespread. Basic **banking hours** are Monday to Friday 9am to noon and 1.30 to 3.30pm, Thursday till 6pm. **Credit** cards are fairly widely accepted – but certainly not universally; independent or smaller restaurants and cafés often don't take them. There can be a surcharge in hostels and smaller hotels.

ATMs and exchange are at the airports, and major stations including: Reisebank, at the Hauptbahnhof (daily 8am–9pm), Zoo station (daily 8am–9pm), Friedrichstr. station (Mon–Fri 7.30am–8pm, Sat & Sun 8am–8pm) and Ostbahnhof (Mon–Fri 7am–9pm, Sat & Sun 8am–8pm).

Opening hours

Larger shops open at 8am and close around 6 to 8pm weekdays and 2 to 4pm Saturday, and often close all day Sunday; smaller shops often open at 11am/noon and keep quite erratic hours. Pharmacies, petrol stations and shops in and around train stations stay open late and at weekends. Museums and historic monuments are, with a few exceptions, closed on Monday.

Phones

Call shops are the cheapest way to phone abroad, though you can also phone abroad from all payphones except those marked "National"; phonecards are widely available. The operator is on ⓣ 03.

Post offices

Post offices are open Monday to Friday 8am to 6pm and Saturday 8am to 1pm. There's a convenient branch at Dircksenstr. 2, Mitte.

Smoking

After a wave of restrictions on smoking in all bars was introduced, a lawsuit from a small bar owner resulted in the law being loosened, and Berlin bars are pretty much almost all back to being smoky or having smoking areas. Expect to get smoke in your eyes in almost all bars that don't serve food. All restaurants are smoke free, but many offer a smokers' lounge somewhere.

Sports and outdoor activities

Bundesliga football (ⓦ bundesliga .de) is the major spectator sport in Germany, with world-class clubs playing in top-notch stadiums, many revamped for the 2006 World Cup such as the Olympic stadium (see p.129). Important matches sell out well in advance; tickets can be purchased from the clubs' websites.

Time

Berlin is on Central European Time (CET), one hour ahead of Britain and six hours ahead of EST, with the clocks going forward in spring and back again in autumn on the same dates as the rest of the EU. Generally speaking, Berliners, like the rest of Germany, use the 24-hour clock.

Toilets

There are a few public toilets (*Öffentliche Toilette*, WC) some of which you'll find in the almost romantic-looking toilet huts in parks and close to the subway. In some, you have to put a €0.50 coin in the slot to open the door. There are mostly free toilets at petrol stations, where

you have to ask the clerk for the key. Also big shopping centres have public toilets normally with a maintenance woman, who you should tip around €0.30–50. Gentlemen should head for *Herren*; ladies should head for *Damen*.

Tipping

If you're in a group, you'll be asked if you want to pay individually (*getrennt*) or all together (*zusammen*). In general, round your bill up to the next €0.50 or €1 and give the total directly to the waiter when you pay (rather than leaving it on the table afterwards).

Tourist offices

The main contact details are: ☎ 030 25 00 25, ⓦ visitberlin.de. Tourist offices at: Hauptbahnhof (daily 8am–10pm), Brandenburg Gate (daily 9.30am–7pm) and Kurfürstendamm 21 (Mon–Sat 9.30am–8pm, Sun 10am–8pm).

Travellers with disabilities

Buses and trams marked with a wheelchair symbol are equipped for disabled passengers, and a footnote on the printed schedule provided at every stop indicates which trams and buses are so equipped. Look for the words *behindert* (disabled) and *ausgestattet* (outfitted). Both buses and trams also have seat-belt-like straps to prevent a wheelchair from rolling during transit.

Festivals and events

Bread & Butter

January Ⓦ breadandbutter.com
Held at Treptow's Arena complex (see p.118), the city's most prestigious fashion event features a dizzying range of brands, labels and designers – and plenty of parties in the evening.

Long Night of the Museums (Lange Nacht der Museen)

January and August Ⓦ lange-nacht-der-museen.de
There are two Long Nights of the Museums, when many of Berlin's museums stay open late into the night – usually until midnight or later – with special programmes and events.

Berlinale

February Ⓦ berlinale.de
For two weeks each year, Berlin turns into Hollywood as the Berlinale international film festival takes over the town. Around four hundred films are shown every year as part of the Berlinale's public programme, the vast majority of which are world or European premieres.

Impro

Ten days in March Ⓦ improfestival.de
Running since 2001, this event is the biggest improvisation theatre festival in Europe. Its goal is to show international developments and take part in an intercultural exchange with different ensembles.

Gallery Weekend

End April/early May Ⓦ www.gallery-weekend-berlin.de
Fifty-plus galleries and small venues dedicated to design and art open for one weekend to present exclusive exhibitions and contemporary international art.

My Fest

May 1 Ⓦ myfest36.de
Kreuzberg open-air festival, with music and cultural events and a lot of food stalls (especially around Kottbusser Tor). Note that May Day demonstrations in the evening in the same area have a tendency to turn ugly, though the daytime is usually very safe and fun.

Berlin Festival

May Ⓦ berlinfestival.de
Acclaimed three-day dance and pop festival held at Arena Berlin. The guests tend to be world renowned – Moby, Peaches, Björk – and the event coincides with other music events, which feature additional shows in clubs across town.

Carnival of Cultures

May Ⓦ karneval-berlin.de
This colourful weekend street festival has been running since 1996, with four music stages featuring acts from around the world, plus culinary delights and handmade arts and craft stands. The peak of the festivity is a street parade with around 4800 participants from eighty nations on Whitsunday.

Christopher Street Day (CSD)

June Ⓦ csd-berlin.de
Held in memory of the first big gay uprising against police assaults in Greenwich Village (the Stonewall riots), Berlin's biggest celebration of gay pride has been running since 1970 and draws around half a million people.

Fête de la Musique

June Ⓦ fetedelamusique.de
Over ninety concerts are put on all over town to celebrate the Fête de la Musique, a hugely ambitious event that happens across 520 cities.

Classic Open Air

July Ⓦ classicopenair.de
Five days of classical music at the beautiful Gendarmenmarkt. Previous events have included London's Royal Philharmonic Orchestra performing the complete James Bond title themes and The Scorpions performing with the German Film Orchestra Potsdam.

International Literature Festival

September Ⓦ literaturfestival.com
Berlin's biggest literary event celebrates "diversity in the age of globalization" and features an eclectic and international selection of writers over twelve days.

Berlin Art Week

Mid-September Ⓦ berlinartweek.de
Started in 2012, Berlin Art Week offers an exciting and richly varied programme of outstanding exhibitions, openings and events at ten participating institutions.

Berlin Marathon

Late September Ⓦ bmw-berlin-marathon.com
First held in 1974, Berlin's marathon traditionally takes place on the last weekend in September. With around fourty thousand participants from around one hundred countries, it's one of the largest and most popular road races in the world.

Festival of Lights

Mid-October Ⓦ festival-of-lights.de
Every autumn, Berlin's famous sights are transformed into a sea of colour and light, including the Brandenburg Gate, the Berlin TV Tower, Berliner Dom and more. The nightly light show comes with art and cultural events around the topic of light.

Berlin Jazz Festival

Early November Ⓦ berlinerfestspiele.de
Running since 1964, the Berlin Jazz Festival is a world-renowned event that presents all the diverse styles of jazz. The full and varied programme is traditional and progressive in equal parts, and has tended to focus in particular on big bands and large ensembles.

International Short Film Festival

Mid-November Ⓦ interfilm.de
The five-day International Short Film Festival Berlin was founded in 1982 and is today Berlin's second largest international film festival. The event showcases numerous competitions across all genres, as well as workshops and parties.

Christmas Markets

December
Many public locations in Berlin, such as Gendarmenmarkt, Alexanderplatz and the Schloss Charlottenburg, are taken over by Christmas markets selling arts, crafts, Glühwein, Wurst, pancakes and more.

Chronology

720 The region known today as Berlin is settled by Slavic and Germanic tribes.

948 Germans take control over the area of present-day Berlin.

983 The Slavs rebel (successfully) against German rule.

Twelfth century Germans take over the land again.

1244 Berlin is first mentioned in written records.

1247 The city of Cölln is founded right next to Berlin.

1307 Cölln and Berlin become known simply as "Berlin", the larger of the two cities.

1451 Berlin becomes the royal residence of the Brandenburg electors and has to give up its status of a free Hanseatic city.

1539 The city becomes officially Lutheran.

1576 Nearly five thousand inhabitants of Berlin are wiped out by the bubonic plague.

1618 The devastating Thirty Years' War begins. Half of Berlin's population left dead.

1685 Friedrich Wilhelm offers asylum to the Huguenots. More than fifteen thousand come to Brandenburg and six thousand settle in Berlin.

1699 Inauguration of Schloss Charlottenburg, commissioned by Sophie Charlotte, wife of Friedrich I.

1701 Berlin becomes the capital of Prussia.

1740 Friedrich II – known as Frederick the Great – comes to power and rules until 1786. He turns Berlin into a centre of Enlightenment.

1745–47 Sanssouci Palace is built as the summer palace of Frederick the Great.

1788–91 The Brandenburg Gate is built by Carl Gotthard Langhans.

1806 Napoleon conquers Berlin but grants self-government to the city.

1810 Humboldt University is founded by Prussian educational reformer and linguist Wilhelm von Humboldt.

1841 The Museum Island is dedicated to "art and science" by Friedrich Wilhelm IV of Prussia.

1861 Wedding, Moabit and several other suburbs are incorporated into Berlin.

1871 Berlin becomes the capital of a unified German Empire, under Otto von Bismarck's chancellorship.

1894 The Reichstag opens.

1918 Berlin witnesses the end of World War I and the proclamation of the Weimar Republic.

1920 Berlin established as a separate administrative zone with the Greater Berlin Act. A dozen villages and estates are incorporated into the city.

1923 Tempelhof is officially designated an airport.

1933 Adolf Hitler comes to power.

1939 The beginning of World War II.

1938–45 Thousands of Jews (and other minorities) living in Berlin are sent to death camps.

1943–45 Seventy percent of Berlin is destroyed in air raids.

1945 The Allies take Berlin, and divide it into four zones.

June 1948 The Berlin airlift sees Allied planes delivering supplies to West Berlin.

1949 The Federal Republic of Germany is founded in West Berlin and German Democratic Republic in East Berlin.

June 1953 An uprising of industrial workers against the Communist regime is brutally put down.

August 1961 The building of the Berlin Wall begins.

June 1963 US President John F. Kennedy visits West Berlin, delivering his famous speech, "*Ich bin ein Berliner*".

1972 Access is guaranteed across East Germany to West Berlin with the Four Powers Agreement.

1987 During his second Berlin visit, Ronald Reagan makes a speech in front of the Brandenburg Gate, demanding Mr Gorbachev "tear down this wall!"

1989 Following mass demonstra-tions across East Berlin, the border crossings are finally opened on November 9.

October 3, 1990 The two parts of Berlin are unified as part of the Federal Republic of Germany.

1997 Peter Eisenman's controversial design for a Memorial to the Murdered Jews of Europe (see p.54) is chosen.

1999 Berlin becomes capital of a reunified Germany and the German government and parliament begin their work in Berlin.

2005 Openly gay mayor Klaus Wowereit dubs Berlin "poor but sexy", which becomes a slogan for the city.

2006 The new Hauptbahnhof is opened.

2008 Tempelhof airport is officially closed; the surrounding area is later turned into a public park (see p.108).

2009 Twenty years since the fall of the Wall is celebrated with a "Festival of Freedom". Visiting dignitaries include Mikhail Gorbachev and Bill Clinton.

2014 Structural work on new Stadtschloss (City Palace) completed; expected to open 2019.

2014 Germany beat Argentina 1–0 in the World Cup Final.

2015–16 Berlin takes in a million refugees.

German

Being the cosmopolitan city it is, it's fairly easy to get around Berlin using English. That said, it's worth learning some basics in case you find yourself needing to communicate in the native language. Needless to say, any attempt at speaking German often goes a long way.

Alphabet

Umlaut: ä, ö, ü are the letters that have the mysterious Umlaut in the German language, which can also be spelled as ae, oe or ue. The ä is pronounced like the English a, the others are comparable to speaking the German o or u with a ping-pong ball in the mouth.

The "sharp S": Whenever the s is supposed to be emphasized in German, the "sharp s", **ß**, is used, which is pronounced like the English double s. Since the spelling reform in 1996 there have been some discussions about whether to retain ß or use ss, but for now both variations are accepted.

Pronunciation

Consonants: "w" is pronounced like the English "v"; "sch" is pronounced "sh"; "z" is "ts". The German letter "ß" is basically a double "s".
Vowels: "ei" is "eye"; "ie" is "ee"; "eu" is "oy".

Basic words and phrases

Yes	Ja
No	Nein
Please	Bitte
Thank you	Danke
Good morning	Guten Morgen
Good evening	Guten Abend
Hello/Good day	Güten Tag
Goodbye	Tschüss, ciao, or auf Wiedersehen
Excuse me	Entschuldigen Sie, bitte
Today	Heute
Yesterday	Gestern
Tomorrow	Morgen
Day	Tag
Week	Woche
Month	Monat
Year	Jahr
Weekend	Wochenende
Monday	Montag
Tuesday	Dienstag
Wednesday	Mittwoch
Thursday	Donnerstag
Friday	Freitag
Saturday	Samstag/ Sonnabend
Sunday	Sonntag
I don't understand	Ich verstehe nicht
How much is...?	Wieviel kostet...?
Do you speak English?	Sprechen Sie Englisch?
I don't speak German	Ich spreche kein Deutsch
I'd like a beer	Ich hätte gern ein Bier
Where is?	Wo ist?
entrance/exit	der Eingang/der Ausgang
Toilet	das WC/die Toilette
Women	Damen
Men	Herren
Hotel	das Hotel
HI hostel	die Jugendherberge
Main train station	der Hauptbahnhof
Bus	der Bus
Plane	das Flugzeug
Train	der Zug
Cheap	billig
Expensive	teuer
Open	offen/auf
Closed	geschlossen/zu
Entrance	Eingang
Exit	Ausgang
Smoking/no smoking	rauchen/nicht rauchen
1	Eins
2	Zwei
3	Drei
4	Vier
5	Fünf
6	Sechs

GERMAN

7	Sieben
8	Acht
9	Neun
10	Zehn
11	Elf
12	Zwölf
13	Dreizehn
14	Vierzehn
15	Fünfzehn
16	Sechszehn
17	Siebzehn
18	Achtzehn
19	Neunzehn
20	Zwanzig
21	Ein-und-zwanzig
22	Zwei-und-zwanzig
30	Dreissig
40	Vierzig
50	Fünfzig
60	Sechzig
70	Siebzig
80	Achtzig
90	Neunzig
100	Hundert
1000	Tausend

Food and drink

Terms and phrases

Breakfast	Frühstück
Lunch	Mittagessen
Coffee and cakes	Kaffee und Kuchen
Dinner	Abendessen
Knife	Messer
Fork	Gabel
Spoon	Löffel
Plate	Teller
Cup	Tasse
Glass	Glas
Menu	Speisekarte
Starter	Vorspeise
Main course	Hauptgericht
Dessert	Nachspeise
The bill	Die Rechnung
Organic	Bio
Vegetarian	Vegetarisch

Basics

Brot	bread
Brötchen	bread roll
Butter	butter
Ei	egg
Essig	vinegar
Honig	honey
Joghurt	yoghurt
Käse	cheese
Kuchen	cake
Marmelade	jam
Milch	milk
Öl	oil
Pfeffer	pepper
Reis	rice
Sahne	cream
Salz	salt
Scharf	spicy
Senf	mustard
Sosse	sauce
Suppe	soup
Zucker	sugar

Drinks

Bier	beer
Eiswürfel	ice cube
Flasche	bottle
Kaffee	coffee
Leitungswasser	tap water
Mineralwasser	mineral water
Saft	juice
Sprudelwasser	sparkling mineral water
Stroh	straw
Tee	tea
Teekanne	teapot
Wein	wine
Weissbier/ Weizenbier	wheat beer

Meat (Fleisch) and fish (Fisch)

Currywurst	sausage served with a curry powder and tomato ketchup
Forelle	trout
Garnelen	prawns
Huhn, Hähnchen	chicken
Kabeljau	cod
Lachs	salmon
Lamm	lamb
Lammkotelett	lamb chop
Leber	liver
Leberkäse	meatloaf

Makrele	mackerel
Rindfleisch	beef
Schinken	ham
Schweinefleisch	pork
Speck	bacon
Thunfisch	tuna
Wiener Schnitzel	breadcrumb-coated cutlet, usually veal but sometimes pork
Wurst	sausage
Zander	pikeperch

Vegetables (Gemüse)

Blumenkohl	cauliflower
Bohnen	beans
Bratkartoffeln	fried potatoes
Erbsen	peas
Grüne Bohnen	green beans
Gurke	cucumber or gherkin
Karotten, Möhren	carrots
Kartoffel	potatoes
Knoblauch	garlic
Lauch (or Porree)	leeks
Maiskolben	corn on the cob
Paprika	peppers
Pilze or Champignons	mushrooms
Pommes frites	chips or fries
Rosenkohl	Brussels sprouts
Rotkohl	red cabbage
Salat	salad
Salzkartoffeln	boiled potatoes
Sauerkraut	pickled cabbage
Spargel	asparagus (white asparagus is particularly popular in season)
Tomaten	tomatoes
Zwiebeln	onions

Fruit (Obst)

Ananas	pineapple
Apfel	apple
Aprikose	apricot
Banane	banana
Birne	pear
Erdbeer	strawberry
Himbeer	raspberry
Kirsch	cherry
Melone	melon
Orange	orange
Pfirsch	peach
Pflaum	plum
Trauben	grapes
Zitrone	lemon

Desserts and cakes

Eis	ice cream
Käsekuchen	cheesecake
Keks	biscuits
Kuchen	cake
Schokolade	chocolate
Torte	cake/tart

German specialities

Knödel/Klösse	poached or boiled potato or bread dumplings
Maultaschen	stuffed noodles similar to ravioli
Quark	a type of strained fresh cheese
Sauerbraten	pot roast, usually beef
Schweinsbraten	pot-roasted pork
Spätzle	egg noodles of soft texture

Publishing information

This fourth edition published January 2018 by **Rough Guides Ltd**
80 Strand, London WC2R 0RL
11, Community Centre, Panchsheel Park, New Delhi 110017, India
Distributed by Penguin Random House
Penguin Books Ltd, 80 Strand, London WC2R 0RL
Penguin Group (USA) 345 Hudson Street, NY 10014, USA
Penguin Group (Australia) 250 Camberwell Road, Camberwell, Victoria 3124, Australia
Penguin Group (NZ) 67 Apollo Drive, Mairangi Bay, Auckland 1310, New Zealand
Penguin Group (South Africa) Block D, Rosebank Office Park, 181 Jan Smuts Avenue, Parktown North, Gauteng, South Africa 2193
Rough Guides is represented in Canada by
DK Canada 320 Front Street West, Suite 1400, Toronto, Ontario M5V 3B6
Typeset in Minion and Din to an original design by Henry Iles and Dan May.
Printed and bound in China
© Rough Guides, 2018
Maps © Rough Guides

180pp includes index
A catalogue record for this book is available from the British Library
ISBN 978-0-24130-626-0

The publishers and authors have done their best to ensure the accuracy and currency of all the information in **Pocket Rough Guide Berlin**, however, they can accept no responsibility for any loss, injury, or inconvenience sustained by any traveller as a result of information or advice contained in the guide.
1 3 5 7 9 8 6 4 2

Acknowledgements

Paul Sullivan would like to thank Neil McQuillian for his assistance on this title.

Help us update

We've gone to a lot of effort to ensure that the fourth edition of the **Pocket Rough Guide Berlin** is accurate and up-to-date. However, things change – places get "discovered", opening hours are notoriously fickle, restaurants and rooms raise prices or lower standards. If you feel we've got it wrong or left something out, we'd like to know, and if you can remember the address, the price, the hours, the phone number, so much the better.

Please send your comments with the subject line "**Pocket Rough Guide Berlin Update**" to mail@roughguides.com. We'll credit all contributions and send a copy of the next edition (or any other Rough Guide if you prefer) for the very best emails.

Rough Guides credits

Editor: Neil McQuillian
Layout: Pradeep Thapliyal
Cartography: Richard Marchi
Picture editor: Phoebe Lowndes
Photographers: Diana Jarvis and Roger d'Olivere Mapp
Proofreader: Diane Margolis

Managing editor: Monica Woods
Production: Jimmy Lao
Cover photo research: Nicole Newman
Editorial assistant: Aimee White
Senior DTP coordinator: Dan May
Programme manager: Gareth Lowe
Publishing director: Georgina Dee

Author: British writer and photographer Paul Sullivan has been based in Berlin since 2008. His words and images have appeared in *The Guardian*, *The Sunday Times Travel*, *The Telegraph* and the BBC, and he has authored – and photographed – guidebooks for publishers like National Geographic, Time Out, Cool Camping, DK Travel and Wallpaper*, as well as a couple of books on Icelandic and Jamaican music. He is the founder of www.slowtravelberlin.com, through which he runs local photography and cultural-historical tours.

Photo credits

All photos © Rough Guides except the following:
(Key: t-top; c-centre; b-bottom; l-left; r-right)

Cover Berlin Cathedral – AWL Images: Francesco Lacobelli
1 Getty Images: Nikada
2 Alamy Stock Photo: JLImages (br); Radius Images (tr). Corbis: Schoening (tl). Robert Harding Picture Library: Norbert Michalke (bl)
4 Alamy Stock Photo: travelstock44
6 Picfair.com: shanelopes808 (t)
11 Alamy Stock Photo: Paul Brown (tl). Robert Harding Picture Library: Karl Johaentges (br)
12 Getty Images: benedek (t)
15 Getty Images: Merten Snijders (tl)
16 Getty Images: Westend61 (t)
17 Alamy Stock Photo: Scott Wilson (b). Corbis: Sylvain Sonnet (t)
19 Alamy Stock Photo: Iain Masterton (b). Corbis: Hans-Peter Merten (b); PictureNet (c)
20 Alamy Stock Photo: SZ Photo / Eckel, Jochen (b)
22 Alamy Stock Photo: travelstock44 (b)
23 Alamy Stock Photo: Digital-Fotofusion Gallery (t); park_Berlin (b). Getty Images: EyeEm / Sebastian Kopp (c)
30 Alamy Stock Photo: AA World Travel Library
31 Alamy Stock Photo: Hemis
38 Kaschk
39 Mogg
40 Alamy Stock Photo: Julie G. Woodhouse
41 AMANO Rooftop Bar
45 Corbis: Massimo Borchi
51 SuperStock

52 Robert Harding Picture Library: Ulf Boettcher
55 Corbis: Wolfgang Kumm
56 Alamy Stock Photo: Ingo Schulz
58 Cafe Einstein
60 Corbis: Jon Hicks
63 Alamy Stock Photo: MBimages
65 Burg & Schild
67 Oliv-Café Berlin: Oliver Mahne
69 Alamy Stock Photo: travelstock44. de / Juergen Held
72 Alamy Stock Photo: LOOK Die Bildagentur der Fotografen
76 Alamy Stock Photo: Yadid Levy
79 Alamy Stock Photo: Radim Beznoska
80 Corbis: JA
86 Alamy Stock Photo: imagebroker
87 Mundo Azul
88 Chutnify
91 Zula
94 Suicide Sue
100 Big Brobot
102 Goodies
107 Alamy Stock Photo: Iain Masterton
111 Alamy Stock Photo: Julie G Woodhouse
116 RosaCaleta: Lena Ganssmann
120 Alamy Stock Photo: Zoonar
122 California Breakfast Slam
124 Aquarium Berlin: Gru üne Baumpython
131 Alamy Stock Photo: Eden Breitz
133 Alamy Stock Photo: Frank Rothe
146–147 Robert Harding Picture Library: Helmut Meyer zur Capellen

Index

Maps are marked in **bold**.